THESE DAYS
ARE NUMBERED

THESE DAYS ARE NUMBERED

Diary of a
High-Rise
Lockdown

REBECCA ROSENBLUM

DUNDURN
PRESS

Publisher: Kwame Scott Fraser | Acquiring editor: Russell Smith
Cover designer: Laura Boyle
Cover image: Anastasia Yakovleva

Library and Archives Canada Cataloguing in Publication

Title: These days are numbered : diary of a high-rise lockdown / Rebecca Rosenblum.
Names: Rosenblum, Rebecca, 1978- author.
Identifiers: Canadiana (print) 20230137687 | Canadiana (ebook) 2023013775X | ISBN 9781459751439 (softcover) | ISBN 9781459751453 (EPUB) | ISBN 9781459751446 (PDF)
Subjects: LCSH: Rosenblum, Rebecca, 1978-—Diaries. | LCSH: Authors, Canadian—Ontario—Toronto—Diaries. | LCSH: COVID-19 Pandemic, 2020-—Ontario—Toronto. | LCSH: Social distancing (Public health)—Ontario—Toronto. | CSH: Authors, Canadian (English)—Ontario—Toronto—Diaries. | LCGFT: Diaries.
Classification: LCC PS8635.O65 Z46 2023 | DDC C813/.6—dc23

We acknowledge the support of the Canada Council for the Arts and the Ontario Arts Council for our publishing program. We also acknowledge the financial support of the Government of Ontario, through the Ontario Book Publishing Tax Credit and Ontario Creates, and the Government of Canada.

Care has been taken to trace the ownership of copyright material used in this book. The author and the publisher welcome any information enabling them to rectify any references or credits in subsequent editions.

The publisher is not responsible for websites or their content unless they are owned by the publisher.

Printed and bound in Canada.

Dundurn Press
1382 Queen Street East
Toronto, Ontario, Canada M4L 1C9
dundurn.com, @dundurnpress 𝕏 f ⊚

For Mark, my mominator, and my 523 friends
who helped me make this book

Introduction

My greatest fear is somehow getting unstuck from the earth and floating away, all alone, and no one knows where I am until I'm too far away to find. This sounds like a metaphor, and it is, but not entirely. I've done some drifting occasionally, and I don't like it. Being woven in tight to earth, to people and communities, is my thing. Sometimes, I feel that fear of floating away if I'm somewhere unusual where I don't know anyone — somewhere no one would look for me. As I walk down an unfamiliar sidewalk to a new doctor's office, or stand in the terminal during an unscheduled layover, that sensation of being unfindable makes me pull out my phone and open my contacts list. Being able to talk to friends, family, co-workers, to offer and receive help, to have a friendly chat about literally anything — current events or where to find cheap vegetables or why we used to love that weird old song ten years ago — makes me feel anchored and real, like I am a part of real life and could never just float away. Other people are my favourite part of being a person.

So, in many ways, the beginning of the Covid-19 pandemic was my worst nightmare, not just because of the disease itself, although of course I worry plenty about that — I'm very lucky with my health, and the health of those I love, and my anxiety doesn't usually operate on that vector. I was scared of illness, of course, but what mainly scared me was what I would do without everybody else during lockdown. There were rules to follow to keep yourself safe, and while the ever-shifting nature of the rules made their utility seem *kinda* farcical, I felt soothed in exactly the way I was meant to, by sanitizing my doorknobs and microwaving the mail. But no one offered a rule for how to feel like a part of society when I had to stand six feet away from it all. There was precious little soothing in the news about how to stay connected and sane and *happy*, if your happiness came primarily from other people.

I mean, I could *see* a lot of people, out there, through the windows. I live in the most densely populated neighbourhood in Canada, at least according to the most recent census data I could find. In 2016, there were at least eighteen thousand people living in the neighbourhood of St. James Town, Toronto, Canada, and probably a lot more now (several large residential towers have been built since that census) in about one square kilometre east of downtown, west of Parliament, between Bloor and Wellesley. My apartment complex alone houses approximately six thousand people in half a block, on a single side of the street.

(The town I grew up in had three thousand people for most of the time I lived there, and the road I lived on was out of town, such as it was — never able to get cable TV, proper internet, or sewers because the houses were too far apart. For some perspective.)

Of course, I'm a writer, and I'm married to another writer, and we have two cats — all indoor creatures who are supposed to be fine with staying home and staring out windows all day every day. But I'm also a publishing professional and my husband is a comms guy and the cats were used to us leaving them to their windows ten or twelve hours a day, before and after all the writing and staring. And then we stopped doing that, and we were all just … here … together … alone.

Before the pandemic, my husband and I didn't really know most of our neighbours — we never really fit in here. St. James Town is famous for being a "landing pad" for new immigrants, including refugees from a number of war zones, which we hadn't exactly realized before we moved here. There are also many students, young families, and people struggling in assorted ways. In the hallways I hear Hindi, Punjabi, Tamil, occasionally French — often I'm not sure what I'm hearing. There are big parties in the park across the street that I can never understand — are they organized by some official body, or do people just start showing up, and then more come, until there are a hundred people in the park, eating off paper plates and playing club music? I've certainly never been invited. Behind the trees in the park where the parties happen, people used to play basketball all through the day and all night until one day, about eight years after it was built and three years after someone was shot there, the basketball court was torn down. (At the very end of my editing this book, after nearly two years of demolition, construction, and constant noise, the basketball court was mysteriously rebuilt, more or less exactly as it was before.)

I don't fit in in St. James Town, but I didn't exactly fit in in my small town, either, and both places were my home. You smile at your neighbours, you return misdelivered mail, you admire dogs and babies, you keep your TV at a reasonable level, you don't say too much to people you don't know too well. I've been happy in St. James Town, but also, pre-pandemic, I commuted to work forty hours a week, travelled regularly, and had lots of friends to visit and events to attend throughout the city. It was a good home base for me, but I didn't think *that* much about it. Then the pandemic happened. And *here* became all there was.

Well, also my husband; also the inside of my head. Also the internet, and my cats, and the people who still talk on the phone. And that's it. Without a yard or a driveway, neighbours I knew, or a brain that could tolerate breaking the rules, that was it for the months and months of endless lockdowns in Toronto. I stopped going to work every day and talking to my beloved colleagues about copy-editing rules, I stopped taking the subway and the bus every day and observing all my fellow commuters, I stopped going to parties and having joyful party conversations, I stopped chatting with strangers in line at the supermarket (although I still went to the supermarket — it is very tricky to get things delivered to my building). No more volunteer work and our noisy, friendly meetings; no more dinners out with pals; no more family potlucks. Introverts crowed about finally dodging all these things they'd never liked, and I mourned — even the subway, even the grocery chats. Every connection lost was something that had anchored me to the world and although I had never felt more stuck, I also felt in cataclysmic danger of drifting away forever.

This book is a selection of transmissions I sent out from my satellite, trying to connect back to earth. I started out just posting "hello" to friends on social media, same as always, but with a little more urgency, since it was now my only way to greet them. And then I started counting the days, thinking it was going to be a very small, finite number of them. As the two-week lockdown that the government originally forecast turned out to be longer, the posts got longer, too — designed both to give myself a little daily task and to engage people, ideally brighten my days and others' too, and give us all something to think about besides lurking germs, handwashing protocols, hospital occupancy, and cordoned-off parks. I wanted people to talk to me, so I kept starting conversations — about the pando, sure, but about anything I could think of: my daily walks, my husband, my cats, my memories of childhood, anything I read or watched or ate or thought about. I wrote about the news, the weather, and the traffic I could see from my window. I wrote about things I had done in the past that now, in this time of reflection, I realized I regretted. I wrote about things other people had written in the comments on the previous day's post.

I've always been a Fairly Online Person, but I have energy enough for Online and Real Life both. Deprived of a path, all my real-life energy went online and exploded into thousands of words of content and answers to every comment anyone was kind enough to offer — and I got so many. I will never stop being grateful to the friends and associates who engaged with me through these posts and kept me tethered to earth during the first two years of Covid times. This book reproduces only my side of the conversation, but it was all written, originally, for an audience of a few hundred pals and associates. Together we kept it together in the weirdest times. This is how we did it.

First Wave

March 13, 2020

It is very ominous to listen to or read or discuss the news today, but also today *is* the news. Everything everyone is doing is somehow part of whatever is going on with this virus thing — "should we go to work, what about vacation, how are you feeling, was there a big line at your grocery store?" We read the case counts every day. There are ten times more cases in the province this week than last week. About four hundred people died of it in Italy in the past two days. That's … hard to imagine. I read a thing in the *Guardian* that hospitals in some regions in Italy are running out of beds and people are just in the hallways or lying in ORs. It's hard to put that in the context of: Should I take the subway and sit next to someone who is sniffling? And yet … I worked from home today, more to avoid the subway than the actual office, so I guess that's my answer. The lines are pretty long at the stores around here, but manageable. People seem a little freaked out, though. Polite, but the veneer is thin. Also, a lot of stuff is sold out, but I am definitely not up for going to more stores. That's it for me and Apocalypse Pasta Aisle. Maybe later, if I'm feeling adventurous, I will go over to my mom's building and stand under her balcony and wave at her.

I am probably going to have to go to work on Monday and, while I'm a bit envious of those who get to enact their social distancing properly, at home, I'm glad they are doing it because it makes it safer for those who can't. Staying at home is ideal, but a subway car just for me would be second best, I think ... [Edit from the future: work did not, in the end, make me commute that Monday ... or ever again.]

March 17, 2020

My parents are very reserved, quiet people. When I was born, they lived in a crumbling house on the outskirts of a tiny town and would have been happy living in an isolated splendour of three in their weird house all the time ... until I learned to walk and my mom noticed that if she set me down in the grocery store, I would run away. I would run until I found another kid and then ... I would kiss that kid. They realized I was lonely and put me in playschool and I have been able to avoid bothering anyone at the supermarket ever since.

This story seems relevant at this time.

March 18, 2020

Have you noticed the shortage of hand sanitizer in your local grocery and drugstores? Has everyone you know been talking to you about hand sanitizer supplies? Have you never really cared about hand sanitizer and just assumed you'd wash your hands with soap and water but now worry that you will die of contamination if you do not get some immediately? Well, I finally found a single, small, eleven-dollar bottle of hand sanitizer at a corner shop ... just in time for the building to shut off our water. How is your incarceration going?

• • •

Update from day 6 of home jail: with both of us working from home, the cats have been somewhat nonplussed, but excited to try napping during the day in the rooms where the computers are. They aren't allowed to do this when we aren't here, owing to their tendency to nibble on wires. Today, with the water turned off, we have filled the bathtub as an emergency reserve and Evan (elder cat) displayed an alarming inclination to death by unsupervised drowning, so the bathroom door is now shut, leading to feline despair.

In human news, I have made enchiladas and am halfway through the four-day process of making bread. Mark started listing all his flaws this morning for no reason but is actually still good company after one hundred and twenty uninterrupted hours. With the gym shut, I've gone back to my seventeen-year-old Pilates DVD, which is still pretty good. Later I may do my nails, one of those things I normally don't have time or patience for, and now I have *so much*. I feel that this period and attendant micro-updates are going to cost me a lot of Facebook friends.

March 19, 2020

Day 7 of this indoor life. Also day 4,017 of shared life with Mark Sampson — our first date was eleven years ago today (the above figure includes leap years). One of my favourite questions to ask Mark is "Is this how you thought the relationship would go?" Presumably, most boring happy couples imagine they are on a grand adventure and we are certainly no exception, but I suppose the important thing is, whether we are crawling on the floor looking for a shard of chipped tooth or trying to jam a cat into a backpack or meeting the Scallop Queen in Digby, we find it interesting. Mark, thank you for being so interesting. I do not want to stay trapped in the apartment with you anymore and am seriously considering spending a couple nights in the ravine just for the change, but that is not your fault. You are the best thing that ever happened to me and I'm just really sorry about the past few days. I hope when Covid-19 is all over, you still want to be married. Maybe you could come live in the ravine with me?

March 20, 2020

Day 8 of severe anti-sociability. Between the YouTube workouts that are too hard for me and the constant barrage of reassuring emails from Galen Weston, I am very sorrowful. Galen Weston, if you somehow don't know, owns a lot of grocery and drugstores, and also somehow has my email address. Normally the stores just use it to send deals for loyalty points and, I dunno, maybe recipes sometimes. During this time of global crisis, Galen has taken over the mailing list to send us his thoughts on Covid-19 and how we are all doing. He is trying to be reassuring but I'm not sure why I should be reassured by a grocery-store magnate. But probably eventually Stockholm Syndrome will kick in, because there are *so* many emails. I guess I'll just wait to feel reassured. Also, it may be raining, which means I can't even go for a walk, which was my *one thing*. Cats persist in embarrassing me on video calls. Starting to entertain fantasies of going to work! It feels stupid to complain when I am safe and relatively healthy, but also is there a better place for stupid complaining than among friends? Believe me, if you would like to bring me your trivial (or not) concerns, I am here for them, and you. By which I mean far from you, but emotionally here. I would also completely understand if now is the time you feel you need to mute/unfriend. I would mute myself if I could.

March 22, 2020

Day 10 of external monologue: just brought my lunch from the kitchen to my desk, forgot a fork, not going back.

This is from yesterday:

> Mark Sampson (making dinner): So Kenny Rogers died.
>
> Rebecca Rosenblum (washing dishes): Oh no — of what?
>
> MS: Old age. Nothing to do with Covid-19.
>
> RR: How old?
>
> MS: Eighty-one, I think.
>
> RR: Well, okay. I wish he'd been older.
>
> (Long, long silence.)
>
> RR: I think we should each prepare three topics to discuss at dinner.
>
> MS: What? Really?
>
> RR: I'm worried I already used up all my organic conversation earlier in the day.
>
> MS: Um ...
>
> RR: You can make the death of Kenny Loggins one of your things, if you want.
>
> MS: It was Kenny Rogers.
>
> RR: Oh.
>
> MS: ...
>
> RR: Well, how is Kenny Loggins, then?
>
> MS: I don't know — I'm not on top of that.
>
> RR: ...
>
> MS: Why don't you google it?
>
> RR (googles; triumphant): Still alive!
>
> MS: Hooray!

RR: Oh, man, remember "Return to Pooh Corner"?

MS: No.

RR: It was a good song. Oh, and "Danger Zone."

MS: I remember "Danger Zone."

RR: And of course the real classic ...

MS: Which is what? I don't remember?

RR: I think you will ... (Clicks on the song, turns up phone speakers.)

MS (listens intently): "Footloose"!

(All humans dance; Alice flattens her ears back.)

RR: This was my finest malapropism ever!

(We wound up watching *Brooklyn 99* over dinner.)

March 23, 2020

Day 11 of the Isolation and we have entered the Noisy Period, as my building is testing the fire alarm all day today, Wednesday, and Friday, because they are monsters. (Mark Sampson suggested it's because they want us to be safe from fire, but I yelled at him until he agreed that it's because they are monsters.) This has been going on for only thirty minutes and I've already taped a pillow over the speaker, which is helping way less than you'd expect. I'm terrible with loud noises and this is probably not going to go well. Expect rage around midday and despair ~2:00 p.m. (all times approximate).

In non-noisy news, we gave up on dinner table conversation last night and just started performing *Waiting for Godot*, passing the book back and forth as we ate. I am Estragon.

March 24, 2020

Day 12 of My Yoga Pants Life: my brother taught my mother to Skype and it is such a gift. Life keeps moving. We broke a glass at a video cocktail party last week (wild night) and elder cat has gotten very good at finding shards of broken glass that escaped cleanup and bringing them to my attention. I am tired all the time despite doing less than I have ever done, day to day, in my adult life. Also realizing that if I can't catch up on the *New Yorker* now, I never will. Sadness.

• • •

I've been getting some sad emails from Canadian Blood Services encouraging me to show up for my blood donation in two weeks. I hope I can, if everyone in my household is healthy.

March 25, 2020

Day 13 of being very sad and worried all the time. Three hundred and nineteen cases in Toronto today, up by thirty-nine from yesterday, and the medical officer has recommended today that all parks and playgrounds be closed so people will stop congregating and socializing. I can't truly fathom it. Fewer places to be; more time at home, alone. The claustrophobia tightens.

What are you all doing with your time in isolation, I wonder? I talk mainly about single little moments but here is where the bulk of my pandemic time is actually going — what about you?:

- My job: It's very portable, so from more or less nine to five daily, I sit at my desk and try to get educational resources published and on their way to students and teachers, who I know will be just thrilled (okay, the teachers will be more thrilled than the students). Focus and internet connection speed are not what they were at the office, but thank goodness this is not a super-busy time.

- Cooking: I had all these projects I thought I'd do "if I had the time" and I've basically done none of them except cooking projects. I made enchiladas where you soak the beans and then cook the beans and then make the enchiladas: two days; I made bread: four days; I made a potato cake and a risotto … We're trying to be really careful with groceries and not buy too much, so I tell myself I'm helping by stretching food to the max.

- I repotted some plants and did some U.S. tax docs at the very beginning of the period, before my resolve went to hell.

- Talking to everyone! The best thing about this isolation is that I actually talk to my friends every day and that is glorious. Man, there is a lot of software available if you want to talk to people virtually — so far, using Facebook, Twitter, Instagram, WhatsApp, Signal, email, iMessage, Mattermost, Zoom, BlueJeans, Skype, FaceTime, Houseparty, and the actual phone.

- Marriage: I think Mark will be relieved when he's not the only human I see in a day, but so far we aren't driving each other *too* crazy. But I do have a lot of attention to really focus on him. The other day he had a mystery scratch on his stomach and I pondered that for ages. Ages!

- Yeah, I'm still writing a novel … kinda. I mean, I am always writing a novel — you'd think Covid isolation would give me extra time to work on this, but not really. Mainly it's just giving me more time to lie on the floor and be worried, then feel guilty that I'm not writing. The only parts I like working on are the parts where the characters move around Toronto and I get to move with them: the Dufferin bus, a rainy night on Queen Street, Lee's Palace, Burger's Priest, a deserted 506 streetcar stop. I'm a little concerned I'm turning my coming-of-age/family novel into a travelogue, but I suppose I can edit some of this out when (if?) I can ever leave my immediate neighbourhood.
- I'm also reading books and magazines, but very slowly. It's so hard to concentrate, especially when I genuinely *have* to concentrate on work for much of the day. I do get things done, a tiny bit, ish. Even TV is a challenge.
- Going for walks: I live in one of the highest-population-density areas in Canada, so this is challenging, but I do try to get out every day and walk gingerly around people for half an hour or so. It's good to see the sky. I fantasize about going to different neighbourhoods (see "novel" entry above). Sometimes I walk to my mom's place and wave at her!
- Online workouts — some are fun, some are too hard, none of them are really suited to being done in the space I have, but I try!
- Picking up my cats and cuddling them until they bite.

March 26, 2020

Day 14 of the most unusual times. I went to a park last night, since they are closing. People seemed to keep mainly to themselves and I walked on the mud a few times to avoid others on the path, but then a little dog came running up to me. It was very cute and I like dogs, plus I know they can't transmit Covid, since I researched it for my cats, but I waved him off out of standard social-distancing instincts. Then a little girl of about five came up behind him and said, "Don't worry, he's friendly," and seemed ready to engage with me and I just ... fled. Poor kid — I didn't know what to do if she didn't know not to come near me. "I like dogs, too, thank you," I yelled over my shoulder as I ran away.

So I totally get why they are closing the parks for the greater good, but it's a big blow. The virus times are making me think a lot about how I count on a lot of common resources in the community, and when the going gets tough, those go away, and we are basically left with what is our own. I've made certain decisions in my life with an idea that my personal space and possessions will be limited, but I will be able to share and enjoy the whole vast city — libraries, parks, museums, concerts, community centres. Restaurants, bars, movie theatres. I mean, I know no one has access to these things at this present moment and everyone is struggling, but I just ... really wish I had a yard. I was very sad in the park yesterday, thinking spring is going to come and I don't know when I'll get to walk on grass.

And I know I have so many friends who would invite me to their yards if they could, but they can't, just like I have been making all this food and wishing I could share it but it isn't safe, and all these basic, kind human instincts aren't working right now. I'm just finding the Covid-19 period sort of ... forces an artificial selfishness on people. And it's so lonely. This is the first time I've cried in this whole period, about the dumb grass, and I get that I'm very lucky, but telling myself I'm lucky not to be in serious trouble is really not holding much water today.

March 28, 2020

Does anyone remember a Joe Ollmann comic that begins, "I'm wandering in the cemetery again, drunk as a lord"? It has black swans in it and I kept the clipping for probably twenty years but it's lost now and I miss it. Anyway, there are no parks now, so we wander in the cemetery now (sober) and it's pretty dark, but interesting.

Day 16 of whatever period this is.

March 29, 2020

Update from day 17 of social sadness: apocalypse swing set. Park report: after responses to my sad post last week indicated that perhaps not every park is closed, today I did a circuit of all the ones I frequent and here's what I came up with:

- The parkette near me has its play structure embargoed with DANGER tape, but you can still stroll through it. It's tiny and not very nice, so there's little point without the play structure for anything but walking your dog, but there is that.
- The parkette slightly farther away does *not* have the play structure or basketball court embargoed. Since today is the first time I've looked at it, I couldn't tell if it had tape on it and someone ripped it down very thoroughly, or if it just never

did. That parkette doesn't even have grass, just the two above-mentioned attractions. The basketball court is extremely popular and people play all day and most of the night, from basically now until snow. While I do not enjoy the constant bouncing and yelling sounds (and someone got shot on the court a few years back [they didn't die] [I don't know if it was a basketball-related dispute]), I know the kids here have basically nothing else like it and it would be a huge loss. I did see some chain-link fencing sections propped up against a pole, possibly unrelated … or a plan for future embargoing.

- Those are my only regular parks in St. James Town. St. James Town is poor and has been zoned in the way so often accorded poor people (wall-to-wall condo and apartment towers, almost no green space). Directly across Bloor Street is Rosedale, wealthy and ancient, and zoned for spaciousness and trees, so I hopped over there and went to Craigleigh Gardens, which is a gated park that I expected to be locked up tight but wasn't! It was muddy but semi-busy! One of the gates is under construction, and it's very hard to get in from that side — basically impossible if you have any mobility issues, are pushing a stroller, or are wearing nice shoes — but from the other end, it's business as usual. Lovely surprise.

- Then, behind Craigleigh, I doubled back down Milkman's Lane and it was open, too! There is a gate there, but it was wide open. However, by this point it was a gorgeous Sunday afternoon after a morning of rain and it was simply impossible to social-distance appropriately on the narrow trail — it was crowded and people weren't really being rude, but they also weren't trying very hard. Sunshine is exciting, I get it. But also I turned around after about two hundred metres because eek!

And that is the report on some parks I know — encouraging! And it's really spring! Also, people need to give each other way more space out there!

March 30, 2020

Day 18, disease event: Notes from a lunchtime walk to go yell "Happy birthday!" at my mom on her balcony:

- I had a brief flash of fear that I was not social-distancing appropriately with a parked car until I remembered we are not being asked to do that yet.
- I stepped into the road to give someone more space and he appreciatively tipped his ballcap at me.
- I saw some pigeons and remembered the following incident from the weekend: Mark and I were cutting through the previously mentioned tiny parkette and there was a woman there more than six feet away, so I paid her no mind … and then I saw pigeons were gathering at her feet, more and more of them. "Do the pigeons … know that woman?" I started to say to Mark, but somehow my voice startled them and maybe eighty or

ninety pigeons took wing at once and it made a
pulse in the air that you could feel and I actually
screamed (not proud, but I've been indoors in silence so much), and the woman just watched me
wryly as the pigeons wheeled around in a flock
and eventually came back to her once we'd walked
away. Later Mark taught me the word "murmura-
tion" so at least I learned something ... *but!* Also
the woman eventually took out a big sack of bird-
seed and yes, the pigeons definitely did know her.

- My mom is dealing with spending her birthday
  alone in captivity with great equanimity, but honestly I am not. She was born during WWII! She
  deserves a birthday hug!

March 31, 2020

Day 19 of the first global challenge we've faced together with the
rest of the world: I'm sad about how harsh landlords — mine and
others I've heard about — are being in the face of the "no evictions
during pandemic" thing. A lot of letters are being sent to tenants
that are basically, "We will find a way to evict you. Maybe not today, maybe not tomorrow, but we'll do it." The banks aren't doing
this about the mortgage relief, are they? I think that might be because banks are regulated a lot more closely than landlords and/or
because even if you are definitely going to be paying a mortgage for
another twenty years, it's relatively easy to move it to a competing
bank, whereas it's very hard to find another apartment.

To be clear, I can pay my rent, now and — as far as I know — in
the future (there's a lot I don't know about the future, though!). This
is just something I'm upset about as a general wrong.

On a lighter note, I dreamed last night that Mark and I had a couple-Halloween costume as carrot and celery, which was nice.

• • •

Something good happened today: St. James Town had the seven-thirty cheer for front-line health-care workers. People went out on their balconies and yelled and banged pots and pans and I think there was some honking, too — very cathartic. I hope the health-care workers felt appreciated, because they are, and also I enjoyed cheering for them. I've been sad that we hadn't had it before but perhaps I just missed it? It was great and loud and long — SJT is excellent at being rowdy — and scared my cats. Well done, neighbours. Well done, health-care workers, and thank you.

April 1, 2020

Further to the park report from a couple days ago, Mark let me know this morning that you can now actually be fined for using a recreational space when you aren't supposed to. Which is … grrr. I'm not sure it helps — people will just walk on the sidewalk and be sadder — but the law is the law. FYI.

April 4, 2020

Eventful day 23 of what is I guess my new life now: our neighbour down the hall dropped by to play with the cats! This was our first sustained in-the-flesh interaction with a non-Sampsenblum person in twenty-three days! She stayed in the hall and we stayed in the apartment, so more than six feet, and the cats wandered between.

I would have been quite hesitant to do this if I hadn't known her slightly from previous pet interactions when I used to let the cats in the hallway pre-pandemic (I've been keeping them in because I know that cats can't transmit Covid, but others might not know and be scared). I wanted to be generous and let her play with them since the cats have been a real help in this weird time and she's a sweet person, but it ended up being a real joy for me to chat with her through the open door. A mitzvah all around!

Other day 23 highlights include cleaning the bathroom with both bleach and vinegar and feeling an inkling it wasn't quite right, so I texted my friends wondering if the bathroom might explode (what would you do?) and a pal kindly informed me that I was in danger of making chlorine gas and should ventilate the room. Which I of course did, and then had to inform my husband that I had maybe created a WWI chemical agent in our bathroom, so he shouldn't go in there for a bit. It was another one of those "Is this how you pictured marriage?" conversations.

These Facebook messages just get longer and longer about less and less, don't they?

April 5, 2020

Day 24 of the great loneliness: Some leftover events from other days include finally planting my seedlings yesterday and cooking something called "broccoli tots" purchased in the early days of the pandemic, when you couldn't really get frozen veg and we took what was available. We got better stuff later, so these have been hanging around and taking up freezer space, so I made them yesterday and they were *dreadful*. Like a tater tot but bad. Neither of us could really eat very many, and we are not a household that wastes food. But I did grab the pan and serving spoon when the seven-thirty cheer went up for front-line workers. As we stood on the balcony, banging our dirty broccoli-tot pan along with the cacophony of St. James Town (some people have figured out how to deliberately set off their car alarms at seven thirty; it's very impressive), Mark said that these were the sorts of things that would get into the history books, which is such a wild thought. I never think of being *in* history. I thought of that old Garry Trudeau cartoon, "journalists write the rough draft of history." This is now — we're in the rough draft, friends. [Edit from the future: Is *this* a history book?]

April 7, 2020

Day 26 promises to be a glamour train because I am *giving blood*, my first appointment other than a video conference in almost a month. I realize my excitement is misplaced but I don't care — people need blood, which I am willing to provide, and I need to *leave my apartment*. It's a fair trade. I am currently wearing a dress and tights, and may later put on makeup. Of course, I will also be wrapping most of my face in a cotton scarf (which matches my dress) until I can get the whole mask thing under control. I have been experimenting with how good I am at breathing through fabric — not great — and it's a fair walk to the clinic. This is going to be interesting. Interesting is fine.

• • •

The clinic was very organized. Everyone was nice. I found it tense, much like I find grocery shopping tense these days, but unlike at the grocery store, you get to lie in a reclining chair and everyone is very kind and no one gets into your space without a mask and gloves. Of course, the staff bends over backward to make it a good experience because the blood is so needed, so they want us to go home and tell our friends and I'm here to tell you: *giving blood is a good experience.* If you feel up to it, I encourage it. At the end, you get snacks and congratulations and the exhilarating feeling of knowing you've done something good and also don't have to go back for another fifty-six days.

On the way home, I was so happy to be out in society, and someone somehow dropped a T-shirt off a high balcony and I watched it float onto Bloor Street and an old man smiled at me for my appropriate social distancing and I was thinking how much I disagree with the people who say self-isolation is great because they never wanted to associate with most people anyway and then a hailstone hit me in the eye. I was so startled I kept looking at the sky and then the ground and then the sky again — more hailstones! I ran to the mall entrance but of course the mall was shut because pandemic. I explained this to a number of other people, but we did not have the rueful bonding conversation I normally would have had with strangers in that situation because pandemic.

Finally I ran home through a waning rainstorm in time for pizza with Mark and the seven-thirty front-line cheer, which I realized is led by someone with one of those ballpark horns who kicks things off at the stroke of seven thirty and stops at exactly seven thirty-five. When St. James Town quieted down, we could hear other neighbourhoods cheering on in the distance. Society, man — I like it.

April 9, 2020

Day 28 — wow, four weeks! I honestly cannot remember how I felt five weeks ago.

I do remember how it felt four weeks ago when I finally did start self-isolating, and that my apartment was the safest little bubble and I was so happy that I could just stay here and work from home and not feel pressure to leave. I guess … I still feel somewhat this way, and I know certainly that I am privileged, but I am also having so much trouble with the constriction. I'm trying to channel past-RR and remember my good fortune in staying in, but, honestly, I had a fight with Mark last night about how to fold sheets and later accused him of seeking vengeance by deliberately kissing me after eating peanut butter and these are not things I do when I'm at my best.

In other news, well … I've started a project to wash and dry my vast collection of scarves and then wear each one to decide whether I should keep it or not, so I guess stay tuned for a lot of scarf news? Some of my seedlings have started to come up, so they are thriving even if I am not. I may make matzoh later — happy Passover, if you observe, by the way.

I'm glad I have been keeping this Facebook diary because honestly it is so hard to remember what happens from week to week. Time is weird!

April 10, 2020

Day 29: Today I walked way north into Rosedale and crossed to another side of the ravine — something I could theoretically have always done but never bothered to do because why would I? I was wandering along, passing all these big, gorgeous houses, thinking about how it really makes sense to be rich during a pandemic, and then I found … a new park! A giant park, with a big, open field and no gate, and although the play structure and hockey rink (?!) were blocked off, the rest was free and you could just go in and walk around if you wanted to, and a few people were doing so, very carefully social-distancing.

If I'm being brutally honest, and I guess that's where these posts are going, my first reaction was furious envy. At a time where pretty much nothing in St. James Town is usable, outdoor space-wise, this hit me really hard. I have the time and mobility to walk and get to this oasis, but who else does? This pandemic is going to make me an urban-green-space advocate.

As I walked through, I passed some parents playing soccer with their little kids and someone accidentally kicked the ball into the road. The tiny girl went running for it and the mom shrieked in terror. I was nearer the ball and raised my arm to signal I'd get it for them and began to jog over, and then I realized that going near the family or touching their toy was no favour and stopped. I watched to make sure the woman caught the kid before she ran into traffic, and then ran away myself, burning with embarrassment. Remember when we could spontaneously help each other?

April 12, 2020

Day 31: I bought some foiled eggs when I went to pick up my prescription last week and asked Mark to hide them for me this morning so I could have an egg hunt. Not normally something we'd do, but looking for any form of entertainment now. It was actually really fun! When I ran out of steam, I asked if I'd found them all, and Mark said no but the remaining eggs were safe from cats, so I could just try again later, and we ate breakfast. I tried to eat a chocolate egg with my cottage cheese and it turns out that I am now officially can't-stomach-chocolate-at-breakfast years old. Grim shock!

Later, we moved the living room furniture around to do a YouTube workout, which is another pandemic innovation, and as we were hopping around, I found a bunch more eggs. I feel like there's a lesson in there somewhere about changing things up and seeing from a new angle to yield treasures — C-19 has certainly given me some new perspectives. I actually later tried to go to that park I found on Friday, coming at it via a different, less circuitous route, and couldn't! Again, something about getting the perspective right, right?

April 14, 2020

Day 33: I have been finding new things to be anxious about as we leave the apartment less and less, which does not bode well. Last night we made a roast chicken et al. for dinner, and it was very nice. As he was packing up the leftovers, Mark said to be careful when I ate them because there might be little bones in there. I said, "Well, then, I won't eat any." This morning I demanded that if Mark ate any, he call me so I could keep an eye on him in case he choked. I remembered the terrifying time I briefly choked on a fishbone in a restaurant and was too embarrassed to say anything until after I coughed it out. Once the crisis was averted, I didn't want to eat the rest of my fish in case there were more stealth bones, and my friend leaned over and cut it all up for me and patted all the pieces and said, "See, no bones!," and I saw his whole future as an excellent father (which was right), and so I ate the fish. Later that night we went to a reading and that was the second time I'd ever talked to Mark Sampson and my voice sounded funny because the bone had scratched my throat, but it was still really nice.

Man, I miss going out with friends and restaurants and readings (and cheerfully letting others touch my food). I watched Mark eat the leftovers and he didn't choke, but can not choking really be the best one can say about an experience?

April 16, 2020

Day 35 (or possibly day 1,000 — no way to tell). Neighbour noise report: my neighbourhood is extremely noisy, but if I delve into that it gets whiny really fast. I have been marinating in noises for thirty-five days, suffice to say.

Inside our building, interestingly, is not noisy. It is one of those old seventies cinder-block constructions where if you can hear your neighbours, your neighbours are doing something unusual. So here is the report on our neighbours, all of whom are 98 percent silent, but I've had nine years to find out what I can and thirty-five days to really ponder it:

- North-side neighbours are a couple and their perhaps ten-year-old (?) daughter. The dad is friendly enough, the mom is very reserved, but the little girl would like to pet our cats and possibly even talk to me at the elevators, so the mom is cordial for her sake. They once had an elderly woman staying with them who paced the hall for hours and slightly frightened me. The only noise we have ever heard from their place took me quite a while to figure out — turned out to be a popcorn popper that was touching the wall for a few minutes. The only noise ever.

- South-side neighbours are a couple with a tiny baby. Although they refuse to be rude, they very definitely wish to talk to me never. Pre-pandemic, I never heard a peep from them, but since I have been home I have heard the baby crying once, someone jumping rope once, and a few things falling on the floor. Also, once, a loud argument that may or may not have been on TV.

- Across-the-hall neighbours are a couple with a miniature dachshund and, they claim, a cat, which I have never seen. I occasionally hear them chatting happily, or their TV if I am in the hallway (the doors are less soundproof than the walls). The previous occupant told me that the apartment is a bachelor, and they have lived there for more than five years and just seem really joyful for two men and two pets living in a single room. These neighbours are pretty friendly but, unlike the other two mentioned, speak English as a first language, so that could have something to do with it. (There is another couple with a miniature dachshund living down the hall; also two men, also friendly — I don't know if they have a cat or not.)
- Upstairs neighbours: These are the ceiling singers. I think there are several of them. I think they are pretty young, but since we don't share a corridor, we can't be sure. They definitely love music, they are definitely mainly untalented, and they have a lot of friends to throw parties for. They are a tiny bit noisy, but since they replaced an abusive parent who screamed and threw things, I appreciate them every single day.
- Downstairs neighbours: No available information. We have never heard anything and never seen them, to our knowledge. Since noise travels down more easily than up in a building, probably we are their noise, although we are really quiet, according to me. I wonder what they think …

April 18, 2020

I find the language about park rules intentionally baffling, and the whole idea of ticketing people for incorrectly using parks really repellent. I read an article that says tickets are supposed to be for people getting too close to each other, but the cops *quoted in the article* admit to giving tickets to people for sitting on benches longer than deemed appropriate. It's a scare tactic and it's working — Mark and I hiked up to the lovely park in Rosedale and then I wanted to leave almost immediately because what if someone came near us and then we got an expensive ticket? Which is bananas, because we were behaving appropriately, and also the cops don't come to parks in Rosedale.

April 20, 2020

Day 39: I keep finding tents in my neighbourhood in new spots wherever I go for a walk. I've been donating to different food programs to support people in need, but it doesn't feel like enough.

April 21, 2020

Day 40: This spring was probably the season I had the most tickets to stuff ever — I was really excited about being out and seeing so much cool stuff. All cancelled now, of course, and I'm embroiled in trying to figure out refunds, and it's breaking my heart. In general, I just wanted my money back and to start all over post-pandemic trying to figure out my life and what I can afford to do in the Great After, but it actually can't work like that. Theatre,

music, and dance companies who have already paid their performers don't have the money to give me. Someone on the phone today
asked me if I'd like to reserve tickets a year from now, and when
I said I couldn't be sure of my plans in a year and could I just get
the refund, they admitted they simply wouldn't have the cash flow
until October. I took the 2021 tickets. Where will we be then?
Immune? Perhaps there will be a fantastic vaccine and we'll all be
immune. I certainly hope so, because I will have a lot of shows to
go to. [Edit from the future: I got my first vaccination a year and
four days after this post, but the show was postponed for a second
year. It was the only ticket I maintained through the whole of the
pandemic except for one that we lost track of and failed to show
up for. I actually saw this show almost exactly two years after the
original ticket date.]

April 22, 2020

I could not get it together to shower before work, so I had to take a
lunch-hour shower, is how day 41 is going for me. Mark wanted to
go for a lunch-walk but I didn't have pants on yet so had to decline.
I have pants on now, FYI.

I think we have reached the nadir of my coping skills. To be
clear, nothing terrible has happened but a few mildly bad things
have, and I just had no emotional resources left to deal with them.
In general, I have limited patience with the whole introvert–
extrovert binary, but there is some truth to the idea that I draw
energy from interacting with other people. No other people = no
energy. Aside from following Mark around like a vampire, watching *Brooklyn 99*, and organizing my scarves, I no longer wish to do
things. I still *can* do things, so it's not as bad as it might be, but I
really don't want to.

Do we predict I arise, phoenix-like, from this situation with more self-sufficiency and resilience? Stay tuned for week 7, starting on Friday, to see if I grow as a person or if Mark takes to wearing earphones during meals.

April 23, 2020

Day 42: I took an early morning walk and it was so unpopulated I went all the way downtown. Wild to see the city of my heart so empty, heartbreaking to see people sleeping rough all alone on the empty sidewalks, but profoundly empowering to walk on these streets again. I missed them.

April 29, 2020

Day 48: Today I saw from a distance two people getting out of a cab and dropping a bunch of things onto the sidewalk. As I walked closer, I watched them pick up most of their stuff but I distinctly saw a small, flat object get kicked away by accident. I promised myself I would check what it was as I walked by and speak to them only if I absolutely had to, though I am constantly dying to speak to everyone and no one else really wants to have conversations with strangers at this point in history. As I skirted past them, I saw that it was a bank card, so I had the unmitigated pleasure of saying, "Hey, man, your debit card!" while pointing at the ground, and getting smiled at and thanked in return — the guy even made eye contact.

Today was a fairly lousy day but that happened, so … something.

May 2, 2020

Day 51: No one tells you that one definition of love is if there is a global health emergency, you will start performing all the basic services for each other that you used to get outside the home, like haircuts. I sort of wish I'd known that when I was dating but wouldn't have really changed anything.

May 5, 2020

Day 54: Friends, I went to the grocery store! One person per visit per household per week is my understanding of the rules, and Mark had already been on Saturday so we were done for the week but ... I left some stuff off the list! And thought of some other stuff I felt like making! And was just generally having a miserable day and I got so mad thinking I couldn't make the meals I wanted because I wasn't organized enough to make the right grocery list four days ago and the store is right down the street and I just ... went there and bought all my stuff. And I feel like a monster, which is why I am confessing to you — I made it nearly eight weeks and now this! *Of course* nothing really happened and I didn't get near anyone at the store, but that is because most people are obeying the rules — if everyone did what I did, the store would be crowded and it would be dangerous. At least most people are good citizens, and I am, most of the time. Oh my God, I did not know I could feel this level of despair over thirty dollars' worth of groceries.

May 7, 2020

Day 56: Today is the last day of the second month of quarantine for me. My Christmas-present concert in June got postponed indefinitely this morning and someone is putting up hateful anti–Hillary Clinton stickers in my neighbourhood again for reasons I can't possibly understand. I did save the pro-Hillary stickers I was given when this last happened three years ago and have been covering up the anti ones, but the thrill of battle is gone. I overheard the neighbours fighting last night. Even the prospect of 1.5 kilos of cheese coming tomorrow morning can't cheer me up.

A cheerier story from the past: a person of my acquaintance (who shall remain nameless, since I didn't ask whether I could tell this story) when a very small child destroyed a towel rack by swinging on it, and responded to chastisement by parents by shrieking, "You *wanted* kids!" Upon hearing this story, Mark Sampson was deeply charmed and has gone on to respond to much spousal criticism with, "Hey, you married me!"

May 9, 2020

Day 58: I wasn't feeling great today, so Mark Sampson brought my mom her Mother's Day gifts in the snow and a mask (zeugma!) and bonus, we got to have this gem of a conversation:

> RR: Was the mask okay?
> MS: Not at all! It was fine inside but as soon as I
> was out in the cold, it made my glasses steam
> up completely.
> RR: Oh no. What did you do?

MS: I kept it on, out of respect for your mom. I just
    walked very carefully, as though through thick
    fog.
RR: Yikes! Did the plastic stay on the flowers?
MS: No! It was very, very windy, in addition to the
    cold and the snow, and the plastic blew off at
    some point, but I didn't see that, on account of
    the glasses fog. When I got to her place, I went
    to take it off like you told me, but it was already
    gone.

May 10, 2020

Day 59: Mark and I ate some of our (excellent) cheese from
Monforte Dairy and I noticed that one of our cheese knives is
missing. Mark says he doesn't know anything about that but of the
two of us, I feel pretty strongly that the person who somehow tore
one of his shoes all the way down one side and is still wearing it a
month later is the one more likely to have lost a cheese knife.

May 11, 2020

Day 60: I feel like this floating eye when I walk in the city now.
Absent a destination, a schedule, or usually anyone to walk with (I
still sometimes walk with Mark, but often it's just too much work
to distance from others as a pair and I go on my own), I feel sort of
invisible, like I couldn't interact even if I wanted to. All I do is see.
I've always felt I'm pretty observant, but since there's really nothing else to do now, I've stared so hard at everyone and everything.
This peering into people's gardens every day for a week, waiting for

a certain flower to bloom, is new. I've also gotten way judgier — it's dumb, and my judgments aren't even good ones, but I invent narratives about people I see and then I decide if I like their narratives or not. The social-distancing bubble feels like such a trap. Yes, it's nice to slow down and really think about whether that bud is bigger than it was yesterday, but it should really be only physical distance, and yet it isn't. Today I smiled at the woman who cleans my building foyer and hallways because I have seen her most days for close to a decade, but she didn't respond because I was wearing a mask and she didn't see.

May 12, 2020

Day 61: I was looking at one of my plants this morning, thinking it had grown a bit but I wasn't sure exactly how much. Then I thought, well, I should count the leaves on all my plants and keep a tally, and then when I update it, I will know how much they've grown. I held this thought in my head for perhaps one hundred and twenty seconds as a reasonable plan, so … that's not great.

May 13, 2020

Day 62: Normally I don't join "community pages" on Facebook because I don't have time and because a percentage of the posts on those pages always drive me up the wall. During the pandemic, I've joined CareMongering since I do have time, and in the hopes that I will find ways to help others. CareMongering is a network of Facebook groups (each focused on a specific city or area) created at the beginning of the pandemic with the idea that people in need of help could ask for it there, and others with the ability to offer food, transportation, information, money, or just plain kindness would offer it there. Instead of fearmongering, these groups would "monger" care. It's nice and — often — these groups work pretty well, in that people do genuinely get help when they need it. My ability to help has been limited — most people need things that involve a car or a bike or knowledge I don't have — but I've been able to do a few tiny things. I have really been awed by the generosity and ingenuity of others on those pages, though — what they have been willing and able to do for others, usually for total strangers, is an inspiration, and the reason I'll stick with the pages and keep looking for ways to help.

However, the things that irritate me about these pages are present in the pandemic, too, and I have time now to really obsess. Will you allow me to vent here, hopefully harmlessly?

> Scenario #1: Someone posts a very specific request for help, like this: "I'd like to get a nice birthday cake for my boyfriend, but it's hard during the pandemic because I don't have transportation and I'm stuck in the east end, plus our funds are very limited and he's lactose intolerant. Any suggestions of a place we might be able to find something good?"
>
> And mixed in with the helpful responses, there's always quite a number like this:

- My sister runs a bakery in the west end that you would love! They don't deliver but it's worth it to go!
- Oooh, I know a really great place that does cheesecakes. I know you said he's lactose intolerant, but maybe he could just, like, eat the crust?
- Cake is terrible for you, and at this time we should all be trying to be healthy. I strongly suggest a protein powder.

- I'm sorry, what is this about?
- Have you tried googling "cake" and seeing what comes up?

Scenario #2: There's a productive discussion going on about a way of handling something or a general best practice that will work for most people. Folks are sharing their experiences and perspectives and trying to include lots of room for variation, but there's always that one person — Captain Awkward calls him Edge Case Bob — who insists we definitely need to include the possibility that sometimes doing something bizarre or terrible might also be right, and derails the whole conversation. Like this:

A: So we agree that, in general, when you get on the subway during the pandemic, you move as far away from other riders as possible and try to stay aware of where everyone is through the ride, in order to give them their space?

Bob: What if someone needs help, though?

C: Of course, that's part of awareness — we would want to pay attention to someone asking for help and evaluate our distance based on what they need.

Bob: What if they have laryngitis, though? What if a person with laryngitis needs help?

A: Well ... we would want to be looking around a bit, too, at least once in a while, to see if anyone is signalling or looking like they are in distress ...

Bob: What if they are wearing a poncho so their
signals are invisible?

A: Umm ...

C: Well ...

Bob: Wouldn't it just make more sense to immediately start a shoulder rub without asking for
everyone who gets on the subway car with you,
while screaming, "Are you okay?," just to be on
the safe side?

D: I'm sorry, what is this about?

May 14, 2020

Day 63: Remember way back at the beginning of the pandemic (oh, attentive readers) when the building turned off my water and I was scrupulously prepared? Well, they did it again and at the end of week nine, I prepared nothing! I saw the signs, I knew it was today, I just didn't connect the water in the building being turned off with me, personally, not having any ... I wonder how many IQ points I have actually lost during the lockdown? Anyway, today sucks. (If you are wondering why my building turns off the water so often, that is a *great* question. Me too!)

May 18, 2020

Day 67: I was sent a gift via Amazon yesterday and I guess it was stolen? I haven't ordered from them in a long time, but apparently now they send a picture of the package by the door and that certainly is my hallway carpet, but twenty minutes after the stated delivery time, when Mark came home, no package. The whole thing is unsettling because while they could have delivered it to the wrong door (carpet is the same throughout the whole giant building), if it was stolen, it was probably a neighbour, because pandemic and no one is having guests. I guess another delivery person could have taken it, but that seems unlikely. My neighbours are largely uninterested in being my friend, but they seem decent enough people and I know them all by sight. Just such an odd feeling. Perhaps the gift will eventually emerge from another floor, delivered by accident, but it seems much more likely that I will never know exactly and continue to feel vaguely suspicious of all my neighbours until, gradually, I forget about it.

May 19, 2020

Day 68: Mark is having a terrible time wearing masks — we have two designs and both slide down his face within minutes of being put on, requiring constant readjustment, which of course defeats the purpose of wearing a mask. Today, after watching this happen for quite a long time (and while my own mask stayed firmly in place):

> RR: It's your tiny WASP nose! It's not anchoring the
>   mask firmly enough.
> MS (hangs head like Charlie Brown)
> RR: If your nose were just a little bigger ...
> MS: No one's nose is shaped like a wasp ... *Oh!*
> RR: ... Really?
> MS: I get it now.

May 20, 2020

Day 69: They tested our fire alarm *again* this morning — our fire alarm is in such tiptop shape; I never realized the vigilance until I was home every day to witness it. That took about thirty minutes and then they started testing one in a neighbouring building and, since it's a lovely day and windows are open, I can hear that, too.

The one person in my work department who is allowed into the office reports that my office plant — Mr. Planty — is doing quite well, and I am very grateful. I will come back for him someday, I will!

• • •

We tried a brief, physically distant visit with friends at lunch in a park today and this very weird thing happened: we were sitting on a low rock wall with the requisite six feet between us, so taking up a lot of space, but there was still a lot of wall left over. A kid of perhaps nine or ten, all but engulfed from forehead to hips in a grey camo hoodie and riding and then carrying a scooter, climbed up on the wall behind my pals — facing me, but sort of glowering over them from behind. I motioned that we should get up because — well, it seemed best, and none of us was really in love with the rock wall (which turned out to have been quite dirty) anyway. The adults responsible for the kid saw us scoot away and called apologies after us, and then started remonstrating with the kid in another language. I felt bad, because while the moment had been undeniably weird, it was only a moment, and kids have a hard enough time knowing how to be with strangers without being pulled out of society for two months. *So* much remonstrating. Man, it must suck to be a kid right now.

May 21, 2020

Day 70: Yeah, gasp: ten weeks. I went for another early morning walk downtown today because as things open up it won't be as easy to do that, I figure. (Also gasp: things are opening up here in Toronto … a bit. Parks are reopening — hooray! Some stores, too … not sure how I feel about that … Non-medical masks are being recommended … okay. On it. Back to the walk.)

When I came out of my building, I saw two security guards talking with someone who was attempting to take off all his clothes and, indeed, had mainly done so already. They were having a low-voiced, reasonable conversation about it. About ten minutes later, walking toward Yonge and trying to change the music on my earphones, I was startled by someone bursting out of a building, yelling and sobbing. He seemed really upset, as if he'd just ended an argument with someone, but when I turned off my music to hear what he was saying, it was about supermodels. I passed the park by Sanctuary, a place that offers meals and sometimes clothes to people in need. The park used to be part of my route to go see my mother, but I haven't been through it in weeks because it is now occupied by a tent city. I saw a car with its window smashed — otherwise undamaged, it seemed to me, but it was hard to tell what had been taken.

It feels so important to look around and really see what is happening in our locked-down city to those who can't lock down, or can't understand what is happening enough to do so, or both. I also saw a few people (more than last time) seemingly briskly setting out for work, a lineup at the Tim Hortons, a lilac tree about to bloom, and lots of quiet, empty streets, of course — but overall, it felt like a tough city today. And honestly, I shrank from it a bit, cut the downtown part of my walk short and went over to Allan Gardens, where a few people were just waking up but by and large it was very peaceful. For a while a guy had set up a hammock in Allan Gardens and was living in it with his cat, but usually that park is more a living room than a bedroom and this morning it was green and quiet.

May 23, 2020

It is day 72 of the lockdown or, seen another way, it is my day 15,341 on earth (yes, I looked up the leap years). And now I am a brilliant answer but no question was asked ... forty-two!

May 24, 2020

Day 73: So yesterday was my forty-second birthday. I have to admit, I was sort of mopey on Friday when, after dinner, I realized there was nothing to do with my birthday eve but watch four hours of television and go to bed. We did watch *Hustlers* off Mark Sampson's curated movie list, which was just great, and then a couple episodes of *Never Have I Ever,* also great — and not perhaps what Mark would have chosen for himself, so I appreciated the birthday forbearance.

On my birthday proper, I got my first ever breakfast in bed — somehow I'd missed out on this my whole life. It was lovely, but then we had to change the sheets. How do people eat pancakes and syrup while reclining and not get it everywhere? Anyway, Mark cleaned up the kitchen (during lockdown, dishes have become my most loathed chore) and I lounged around and then we set off for the park. We ate and read and hung out in the sun until everything in the cooler melted and then headed home for more lounging, calls, a distanced visit with fam, fancy dinner on the balcony, and Zooming with friends. I did my once-a-year experiment with drinking Bellinis (as most people know, I never got the hang of alcohol and don't actually drink) and ended up collapsed across Mark's lap by nine thirty.

• • •

Oh my goodness, I almost forgot the actual best part of my birthday. We were eating our picnic, which was basically bread and fancy cheese, and oranges, and Tim Tams that melted in the sun. And saying how people talk about cheese the way they do about bands, and everyone wants their favourite to be the one no one else has heard of — the more obscure and hard to find, the better. And then right as we're closing out that conversational avenue, Mark Sampson throws in, "And brie is Coldplay."

May 26, 2020

Day 75: A sub-isolation within the original isolation: owing to heat and noise from jackhammers, I can't work in my office anymore, so I'm sealed in the bedroom where the air conditioner both cools and is loud enough to drown out the rapture.

May 27, 2020

Tonight around twilight, I was wandering in Rosedale, chatting with my mom on the phone, when I saw a little kid of perhaps three coming down a driveway solo, slurping a freezie. I paused to watch since he was alone, and sure enough, he came right to the edge of the road. I shook my head at him — usually kids are intimidated enough by disapproval from a stranger. But he stepped down into the street!

RR: Oh no, don't do that!

Mominator: What's wrong? Are you okay?

Kid (walks across the street)

RR: Oh, just this little kid, wandering in traffic.

Mom: *What?*

Kid (totally blasé)

RR: Well, it's Rosedale, there's not much traffic, but he's in the street.

Mom: Where are his parents?

Kid (heads down the sidewalk away from RR)

RR: I don't know, there's nobody. I'll ask him where they ... nope, pandemic, can't talk to strange kids.

Mom: You can't leave him all alone.

RR: Oh, he's headed toward some women coming the other way — maybe these are his people.

Mom: Oh, good.

RR: Uh-uh, walked right past him. And they didn't seem weirded out by a lone three-year-old out for a stroll. Rosedale is weird.

Mom: ...

RR: Well, I'll just follow him and make sure he doesn't get kidnapped. Maybe he knows where he's going ...?

Mom: Okay, you watch him.

RR: Oh, no, he noticed me, now he's afraid of *me*. I am a toddler stalker. I need to drop back more.

Mom: Don't lose him.

RR: I lost him.

Mom: Oh no!

RR: He went into one of these yards ... Oh, there he is ... He found some women, they seem glad to see him ...

Mom: Is he glad to see them?
RR: Seems to be — okay, they're looking at me. I
guess I peace out now.

What *is* Rosedale? I mean, I'm not a parent, there's much I don't know, but surely most people in most neighbourhoods wouldn't tell a kid that young to cross the street and walk half a block alone if they got lonely … Would they?

May 30, 2020

Day 79 is the #NotAnotherBlackLife protest in Toronto. I'm in awe of the organizers — people working for Justice for Regis Korchinski-Paquet, the young woman who fell from her balcony a few days ago while police were in her apartment, as well as all the activists for racial justice in this city who have helped organize today into a strong and peaceful protest. And those attending today. I'm also desperately sad about the need for it. I won't be attending — I've found street actions overwhelming at the best of times and I can't imagine going alone today and trying to keep proper distance from everyone, after not going anywhere but quick errands or the park for seventy-nine days. I feel guilty about making the choice — it is certainly a choice — not to go, but this post isn't *just* guilt vomit. I usually give money when I am not showing up where I feel I should actually be, and I did that today, contributing a little bit to the legal fund for #JusticeForRegis Korchinski-Paquet. I'm sure the little bit I gave isn't going to do much, but the point for me is to do something rather than nothing, to feel implicated. It is easy to feel helpless and I often do, but this is my city, too, and I owe it whatever I can manage to push for what I believe is right.

June 2, 2020

Day 82: In honour of #BlackoutTuesday I will not be posting my usual nonsense. It has been hard to watch the events of the past few days in the U.S. — Trump is still threatening to send the military to states where the governors cannot stop people from protesting in the streets over the killing of George Floyd — and here as well. I don't have anything insightful to say, but I'm trying to pay attention, read and watch as much as I can, not look away from the things that are burning and broken, and to think about ways to do better, myself.

June 4, 2020

Day 84: Twelve weeks, friends. If the lockdown were a pregnancy, we would be ready to announce the news! Three hundred new cases today and forty-five deaths yesterday in Ontario. Despite being incredibly sad and worried about so many things this week, I have a natural personality pre-set of being fairly focused on minutiae (did you notice?) and the weather has been so warm this week, so although I remain worried, this morning seems … nice. Here is the minute news of the week at my house:

- Mark went to *work* yesterday and will probably be working from his office one day a week from now on, the emergency stay-at-home order in Ontario having ended earlier this week, as the above numbers are part of an (alleged) downward trend. It was wild to spend a day alone in the apartment, and to wait until Mark got home to tell him stuff. I think the cats were a lot calmer without their celebrity heartthrob to follow around.

- The fire alarm went off in the middle of the night for forty-five minutes on Tuesday, and also the building across from Mark's work had an explosion(?), so I'm feeling a little targeted by mysterious forces.
- Masks are not mandatory in Ontario but they are "recommended by health officials." I love listening to health officials and we have managed to get a range of masks now, so we are ready for more workdays or whatever may come. I am ranking the masks from hardest to breathe in to easiest, and a new wrinkle came up yesterday when someone tried to talk to me in my mask for an extended period (normally I wear them mainly at the grocery or drugstore, the only indoor places I go, and no one chats) and I sucked quite a wad of fabric into my mouth trying to speak, so now I need to reorganize my ranking by ease of speech.
- I've finished day nine of Thirty Days of Yoga and am really enjoying it. I'm trying to do some other yoga every day and also some breathing exercises and generally just *calm down*. The only thing that sucks is realizing that when I finish the thirty days, if I skip none (unlikely that I won't wind up skipping eventually), it will be day 105 of the lockdown. I mean, could that happen? Really?
- When people say "decimate," do they mean "lost one tenth of" or do they mean "lost most of"? I try to be really chill about evolving language, but I feel that one actually evolved into meaninglessness and now we just can't use it anymore because no one knows what it means.

- Could my good mood be coming from the fact I walked to a park last night and saw a friend and his entire family to give them a seedling? Quite possibly. It's good to see friends!
- Toronto is still stuck in pre–stage 1 reopening for at least another week, but soon maybe the patios will reopen? And weddings and funerals and drive-in movies and "animal attractions," whatever those are? I will probably go to none of those things out of an abundance of caution, but then again, maybe I will … It would be nice to have the option …

June 7, 2020

Day 87: Evan has taken to sneaking into the closet and crawling into his kitty carrier, where he remains until forcibly removed. I don't think any of us want to be here anymore.

June 8, 2020

Day 88: What is with dudes announcing to strangers they see in passing that "you shouldn't bother with a mask." I saw this twice in three days (once directed at me, once at someone else). What is a good answer when someone whizzes by me and says, basically, "Try less hard to be considerate of others"?

June 11, 2020

Day 91, thirteen weeks complete. If ninety-one does not sound like it should be divisible by anything, it's because they did not teach thirteen as a multiplier in grade school — we are beyond the times table, baby!

This week was a minor nightmare for me — it was very hot in my apartment, there was constant jackhammering during the day and often loud music and/or shouting at night, and I couldn't muster focus for almost anything. Because of the heat, even cooking, a reliable pleasure usually, was largely unpleasant. Plus a division was sold off at work, leading to a lot of people leaving and uncertainty and sadness. Plus the dawning realization that no matter how flexible we are with our timing or how we plan it, we really are probably not going to be able to go to Charlottetown to see Mark's family this summer … Plus I am mainly just out of resiliency. A mildly snippy text sends me into a tailspin for hours; the fact that when Mark is unavailable the cats hang out under the dining-room table rather than with me hurts my feelings; and I have become so alarmed by all the warnings in my Instant Pot manual that I still haven't used it in almost three weeks (I have helpfully scattered the pieces all over my living room, though).

I get that the paragraph above is not a list of problems so much as symptoms of a problem, which is a dearth of coping mechanisms. My usual coping mechanisms are just so … interactive, though. I suppose I will eventually develop some new ones, but honestly, I would have hoped to have done so at least a little in ninety-one days.

June 12, 2020

Day 92: I got another email from Galen Weston this morning —
is he becoming too important a person in my life? Stockholm
Syndrome? Why do I keep reading the emails? Well, these are some
good questions to consider, but, anyway, I read it right to the end.
In the last bullet he announced that the pay bump that people in
the PC Optimum family of stores had received at the beginning of
the pandemic is going away now. On the one hand, it's still far, far
more dangerous to have that job than it was when most of those
people signed up, which isn't fair, and yet they keep showing up and
largely being excellent. On the other hand, things are ostensibly
improving and getting safer for us all (but are they?). Actually, I
probably do have an opinion here: that they should have gotten to
keep the raise, as grocery-store jobs were never overpaid to start
with and now they are much more onerous and scary. So that's what
I think. Anyway, I thought I should share this, since perhaps not
everyone reads every word of these emails with the devotion I do.

• • •

No more jackhammers. I live in the park now.

• • •

It finally happened: through a complex web of gaslighting and mayhem, the cats got themselves two dinners. Bravo, cats. I hope they
don't puke.

51

June 16, 2020

Day 96: Yesterday was pretty pleasant because there was no jack-hammering at all in the morning. The construction crew was doing other noisy things, but all at least somewhat less noisy than jackham-mers. I'm not sure why — possibly to give the people who actually live in the building being jackhammered a break. (Yes, they are still there; I can see their lights go on in the evening — I feel for them a lot!) And then in the afternoon they started up again, but I had some white-noise tracks and then, only a couple hours in, the build-ing caught fire and they had to stop. Obviously, this wasn't a good outcome, and there must have been real concern because there were half a dozen fire trucks and the street was blocked off (also many sirens, which weren't exactly quiet), but the building wasn't evacuat-ed, so it couldn't have been that dire, and it did end construction for the afternoon. Unfortunately, this seems to have put things behind schedule, as the jackhammers were back first thing this morning.

Forgive me for talking so much about the construction — it is so loud I think about it constantly. Also, there is little else going on. I'm on day twenty-one of the yoga challenge, it's going well, and day six of the meditation, which is off to a slower start but seems to help a bit. I took the winter blankets to the dry cleaner, so that's progress and also a new place to go.

June 17, 2020

Day 97: So Saturday will be one hundred days of lockdown.

In good news, the jackhammerers seem to have gotten quite a bit done while I was in the shower this morning — I think they are starting to cut some corners, but I'll take it. They are nearly done the balcony-edge smashing they have been working on since last week, and I don't know if that could be the end of the loud part of the project or if that's too much to hope for. It would be crushing if the next phase were sandblasting or yodelling or something. My building also tested the fire alarm this morning because of course. Mark Sampson is at work today; cats seem morose.

• • •

One of the relatively minor casualties of the pandemic for me is eavesdropping — I love to hear other voices, random snippets of conversation, other lives. I popped into the corner store for a drink and a snack, something I haven't done in months but I was feeling sorry for myself, and was rewarded with this gem:

> Cashier (middle-aged woman with thick accent): Hello, hello, it's good to see you. It's been a long time!
> Patron (middle-aged woman with thick, very different accent): Yes, yes, it is good to see you, too.
> C: Soon your husband is coming, yes? Then you will be so happy!
> P: Oh no, no, he is here now! He came already!
> C: Oh, really? Already?
> P: Yes, yes. He works with me in the hospital.
> C: Wow, you must be so happy!
> P: Yes, I am very happy! You never meet him yet?
> C: No, I don't think so.
> P: You will sometime. I bring him.
> C: Maybe he come alone and I didn't know it was your husband.
> P: No, not alone.

C: No?
P: No, he can't go alone. He new.

June 18, 2020

Day 98: I think I have perfected my morning routine.

Wake up, do waking-up meditation with app, take myriad supplements and pills, put on gym clothes, go out on the balcony to water plants/make sure squirrels haven't eaten them, feed cats, get cottage cheese, eat cottage cheese in Mark's office while interrupting his work, do yoga, do some other exercise, shower, get dressed, get coffee (or have Mark bring me coffee), eat some other breakfast to supplement the cottage cheese, start working ... less interesting from there.

Having these little set-day challenges for the meditation and yoga is really helpful — I love a structure. The meditation app emailed me this morning to let me know I'd done ten days in a row (I certainly knew that) and to say that if I did fifteen days in a row, I would get a prize, which is basically catnip to me. I feel fairly certain that the prize is some other kind of meditation or possibly just an email from the app saying congratulations, but I don't care — I want it. We all need something to strive for.

• • •

Now in noise news: the jackhammering on this side of the building across the street did not take place today. I don't want to speculate on whether it's over, because the disappointment would be too great if it isn't, but we got a day off anyway. There was jackhammering somewhere nearby, possibly the far side of the building, but it was much more tolerable from that distance. There was also:

- actual hammering
- a truck backing up on and off for close to an hour
- several sirens, including one at 3:00 a.m.
- a melodramatic but brief argument in the park
- an unhappy dog

So, a relatively quiet day for this area. I want it noted for the record that, pre-pandemic, I had a pretty high noise tolerance and used to live in front of the spot on Spadina where the streetcar went into the tunnel, and I never cared. Lockdown in St. James Town is a whole new level!

June 19, 2020

Day 99: It turns out that tomorrow is, in addition to day 100 of lockdown, summer solstice. It's at 5:43 p.m., if you are into that. So two friends and I have decided to go to a park in our masks and form an equilateral triangle with six-foot sides and enjoy the moment together. Then I will go home and Mark has promised to make me a fancy milkshake drink that involves crumbling a cookie inside the drink. I made the cookies yesterday, so as long as it doesn't rain, everything is coming together.

June 22, 2020

Day 102: Weekend was okay, though hot. Had a nice picnic, noticed Mark Sampson had brought all our cheese knives except the lost one, restarted argument about Mark losing the knife. Another (distanced) picnic participant pointed out that it could have been me who lost the knife, which caused me to begin listing other things Mark has lost or destroyed, as precedent for the knife probably also being his fault. Conversation was able to proceed to a better note, others eventually left, and I felt guilty for constantly harping on this issue.

> RR: It doesn't even matter — people don't need cheese knives.
>
> MS: I like cheese knives.
>
> RR: We could cut and spread cheese with butter knives, our lives would be the same.
>
> MS: I like the cheese knives! I didn't mean to lose it … if in fact I lost it! And we still have three …
>
> RR: Yes. I should dwell on the three cheese knives we do have.
>
> MS: Come on, fold up the blanket — it's time to go.
>
> RR: And yet the three cheese knives aren't making me happy. It's still a pandemic. I'm still a sad woman on a blanket.
>
> MS: …
>
> RR: This blanket is twenty-three years old.
>
> MS: It is?
>
> RR: Yes. It was my bedspread in first-year university. I never lose anything.
>
> MS: Well …
>
> RR: Pretty much. But having a twenty-three-year-old picnic blanket is not making me happy.

June 23, 2020

Day 103: Tomato plant tipped over; cat unplugged the router; got caught in rainstorm; mis-entered Excel formulae; caught mask elastic in earring and could not remove until home and rescued by husband; jackhammers; missed opportunity to be voice of reason in argument and now argument fully committed to being unreasonable; today would be parents' forty-eighth wedding anniversary if father were not dead.

But! I made a reasonably successful quiche, got some nice texts and emails from friends, and am probably overselling my ability to be the voice of reason in any argument, anyway. I also managed to accidentally lock myself out of some software that was upsetting me, so it's actually better I can't get back in, and I can't be the first person, nor the last, to become hopelessly enmeshed in my mask (would be great if anyone else has a story?). Umm, still super-worried about that tomato plant ... but the quiche was really good. Think I'll call my mom now.

June 24, 2020

Day 104: I found an anti-mask postcard in my elevator last night — like, professionally printed; someone went to that level of trouble. It had a list of ten reasons masks are bad, most of which were fully bananas, like somehow masks give you "high blood acidity," which is ... what? It had no sources and sounded like it was created by Russian bots to sow discord in Canadian society ... Maybe it was.

June 25, 2020

Day 105: The meditation app has gone berserk (not a sentence you see every day) — it and I agree that I started using it on June 11, but it keeps congratulating me on my "twenty-eight-day streak" of meditations, which does not conform to the space-time continuum.

That said, it's been pretty enjoyable and easy to use, although I don't know if I'm getting any calmer yet. Maybe it takes longer than fake-twenty-eight days.

• • •

Oohh, a Facebook memory of the problematic screening process at Canadian Blood Services just came up and reminded me that a couple months ago, it got me. When I donated (remember? I was so excited and happy that day!), their tests gave me a false positive for a blood-borne disease. The letter they sent me all but admitted that the test is pretty faulty and I probably didn't have the disease, but it was still scary and I had to run around town at the beginning of the pandemic and get retested.— surprise, I'm not sick. Whew.

So I called them and said I had been cleared and had paperwork to prove it, so they could put me back on the donor rolls for the future, and they said nope, I'm now banned unless the rules change. I'm like, "But it was your test that got it wrong, and you said yourself there's problems with the test, and I can prove I'm not sick and never was ..." and the blood lady was like, "Them's the breaks, kid." They said there was no amount of testing I could do to get back into the acceptable category at the moment — on paper, I'm tainted, even though everyone knows that of course my blood is fine. Maybe in the future, the rules will change ...

This is a really small thing, but I was just so upset. I like to do good things, I like to help, and there are so many things I'm not capable of, but donating blood is something I can do, and they threw it in the garbage and banned me. Obviously, queer people and immigrants have been treated like this by Canadian Blood Services for a long time and I've always been upset by that, but now I get it a little more viscerally.

June 26, 2020

Day 106: On time and its new meaninglessness: I have always worn a watch when I am out of the house. When I was a little kid, my parents weren't keen on buying me things, but I always had a cheap digital watch, which my father endeavoured to keep set to the right time. My father was absolutely maniacal about timepieces and their settings, and my mother always wears a watch to go out as well. In our family, a woman has a plain everyday watch and then a second, pretty watch that is really almost like a bracelet that tells time, for wearing with dress clothes when the plain watch won't do, because of course you can't go to a fancy party or a show without a watch. For my fifth birthday, I received such a watch, a little gold Cartier one, which I wore on special occasions for close to twenty-five years (you don't give a child a gold watch unless you know that is a *very careful* child), with several band changes. At that point, I switched to wearing my maternal grandmother's "good watch" and wore that for a number of years, including on my wedding day. (I suppose it seems weird that I felt I needed to wear a watch on my wedding day, but it actually seems weird to me that some people don't!) Gradually that very old watch stopped keeping even sort of approximately the right time. I'm sure it did well by my grandma, and by me for a long time, but it was often more than twenty minutes off at the end — hopeless.

Over the years, my everyday watches have been a variety of Timexes, Fitbits, whatever was on sale at Zellers. Once, when I had a skin irritation, I actually tried not wearing a watch for a bit — after all, phones tell time. However, when people take out their phones to check the time, many of them turn into rude monsters who ignore whoever it is they were just talking to — it turns out I am no exception. I bought another Timex, this time with some prize money from a literary award, which makes me happy. But for ages I didn't have a good watch, so just before the pandemic started, I told Mark I would like a new one for my birthday this year. He got me a really pretty one, although by that point I hadn't been wearing a watch at all for months — I'm always home, near a clock or my computer, and there's no one here to offend if I accidentally get distracted scrolling on my phone. This is the first year I haven't had a pale stripe in my tan on my left wrist.

I've had the new dressy watch for a month and not worn it anywhere, so yesterday when I went to Canadian Tire to get tomato stakes and potting soil, I wore it there. I don't think anyone was impressed, but I felt fancy, and it kept great time. I hope we are heading back to a world where time matters, sooner rather than later.

Summer Dip

June 28, 2020

Day 108: Toronto is in stage 2! This means that malls are opening! And restaurants with patios! Hair salons and barbershops! Drive-in cinemas (how were these ever a problem, Covid-wise?)! Aquariums! Zoos! Libraries, but only for a few limited things! A bunch of things that don't affect me, like splash pads and day camps! In celebration of stage 2, we went to a restaurant patio last night! The last time we dined out as a couple was March 7. I was hesitant to dive headlong into all the stage-2-ness, but Mark wanted to try and I sort of did, too, so we did. It was good! The restaurant had hand sanitizer at the gate and pretty much ordered us (warmly) to use it, and instead of menus had QR codes so we could read the menu on our phones without touching anything. The tables were well spaced apart, though I didn't think quite six feet. The food was great and the staff all wore masks and seemed cheerful. I felt very strange not wearing a mask myself but, of course, we were eating so we couldn't. Everyone eating seemed very cheerful. We were near the Village and it seemed most people were celebrating Pride. Everyone seemed very friendly.

I think many people will feel it's too soon for them to be out at restaurants and if that's your call, it's reasonable — I could yet backtrack and decide it's too soon for me, too! If you choose to be out, I think it's worth supporting businesses that are trying to make a go of it in a very hard time — I've seen some really nasty calls for small businesses to just give up and not reopen because of the risks involved. My compromise is spending money thoughtfully, and tipping a lot. Our charming, cheerful server did not sign up for a job with that level of risk and challenge when he was hired, and we tipped in recognition of that. As Mark put it, "You can't not be generous."

We probably won't dine out again anytime soon — I had a nice time, but it was so stressful.

June 29, 2020

Day 109: I rode the subway yesterday for the not-very-manyth time of the pandemic. If you, like me, used to ride the TTC most days and are now down to a couple times a month, FYI, there are posters advertising a new policy saying that masks will be required on TTC vehicles starting July 2. It could be I'm just really out of the loop but I didn't know anything about this before yesterday — I don't think the policy has been well advertised outside of TTC properties, which, as I say, I no longer frequent.

I'd say that, last night, about half the sparse number of travellers on the TTC were masked, which brings up another point: who among TTC staff is well paid enough to intercept every second passenger and argue with them about mask wear? [Edit from the future: no one.] Also, if someone is rushing to somewhere important and has no mask but would be willing to wear one, will the TTC provide it? [Occasionally.] Or will they actually be prevented from travelling? [No, never.] Because I see that going poorly. Mark saw a brutal reaction from someone who was being prevented from shoplifting this weekend, and everyone knows you can't shoplift (though I wish that had gone differently) — being prevented from doing something you thought was okay is likely to elicit a lot of strong reactions. There's also a footnote on the posters that you don't have to wear a mask if you have a breathing problem, but no info on how you prove that, or if proof is even required. [It doesn't matter. People just did whatever on the TTC the entire pandemic and the most staff could ever do was offer them a free mask.]

June 30, 2020

Day 110: I took a flattering photo of myself with Maybelline Matte Ink lipstick on yesterday and was pleased about being able to wear it with a mask with no smudges. And I haven't generally felt I looked cute in a while and have been so worried about masks and it all just felt like a big victory and culminated in me scrolling the Maybelline New York Instagram page to see if they've figured out that those lipsticks don't rub off on masks. They didn't seem to realize so I ... wrote Maybelline a DM letting them know, and urging them to share the good news so more people would wear masks. I even wrote them a little tagline they could use, which I will not be sharing here because it's very embarrassing.

This all happened over the course of a ten-minute work break yesterday afternoon, and then I didn't think much more about it. Yesterday was actually a pretty good day for pandemic me ... I thought ... and then seven hours later, Mark and I were un-winding at the end of the day, and I told him about it. It was only as I heard the words aloud that I realized, "Oh no, that's bananas." I asked Mark if he'd ever thought he would end up married to an adult woman who would be writing to one of the largest brands in the world, for whom she does not work, to offer them unsolicited marketing help. I started the message "Dear Maybelline." *Help!*

If you had told me I'd be in lockdown for 109 days, I would have known it would be bad but not bad in this exact way.

July 2, 2020

Day 112: Good lord, it's July — also, today is the last day of week 16. If you are keeping careful track, you'll note I was miscounting earlier in the week but forgive me, it's very hot and the count is very high now. We used the day off yesterday to have a picnic because what else is there to do, really? At least we tried a new park, for variety's sake — this one was filled with young families and kids, unlike our usual, which is more hipster-y. I ended up watching the kids and their parents like TV — I've really missed hanging out with small people over the past sixteen weeks! There were a lot of hijinks and a lot of parents trying hard despite clearly being over everything after a 112-day parenting marathon.

Highlights include:

- A little girl whose parents were trying to pick a good spot for a picnic, who said every area they considered was "a secret spot." She also said to another child that she had "super-fast legs for running." Her bangs were ruler-straight.
- Children trying to fly a kite with modest success, attempting to run around a tree and not knowing why they couldn't get any farther — when do children begin to understand how ... objects work?

- A British child saying, "Daddy." He was actually complaining about his bike, but it sounded way fancier to say, "Daddy," thirty times in a row with an English accent.

- When the little girl from the first bullet realized she was not going to have much fun at her picnic because her parents' other child was a newborn, the father called over some slightly older neighbourhood children he appeared to know slightly and asked if his girl could run around with them. They agreed and he instructed, "Don't take your eyes off her," and as they ran off, one kid appeared to take this extremely seriously, sprinting while darting his gaze back and forth between the path ahead and his new companion every second or two.

- The British family had *three* children under six and the littlest one, of perhaps two, broke free and got pretty far without anyone noticing. I panicked when he appeared determined to throw himself off a low retaining wall, and was about to recruit Mark to go scoop him up when a dog squabble broke out at the base of the wall and the little one wisely retreated. The second time he made for the wall, his father noticed and ran after him in a panic, so I think I was not inventing drama.

- Speaking of dogs, a small schnauzer attempted to join our party briefly and its owner called him away by saying, "They have important things to talk about." (We didn't.)

- Several families had this strange kind of bike with two wheels up front and a sort of bin in between the front wheels, into which they'd put picnic trappings but also small children. At first I thought the babies were simply loose in the bin, but eventually I saw there were actually straps to secure them in there.

- There were some hipsters in this park and they were talking about their young-people drama behind us more or less throughout our visit, but I did not care and forgot to eavesdrop — kids are where it's at.

July 3, 2020

Day 113: I really oscillate between trying to focus on the good I see in others and the good I can do myself and just being overwhelmed by how much isn't good right now. Even if things are largely okay for me (eh), it's hard to see others struggle. Yesterday a young woman turned to Mark in our elevator and just started weeping. He asked her if she wanted to talk and she did, so they got off on a floor and talked for a bit, and then he came home. It took me a long time to understand the story — I kept asking where she lived, what was her name, when would he see her again, what she needed him to do. I'm all about the action items! It turned out it was really just one of those moments when someone is falling apart and they just need someone to be kind to them. I'm so glad Mark was there and that he is kind — the right person to ask. But I worry about all the other people out there, crying in their own elevators (probably a metaphor) and will they find anyone to talk to? Take care out there, friends.

July 5, 2020

Day 115: Friends, I saw my mom! I started lockdown on March 13 and she was supposed to come over for dinner on March 14, so that was the first loss for me … One hundred and fifteen days later, after most of our interactions being on the phone or on Skype, and a few being me yelling up at her balcony and scaring passersby, my brother and I wore masks and sat with her outside her building and chatted for half an hour and it wasn't too scary … If it wasn't for us sitting weirdly far from each other, and the masks, and the looming sense of terror, and the lack of food or drink, it was sort of like something we would have done previously. Yay, Mom! If you know her, she's still about the same …

• • •

What we talked about at dinner tonight, pandemic + heat wave edition:

- The books we are both reading, and what the characters have gotten up to since last we checked in on our respective reading.
- So, it's still hot, I guess.
- The food we are eating, how it tastes, how it was made, other ways it could have been made, ways it could have been better, what we like about it, was turning on the oven worth it.
- My need for yoga mat cleaner, whether that is a lie the internet told me, my plan to make it myself, the trouble and expense of getting the ingredients, the trouble with getting the pre-made kind, the kind I finally found for a reasonable

price, the other things I bought to make up the free-shipping minimum, will those things be enjoyable.

• Hey, it's the seven-thirty cheer, it's pretty lacklustre, are people just hot or losing interest, this has been going on a long time, remember when we were so happy to hear it at first, also: WHOOOOOOOO!!!!

• Me apologizing for the yoga-mat-cleaner story, which was actually even longer than the above makes it out to be.

• Reminiscing about yesterday, when we had (distanced) dinner with other people.

July 7, 2020

Day 117: Tonight: I made scape pesto from our farmers' market box. As I was making it, I called my mom to arrange to drop off her stuff from the drugstore and offered her a little pesto — I thought it would be a fun treat since scapes are so hard to get. Except it didn't turn out that great. I was very sweaty when I turned up at my mom's and we tried to enjoy the rare pleasure of talking to each other but were both having trouble hearing and speaking in our masks and standing beside traffic. I was *much* sweatier when I got home, and excited to see Mark just turning on the air conditioner. I sat down to wait for this to happen … and a fuse blew, which has never happened in the nine years we've lived in this apartment. Mark tried to fix it for a while and I sank into sweaty despair — the Wi-Fi was out, all the rooms where a person could conceivably sleep had no power for fans … doom doom doom. Finally Mark called the after-hours super and I … took a bath. I'm not proud of this, but I was just so hot and I figured the super would take hours. He came about ten minutes later and showed Mark where the spare fuses were (inside the box! did anyone ever tell us that?). I had to hide in the bathroom since I hadn't even been clever enough to bring clothes in there with me. This evening was a real low point and we will be charged thirty-five dollars for it, but for now everything is okay and the blessed blankness of unconsciousness awaits …

July 8, 2020

Day 118: I've been ranting to friends a bit about masks but I'm planning to stop. I think people should wear them, I think those who protest are ridiculous and harmful, but I also think I have maybe gotten a wee bit obsessive about this one small measure against a sea of chaos. I've been really struggling with my vision of society as a strong fabric and myself as a bright stitch and perhaps I overidentified that struggle with the masks a little. I don't know that that's a bad idea, but it's not going to save the world exactly and I need to calm down …

July 11, 2020

Day 121: It is moderately cooler after last night's rain, to the point where I ate breakfast on the balcony and felt okay about it. After cleaning the apartment — and, like, I didn't really put my all into it or anything, since we are definitely not having company — I am drenched in sweat. Checked to see if the air-quality alert had lifted, as it is definitely bothering my lungs, and times of a respiratory virus are not times you want anything bothering your lungs. Now the advisory on the Enviro Can website is for tornadoes. Amazing. If you could promise me no one and nothing of value would get hurt, I would actually like to see a tornado someday, but since no one is in a position to make such promises, I guess if a tornado approaches, I will have to hide. Disappointing.

Alice has been making some cautious overtures toward the air conditioner. It's interesting to see her tiny brain grinding toward her own best interest, but she is getting there. Efforts to help are met with panic and fury; she's got to do it on her own. If you haven't had the privilege of meeting Alice, she is eight years old and weighs six pounds, largely eyes and whichever organ is responsible for purrs.

• • •

My in-laws redid our balcony last summer and that, along with my brother fixing our Wi-Fi in January, has probably been the biggest unknowing gift to our pandemic life. I contributed the plants: cherry tomatoes, pea sprouts, little basil, big basil, kale, arugula, other kind of cherry tomato, Roma tomato, raspberry.

July 12, 2020

The upstairs neighbours seem to have acquired a bass guitar that they don't know how to play and I'm sort of here for it. Go, ceiling friends, go. Your confidence is inspiring!

July 13, 2020

Day 123: It was too hot to walk to the public raspberry bush last week but I made it today! The berries maybe aren't as robust as they would've been without the heat wave, but they tasted good. Exactly half the bush had been picked clean by some thorough but fair-minded person. I ate a handful from the other half — plenty left if you are in a berry-picking mood.

July 15, 2020

After 125 days of lockdown, I went to my office! This is the longest I have ever been not there in the nearly thirteen years I've worked at the company (in the usual way of things, my personnel file had me celebrating my ten-year anniversary last Saturday). I was very excited and meant to take photos but in the end it was frazzling and stressful and I took none. Here are impressions instead:

- I was driving a borrowed car, and this was also my first time behind the wheel in a while and I expected to be super-anxious but was so happy to be back in Scarborough, travelling the familiar route, that I forgot to freak out!
- The LRT is coming along! When last I saw it, there were grooved tracks in the intersections (like streetcar tracks) but now there are raised tracks everywhere else (like GO tracks) and even little signals in places. It's still a construction zoo, but looks like … it could actually happen?
- The parking lot was largely empty but there were perhaps ten or twelve cars there, as the warehouse is still operating and some people have to come in for other stuff.
- I had to call from the parking lot and a facilities staffer came out to get me. We were both wearing masks. Then I went inside and there was a little cart set up with hand sanitizer — I had just

put some on, but I used more to set my colleague at ease — and nitrile gloves, plus a sign-in sheet. *Very official.*

- In my department, a couple people I know were there! It was so exciting to see them and we were yelling but then I realized I was taking up someone's time to escort me to my office, so I had to say goodbye.

- Everything looked the same, except the lights were off. Of course, everyone left thinking they'd be back pretty soon so nothing was boxed up or even tidied. It was like coming in real early on a Monday. There were some printouts on my desk that someone had probably left for me when I started lockdown slightly early owing to my TTC ridership.

- I couldn't get the lights on, and my actual purpose in the office was to get the big monitor off my desk (finally!) and it plugged in in three different spots, so it was all very challenging. There was some concern about me taking such an expensive item away, but no concern about crawling around on the floor yanking cords in the dark.

- While I was on the floor, I found my spare pair of office shoes. It was like winning the lottery, since my other shoes have taken the opportunity of the pandemic to disintegrate. To last the summer, I am down to a pair of flats from Zellers and a pair of sandals from Nine West, both stores that no longer exist, both pairs of shoes that shed parts of themselves every time I wear them. This find was a 50 percent increase in shoes for me! I shoved them into my bag.

- Other things I took from my office.(I would have taken everything if I hadn't been wasting someone else's time): prescription drugs, two plants that were in surprisingly good shape (our VP has been watering them occasionally), a gift my niece wanted in February and now will likely be mystified by.

- R from facilities got the lights on and I was finally able to disconnect the monitor from the tangle of other wires. It would not fit into the bag I had brought for it and I couldn't carry it with everything else, so R had to carry it — I felt like a gender stereotype. Also, my office looked like it had been robbed by someone having a stroke and I longed to clean it up but we had to go.

- We lugged everything downstairs and I signed back out, then R put the monitor in my car and I hauled over the plants. Goodbye, office — I don't know when I'll see you again!

- I had meant to go berry picking at a bush I know about near the office, but someone had scheduled a meeting! So, no berries. I did stop and get drive-thru, because I drive so seldom and it's such a treat. It took a while but I got a ninety-nine-cent Frosty, which is in itself an icon of Scarborough summer to me, along with a relatively healthy salad from Wendy's.

- It took me two trips to get everything upstairs in the elevator. On the second trip, I had the plants and I had to very carefully press the button for my floor with my elbow. The guy in the elevator said, "Do you want me to do it for you? Oh, you did it!"

I shrugged modestly and said, "I've been working on my moves."

- Mark is at work today and now we've had a day where we both went to work and when he gets home, we can talk about it — wheeeee!

July 18, 2020

Day 128: As perhaps you've noticed, these posts concentrate mainly on things that I find fun or interesting or challenging to write about, so let's concentrate on the negative for a moment. On Thursday evening at about the nadir of my sorrow, it was raining and we had pretty much given up finding a socially distanced restaurant patio that wasn't soggy and actually nice and settled for diner burgers, and I was pretty miffed about being dealt this hand. At this particular place, you ordered and then sat to wait for things to be brought. A young server came with my drink. I looked up, smiled, and said thank you, as I was raised to do, and she grunted and stomped off.

This was exciting! The surly teenaged service staff is a trope you see often in movies and TV, but you rarely encounter in real life — most teens are actually quite polite to strangers who might tip them, in my experience. Also, in movies and TV and books, you often see a character moving through the world encountering only other characters in the exact same mood that she is in, like pathetic fallacy but with people, which is dumb in writing but very pleasant in real life; I felt briefly in tune with the universe in my bad mood. It was very satisfying. It was also satisfying to see someone resolutely not try at something, since I am always so worried about everything and it's exhausting.

When she returned with the food, instead of setting it on the table, she simply loosened her grip and let it fall! Amazing — I wished I could have filmed it (it was burgers wrapped in paper, so they weren't harmed — it was just such a jerk move, though).

I am not going to start doing the my-life equivalent of dumping burgers on people's tables, but this surly teen was fun to watch in a grim sort of way, and reminded me that being kind is a choice, so if I do it, I choose it. Sometimes I forget that.

July 19, 2020

Day 129: Did you at some point agree to "forsake all others," not realizing that you'd encounter a pandemic with this degree of forsakenness? Have you spoken mainly to your spouse or partner for 129 straight days? Would you like some tips to liven things up? Well, this is not really going to help, but here you go:

- Play the occasional game of Scrabble until the one of you who never wins wins, then never play again.
- Talk about investigating whether the Wii still works so you can play wakeboarding for the first time since 2017, but don't actually do it.
- Talk about which of your friends and family you'd like to emulate in life while sitting on the couch and eating chips.
- Fight about a picture being askew.
- Fight about which rooms plants go in.
- Fight about which of you has too many shoes.
- Read the same book at the same time so you'll have something to talk about, discover neither of you really likes the book, and have all conversations degenerate into kvetching. Have this happen twice, then give up.

- Ask each other a lot of concerned questions each time anyone coughs, even if it's clearly because of dust.
- Step up your pet-grooming routines to the point that pets are enraged.
- Brainstorm meal plans despite the fact that one of you doesn't care, so that it becomes a meal plan monologue.
- Brainstorm rich interior lives for pets.
- Brainstorm rich interior lives for neighbours.
- Brainstorm rich interior lives for actual rich people as you stroll around their neighbourhoods day after day, peering into their yards, garages, and windows.
- Brainstorm what you would do yourselves if you became rich. Make plans for what would go behind each of those many windows. You can't be too prepared for this sort of thing.
- Embrace and then immediately comment on how sweaty the other person is.
- Discuss the latest literary explosions on Twitter (note: ideally one would discuss such things only with loved ones, and not ever on actual Twitter).
- Fight about kinds of tofu, and whether they exist.
- Fight about kinds of laundry detergent.
- Fight about whether one can buy a nice gift at Staples.
- Spend some time in separate rooms.
- Agree that you are lucky to have found each other, because who else would put up with all this?

July 21, 2020

Day 131: I dreamed last night that I had a bad cough but I went in to work anyway. It was like that dream where you forget you're taking the course until it's time for the exam — I forgot there was a pandemic until I had been at work almost the whole day and then all of a sudden, I drew up short in horror and shame, realizing I wasn't supposed to be there, trying to remember who I'd seen, where I'd been. No one had said anything about me coughing, but I figured they were just being polite and were privately furious and/or terrified. In the dream, it did not occur to me to wonder what I was actually sick with; it was purely a social failure on my part.

I do not have a cough and I cannot go to work. I did not sleep well last night.

July 23, 2020

Day 133: OMG, after months of nowhere to be, I had a dentist appointment on Monday and was pretty stoked. Yesterday they called to confirm and also asked if I happened to be free to fill in a cancellation at 4:00 p.m. ... Friday? I thought Friday. I said sure, as I'm off Friday afternoon. They just called to see where I was, as apparently it was for today. I don't think I've ever missed a dentist appointment in my life. They were sort of decent about it, but I feel like a jerk. I also wonder if they are going to send me some sort of no-show bill — isn't there often some kind of penalty? *I don't know these things because I always show up for everything!* Pandemic, you are ruining me!

Also, now my dentist appointment is on Tuesday and I'm going to be worried about it until then.

• • •

In order to keep myself organized, I tried putting all our modest stage 2 plans (and stage 3 starting July 31 — playgrounds and libraries, baby!) into Google Calendar, which I haven't opened in a good long time and, oh, it was very sad to see all our old plans, long since abandoned, still living on, so foolish and naive, in Google Calendar.

• • •

Some brilliant history teacher I had back in the day actually taught a lesson on the concept of the scapegoat, the people in society whom those with *actual* power urge everyone to blame when things go wrong.

July 26, 2020

Day 136: According to the meme going around where your quarantine name (which is for what, exactly?) is the last thing you ate plus your high school team, mine is Chip Royals, which is great.

Started rereading *The Bell Jar* on a whim. It's about a weird, claustrophobic summer in the city (at least the first part is) and I'm enjoying that and also squirming. Also haven't read this book in a long time and I find when I do that, I read over the shoulder of my younger self, the reactions I had then mingling with how I actually feel now, you know what I mean? I read this book first when I was fourteen. That was an age when I was famous for reading funny books dead seriously, but Plath made me laugh even then. I'm excited for how I'll react this time, and to re-encounter young RR. I'm also reading poetry for the first time since the beginning of the pandemic, so things are looking up.

Walking in St. James' Cemetery continues to be lovely and calm, though walking anywhere is of course very hot. Cats, obviously, are melted and hiding.

July 27, 2020

Day 137: I was admiring the complicated tie Mark Sampson did on the back of my sundress to keep it from either strangling me or falling off and thinking about how, when I was young and living alone, I used to occasionally go into work with the back of my dress half-zipped under my cardigan or with my necklace in my pocket and get one of my colleagues to help me before the day began. I've always thought colleagues could be friends, though I've learned to modulate that over the years to accommodate what others think (colleagues should think well of each other but not talk too much; colleagues should talk only when necessary; colleagues should never, ever help each other get dressed). I suppose I should regret expecting my first office to be pretty much the same as my first-year university residence but ... I don't — or not enough, anyway. I have so many great friends from both periods of my life, and my work — which I'm happy to do and believe I contribute to meaningfully — is a pretty sad main dish all by itself without the delightful sauce and garnish of other people. That is one thing the pandemic lockdown has really underlined for me — though I already pretty much knew. Miss you, work friends, past and present.

July 28, 2020

Day 138: I made it to the dentist — it was fine but very tense. I feel like the genuine friendliness that a lot of transactions — shopping, restaurants, dentist appointments — used to be edged with has given way to a sort of "I know you're a nice person but I'm seriously worried about my health and also my livelihood, so I'm going to smile and say one pleasantry, and that's just the best I can do right now." I get it — it's sad, but I do get it. I so look forward to these interactions but they end up being so strained and I feel like the kindest thing I can do is just not talk to people much.

Also! Someone fired a gun at my grandfather's condo complex in Florida. Important information is that my grandfather has been dead since the 1980s, but my family still owns his condo and rents it out when we can, which is notably not in July in Florida during a pandemic. So no one we know was there and I believe no one was hurt, but still — this is the closest I've ever been to an active shooter situation, which isn't very close, but still. But still. Also, active shooter situation = a person with a gun who is firing it. Interesting language choices, modern times.

Also, our building is doing a giveaway for "fun summer meal boxes"! They call them "summer" boxes as if there have been other seasonal boxes, but this has never happened before. I'm super-confused about what is happening here — is this a treat or is it charity? If it is a treat, I want it — treats are not a thing our building is known to provide very often (though I'd rather have them fix the sink), and also maybe it's a meal so I won't have to cook. On the other hand, if it's charity, I shouldn't take it, since there are people here who genuinely need it and we don't. Charity is actually not something this building is known to provide, either — their official stand on pandemic evictions was "maybe not today, maybe not tomorrow, but soon," so I just have no idea what is going on ... I'm going to sneak down to the box distribution and see if I can cagily assess without committing to taking one ...

Wow, there is a lot going on today! I'm not sure how to feel about this level of mayhem.

• • •

So, update on the box: I couldn't figure out what it was before I got it, as they were branded (the property company) and sealed cardboard boxes and you had to go to a special room to get them, which was crowded, so no one was lingering to open them. I decided to take my chances and take one — special preprinted boxes, so fancy! You had to register with your unit number, one per unit. Okay!

It was maybe seven dollars' worth of basic grocery items? Like, two packages of dried pasta and three different kinds of tomato sauce. So, charity and not a treat, but also just very bizarre to give this to everyone in this complex — literally several thousand people. I am not scoffing at the food — it's perfectly nice stuff and I could make a few decent meals with it — but it is bizarre to give it to everyone when many of us are fine buying our own groceries and many of us are really not. Why not take the sizable investment in getting and distributing food to many people who do not need it and use it to fund rent relief to those who truly *do* need it? I mean …

Or, no, you're too committed to capitalism to do that — fine, take the cost of the thousands of branded boxes, which I know from work is not nothing, and just buy everyone a popsicle on a hot day — a fun, festive memory of how the property management company was nice that one time. Which a ninety-nine-cent bag of penne just does not accomplish.

I do not understand this. I feel bad for having taken the food and will give some money to Daily Bread to make up for it (and then some — I won't just give them seven dollars). This was clearly some sort of (admittedly misguided) charitable endeavour that I mistook for a fun snack and now must redirect funds back into the charitable arena. But also, can anyone explain to me WTF?

July 29, 2020

Day 139: Last night we had a distanced park date with friends and while we just brought a cooler of ice cream sandwiches and planned to sit on the ground, our much classier friends brought a proper picnic blanket, wine and glasses, and, best of all, a bounty of interesting conversation that we had not already encountered nine times this week. It was so great and we ogled so many dogs. While we were picnicking, our neighbour — one of the few neighbours who actually will talk to us on purpose and not just when cornered in the elevator — came by and chatted for a while, a rare instance of feeling like we live in a community again. I was very happy.

July 30, 2020

Day 140: Twenty weeks, fellow babies. I've started to adjust to lockdown life, but maybe not in a good way. Yesterday I walked to a little takeout place I like to buy lunch from and it had gone out of business; en route to my backup lunch place, I saw that another place I like had closed as well. I found out the person shooting the gun at my grandfather's place was alone in his apartment, shooting at no one, having a mental-health collapse (presumably, most people who shoot at anyone are having some form of mental-health difficulties, but this seems clearer cut) and you just hear about random, stupid awfulness here and there because people are so sad and on edge and turn on each other. Times are tough, my friends. I hope you are all doing okay.

We ate some of our pasta and sauce from the box of weirdness last night and it was pretty good. Also, my giant tomato plant tipped over and as I was righting it in semi-hysterics, I noticed a red tomato I hadn't seen, down near the bottom. My mom said the first red tomato always comes by August 1, and I guess some things don't change — mainly my mom being right about stuff. The tomato was the size of a gumball but Mark and I split it and it was good.

August 2, 2020

Day 143: I saw a fight last night. A guy was yelling across the street at another guy, which I am somewhat used to, but then he crossed over so they were face to face and things became more heated. The argument didn't make much sense, which I am also used to — sample dialogue includes "I'm not a mean person, I just want to smoke cigarettes" and "Well, you're always taking my stuff." In fact, that was most of it, repeated over and over, very loud. But they were agitated, and then the "you're always taking my stuff" person punched the "not a mean person" person. I haven't seen a ton of punches in my life, but even from kitty-corner across the street, I could tell this was not a jim-dandy. The recipient sort of flopped back a few paces and then staggered right back and kept yelling.

We were waiting for a bus and kind of trapped, which was definitely not where I wanted to be on a Covid night — I've been trying to avoid buses and the TTC in general but there were a few transit failures and I didn't expect it to be busy at nearly midnight, as indeed it wasn't, but the seven-minute wait was something else. I wasn't scared exactly, even when I dropped my umbrella with a crash and everyone looked over at the sound. But then the two men started wandering back and forth in traffic, yelling at each other, while a woman standing on the sidewalk yelled at them both to stop. Then a worker from the fast-food restaurant behind the bus stop also came out and began yelling at them to stop, or at least get out of the road. Then, for no reason, he came over to the bus stop and told us they had been at this for an hour. I was very surprised no one was dead, as multiple cars had to screech to a stop to avoid harming them. The fast-food guy was sad the cops hadn't come yet, and then they did (keep in mind, all this in seven minutes!).

The fighters seemed very committed to (a) continuing the fight and (b) walking in front of moving vehicles. At one point, Not a Mean Person started to storm away, walked maybe twenty paces, spun around, launched himself right back into traffic to cross toward his nemesis and screamed, "I'm not a mean person, I just want to smoke cigarettes!" This caused a car to jerk to a stop and honk at him, and the other guy to hop off the sidewalk where he'd been talking to the woman, to rebut, and the fast-food guy led the cops down to where they were. I heard one of the officers demanding, "I don't know what you want us to do." I didn't hear the answer, but I hoped the cops would at least prevent anyone from being seriously injured that night. I mean, any number of pedestrian laws were being broken right then and surely the cops could urge compliance with those laws …? Just until whatever was causing the feeling of invincibility faded?

The bus came. There was someone flailing and kicking his legs all the way to our stop, and a woman screaming in the distance about someone being a bastard as we walked home. I will think twice about being out so late or tangling with TTC again this Covid summer, although honestly parts of this are just things you see in the city, because life is hard and weird no matter what. But I think this is a tougher summer than any I've seen previously.

August 3, 2020

Day 144: We went to the beach today and it was great — I just waded a little but I think next time I'll wear a swimsuit and consider going in, it was so nice. We saw Canada geese, swans, and even a loon. I also felt way less panicky about people walking too close to me than the last time we were there, though some of that remains. We walked up to the place in the park where we got engaged and then had brunch on the patio at the restaurant where we had our first date (the beach has big Sampsenblum energy) and it all felt really, really normal — something we would have done on a holiday Monday any summer. I did have the pleasure of watching Mark encounter a foot-operated hand-sanitizer dispenser for the first time, which wouldn't have happened another year, but that was a net gain.

August 5, 2020

Day 146: Have I mentioned I live above a roti shop? Like, way, way above — I'm in a high-rise and the shop is on the ground floor. It is relatively new and then had to close down for the first few months of the pandemic, so it's been only recently that I realized they make their curries first thing every morning, I guess to have them ready for the lunch rush. The smell rises all the way up here, which I didn't know when I was working far away every day, and it is an olfactory *gift*.

For years, there was almost nothing to eat in this neighbourhood because everything was scaffolded off for future construction projects or actually under construction. When we saw that the roti shop was coming, we were so excited and we went as soon as it opened, and then ... it wasn't good. Tragedy. Then a month or so later, it smelled so amazing, and we wondered, what if it was just opening bumps, and tried again, and it was very good — hooray! It's a legit sort of roti shop where I can't order any kind of spice at all and even the spice-free version leaves me a bit sweaty — best! The vegetarian special has pumpkin, chana, spinach, and eggplant, and it's all I ever order, but they have hard-to-find things like goat and oxtail on the menu, too, as well as chicken, etc. If you are in our neighbourhood and hungry (and not eating here for some reason), highly recommended.

This post brought to you by the smell through my window right now.

August 6, 2020

Day 147 started at 4:30 a.m. as they all do, with Mark's stupid alarm clock. I was freezing, which was at least novel, because the blanket fell on the floor in the night, so Mark put the blanket back on the bed and left, and I went back to sleep. I was reawakened about half an hour later by a very young woman excoriating her boyfriend, Alex, for "getting with whores," which she knew about from the scratches on his ass. This was obviously happening outside and down many stories, but it felt closer. It was an even more circular argument than the "I'm not a mean person, I just want to smoke cigarettes" one on the weekend — both parties kept saying the same things over and over, the level of fury did not abate, and no one seemed interested in walking away. It makes me doubt the value of verbal argument. It was also so loud and so early. I have no idea where they were. There used to be a large, open courtyard below my window, where you could see many interesting things (two highlights from those years are a group of LARPers having a sword fight and some teenagers setting something on fire, having it get out of control, and running away! I was worried about the second one, as I watched from my office, but security guards put it out). In more recent years, the courtyard has been walled off, so either they climbed a wall or they were just on the street outside it, screaming their intimacies.

I guess they could also have been on a nearby balcony, but the echo didn't sound right for that.

Anyway, I guess they eventually stopped or went elsewhere and I fell back asleep and dreamed I found a new climate activist group to volunteer with. In the dream, an older guy was having an affair with one of the younger volunteers and it was all a bit sketchy — he wouldn't even tell her where he lived, which was somehow important for her to know. Then it was revealed that he was from my hometown. I offered to help her figure it out, since the town is so small and I "know practically everyone," a bold claim that hasn't been true in years, Dream Rebecca. Then Mark chose to watch a noisy pre-dawn YouTube video and woke me up *again*, so I had to get up and put a stop to that.

I finally got a tiny bit more sleep before my clock radio woke me up at the actual appointed time of six thirty with, for some reason, the Twisted Sister classic "We're Not Gonna Take It" sung in French.

Today has already been going on for a thousand years and I'm so tired and it is 9:22 a.m.

August 8, 2020

Day 149: Yesterday Mark Sampson forgot to mute himself during a work meeting before soothing an irate cat by singing a little song.

Yesterday part two we went for dinner on a patio and were seated near some people who worked as some kind of staffers in the Ontario premier's office. I know this because they were also the loudest people on earth — we were properly socially distanced, but if someone is eight feet away and you are screaming like an airshow announcer, they will hear you say where you work. They will also hear you call the CBC "The Moscow Times" and describe someone you met as "so Jewish-looking." I admit to having a grudge against Ford and his team for their lack of care for the lives of ordinary Ontarians, most lately with regard to education, but there are plenty of other examples. Still, they didn't have to so thoroughly live up to my worst imaginings.

Today: I just heard a 1-800-GOT-JUNK ad on the radio that quoted T.S. Eliot, so I just don't know what's going on anymore.

August 9, 2020

Day 150: Observations from SJT this weekend:

- The person in front of us at the grocery store was wearing: black plastic shower slides, black basketball shorts, what appeared to be a loose-fitting black Lycra tee until they turned around and the back was completely sheer with nothing underneath, and a black terry cloth headband with little Mickey Mouse ears. This could have either been a laundry-day accident — because no makeup and hair in a messy pony — or the result of a lot of careful planning, because this person looked completely fantastic. Really made my trip to FreshCo a lot less grim.
- There sure are a lot more people riding their bikes on the sidewalk in SJT during this pandemic and it is very annoying. I won't say anything to them, but I also won't make it easier for them to do this. Sometimes they *ring their bell* to indicate that I am in their way, hoping that, perhaps, I will step into the street or bike lane so they can pedal along the sidewalk? I would love to know the thought process there, but I suppose I'm never going to.

- Best for last: *Huge news!* There is a sign outside the SJT community centre that there is a swimming pool to be built in "winter 2019–2020" and a fenced-off pile of dirt, which hasn't moved in a year. SJT construction does not move fast and is full of lies, so I wasn't surprised by this, but this is the first time in a long time that we stand to benefit from the construction, so whatever it takes. Witness the time the No Frills got knocked down and for three years there was no grocery store in the neighbourhood at all, and then they built a new No Frills farther away, and then the FreshCo came two more years after that in the spot where the old No Frills was. And that's the *best* construction story I have to tell. *Until now!* I was walking past a building adjacent to the community centre that I thought was part of a townhouse development and I peeked in a window and, friends, *the pool is in there.* It's done — they snuck in a pool without me noticing. You all need to take back all the nice things you said about my powers of observation because I missed what appears to be a very large and nice public swimming pool two minutes from my home. It's an indoor pool, so I guess it got finished during the pandemic and was unable to open but it's all filled with water and ready to go — it even has lane ropes. *And it's gorgeous.* They finished it on schedule and it was just the global health emergency that wouldn't let us swim. Friends, I am just *blown away.* Someday, when the world gets a little better and it feels safe, you can come over to my place for lunch and a *swim.* Whoa.

August 11, 2020

Remember day 6 of lockdown, which was my first-date-iversary with Mark Sampson and I said something fun and glib about how I love spending time with him but could use a break? And now it's day 152 and here we are, on our eight-year wedding anniversary and, wow, 146-days-ago RR had *no idea*. We joke that we have really sped up the no-boundaries process of marriage by spending so many hours per day together (all of them. We spend all the hours in the day together unless someone goes for a walk or a distanced visit, we are always together, OMG) but thank goodness, there are still things left to learn.

I know the anniversary date is a time to celebrate the marriage and all the joy it has brought to my life — *so much* — but also, this year especially, I feel like celebrating *the wedding*. We had exactly the wedding we wanted, in a converted train station run by Laborers' International and the ceremony conducted by a poet friend with the legal bits taken care of by a rando from the internet. We had exactly the right music and food, and looking through the pictures, I am again and always so touched that so many people we love came from near and far to celebrate with us — I'll always be grateful. Although in the eight years since, I've made and deepened so many more friendships and I wish so many other people could teleport back in time to be there, too, and that's why we'll have to do it all over again someday, and honestly, I think we will. If the pandemic has taught me anything, it has taught me to never say no to doing something awesome, because what if tomorrow there are no awesome things to do?

There is only one other person who would have wanted exactly that wedding with me, from the pen favours to the book cake topper to the flower girl who was actually the boss of everything. Thank you, Mark, for proposing, and marrying me, and having that great wedding with me, and not having even one puff of a cigar with your friends so I could still kiss you at the end of the night. I always want to kiss you.

August 13, 2020

Day 154: So my household is trying to do limited necessary excursions so we can also do limited fun excursions. Like, we work from home and do home or outdoor exercise and then we occasionally eat on a patio or see friends in a park. Seems like a good balance of risks. But I feel we are being thwarted. I took my winter coat to the dry cleaner, which seemed like a low-contact activity but I've been back twice now and things keep going wrong and I still don't have the coat — and I keep having to hang out at the dry cleaner's while this gets discussed. Mark went to the dentist, which seemed like a reasonable risk, and came home — with his fly inexplicably open, which seems like a needless risk on the subway — with two follow-up appointments, one with the dentist for a cracked tooth and one with an actual surgeon for biting his lip. I do not like this. I just want my winter coat back in the middle of a heat wave and for Mark to do up his pants and suffer in silence with whatever is wrong with his mouth and then later we will get to go do something fun. I mean, that's not actually what I want. You know what I mean.

August 16, 2020

Day 157: We have a portable air conditioner in the bedroom, which, when we first got it, worked great but leaked all the time. We couldn't get it to stop so I pulled out the leaking plug, measured the nozzle, and bought a length of tubing to drain it into the mop bucket. It worked great and was probably my handiest contribution to the household, with the only downside being that you can't mop and run the air conditioner at the same time. We figured this would be fine as we run it only while we sleep, on very hot nights.

I think you know where this is going.

Mark Sampson got up in the pre-dawn to feed the cats because he is a nicer person than me, and then woke me up by rubbing my foot, which felt pleasant until I wondered what he was doing at the foot of the bed on my side — turning off the A/C and taking the mop bucket because, of course, the milk had exploded in the fridge in the night, leaked out the bottom, and was now all over the kitchen floor. I offered sleepily to help but he said it was okay and left.

I waited about ten minutes but then felt too guilty and went to investigate. It turns out Mark's exploded-milk protocol is a lot like his broken-glass protocol but with a mop instead of the vacuum cleaner: turn on every light, put on your shoes, pull the appliances out from the walls, mop the floor, mop behind everything. Then we started taking apart the fridge shelves and washing the milk off those except (a) I was very sleepy and (b) the floor was wet and I kept slipping, so I was pretty quickly sent back to bed. Mark was gone much longer. He was very determined that the kitchen not wind up smelling like sour milk when the day got hot, and to his credit, it does not.

I'm not sure if the lesson we need to learn here is that we need a second bucket or that inanimate objects will betray you every chance they get. Maybe both. Definitely that Virgos are thorough.

August 17, 2020

Day 158: I have noticed people using the pandemic as an opportunity to talk about how great us older people had it with our unelectronic, unscheduled childhoods and how now kids are finally getting to enjoy what we enjoyed — outdoor time, imaginative play, no time constraints!

Hello, I was a country kid who did not live within walking distance of anyone my family was friends with besides (sometimes) a couple horses. I lived across the street from a fallow field and in front of a feed-corn field and our own side lot was planted with rye in which, when it grew tall, my brother and I could lie down and hide. My dad was a prof who was home all summer and my mom did not work outside the home and we did not have any other family in Canada. Sometimes in the summer I would be driven to see a friend but there were also entire summers where I was not. It was dangerous to ride bikes on our road and there weren't side-walks. Sometimes, this pandemic lockdown feels very familiar to me.

What did we do? Well, we played in the yard: we ran around, we had a swing set and a sandbox and a little wading pool. We had a vegetable garden and were put to work a lot weeding and watering, we raked grass clippings and picked raspberries, we rode our bikes the tiny bit we were permitted. Depending on how old I was, I read through various library books or books I was given for my birthday or my parents' books or some combination. We played a few board games and a lot of chess and, yes, imaginative play together and alone — I had a dollhouse in the basement that I obsessed over. Also Ping-Pong.

But also we had a wood-panelled Atari and, later, two different Nintendos that were very important to me — all versions of *Mario Bros.* were important to me. Hours at a time, every day. Also, TV! I liked the courtroom dramas the best: not the real-life ones like *People's Court* — those people were too messy — but the scripted, orderly ones like *Divorce Court* and *Superior Court*. I also liked *Price Is Right* but, come on, everyone liked *Price Is Right*. And it was a whole hour long, every day at eleven — killed so much time. Then there were the weird afternoon shows — I never got into soaps, so that made the pickings slim, but there were sometimes sitcoms in the afternoon; strange, unpopular sitcoms like *Platypus Man* and *Pig Sty*. You could figure something out. I didn't like *M*A*S*H* for a long time but finally I started liking it and that opened up a world of reruns. And then by 4:00 p.m., the better, normal syndicated reruns would come on, like *Facts of Life* and *Night Court*. We didn't seem to ever get *Charles in Charge* at home but sometimes we'd take a trip to somewhere that show was on.

I have a lot of really sweet stories from my childhood, and we did tons of cool things, but if you got my family on any given day in the summer in the 1980s, it was likely a screen-time jamboree. The good old days weren't better, in my opinion — I mean, there wasn't a pandemic back then, so I guess that *was* better — but otherwise, different channel, same show. Nostalgia takes me only so far (in other words, I remember where all the best raspberry bushes were, but I also remember what channels ran the shows I liked).

August 18, 2020

Day 159: Tough day but I finally went outside at the end of it, both to go for a walk and to pick up cat treats after a small kitty revolution. When I came home, I saw the one neighbour who has ever paid us a social call — actually to visit the cats, but I'll take it — at the end of the hallway, with a brand-new cat of her own. I was so happy for her and really wanted to meet the cat, who was scared of me … but I had a bag of cat treats with me and won her right over via bribery, and the three of us had a lovely visit. One of the nicest chats ever in my socially challenged hall!

August 21, 2020

I got into the elevator to find a man huddled facing the wall with a dog in his arms. I didn't ask any questions and we proceeded downward. At another floor, a woman with a dog in a more normal position — on a leash on the floor — attempted to board, but the guy looked over his shoulder, indicated his little dog, and shook his head pleadingly. The woman and dog backed away.

> RR (trying to look over at the dog-in-arms): Is it a
> puppy?
> Guy: No, but it's a rescue. He's got issues.
> RR: Fair enough — we all do.
> Guy: Yeah, well, his predominate.

August 30, 2020

Day 171: So I spent days 165–170 of the pandemic on vacation up north. It was very nice, the area was very pretty, lots of nature, a great change from Toronto, *we saw a bear* (also ducks, a groundhog, a loon, chipmunks, and squirrels that didn't look murderous and thus very different from Toronto squirrels), we had some really nice patio meals, and everyone was friendly (by everyone, I mean people who sold us things as, of course, no socializing ☹).

The problem is that the nice parts are quick to tell and the not-so-nice bits are funnier and take a few paragraphs. Please don't take the word distribution here to indicate I had a miserable time — it was fine, but really we wanted to go to PEI and just not have a pandemic and this was the vacation we could have, you know? We just really needed a break and figured as long as the weather was nice, we'd just sit on the beach and read and swim a bit — our sights were not set too high — but the weather was not that nice for several days. Because pandemic, I didn't feel comfortable lingering in indoor cafés and our hotel was *amazing* but hard to spend tons of time in during the day, both because that's sad and there was construction going on (*of course there was*). It was road construction so I couldn't even complain to the hotel people (at press time, I remain in command of myself and have not complained to anyone besides Mark).

So we went hiking, which I always forget is not just going for a walk with more trees but actually more like climbing at times. I did not fare well. Mark turns out to be great at hiking and extremely agile at scrambling among the rocks and tree roots, which may come as a surprise to people like me, who have seen him trip over nothing many times — I guess sidewalks are just insufficient challenge? He would have had a great time if he didn't have to turn around and go back every five minutes to prevent me from falling onto a rock, face first. I was happy at the end only in that I did not die and because I could stop hiking — then we saw the bear, which was exciting.

Unfortunately, the next day, it rained and we decided we would mini-putt in the rain because it was all we could think of and we'd waited all summer for this vacation so we were going to have some sort of fun, but the mini-putt had other ideas and closed, because perhaps other people are not as driven to hit balls into comic figurines as we are. So we sat in the parking lot outside the closed mini-putt about which we were never that excited in the first place but were now in despair because we could not access it, and googled "things to do near where I am" and found a waterfall that was apparently close to the highway and had a staircase to the top. Reader, the waterfall *did not* have a staircase, so it was hiking again. I climbed as far as I could until I could see death behind every tree branch (this was not very far) and then Mark climbed the rest of the way on his own and I stood at the edge of the trail, reading, and politely and with great shame letting people go past as needed. Mark climbed to the top and then came directly back down to tell me about it. By the time he returned, I had figured out that no one else had come back down and that those people were probably not *all* dying in the falls but making a circular trek and coming down another way and what if that way down was easier? So we went back out to the highway and crossed a culvert over the egress of the falls and went back up the other way and it *was* easier and with Mark's help and patience, I was able to see the top of the falls and it was quite pretty despite the spitting rain but also jeez louise, you know? Then we went and had takeout pizza in the room because we'd both had quite enough of everything.

Thank goodness Friday, our last full day, was perfect, insofar as our low-expectations original plan was met — beach, reading, even a fun conversation with some ducks!

It takes quite a bit of energy to do anything in a pandemic, even have fun.

September 4, 2020

Day 176: It's been a while since we had one of these ...

(Eating lunch on the balcony.)

RR: Do you think Dollarama will still have cat Halloween costumes this year?

MS: I don't know.

RR: Because I'd really like to get them some new ones.

MS: Okay.

RR: The old ones are great, too, but I'm just thinking about —

MS: Hey, you never told me if you're interested in watching the new season of *The Mandalorian*.

RR: *Is that your answer?*

MS: What?

RR: You think Evan should be Baby Yoda for Halloween?

MS: Well, no, but it might be —

RR: *This is the best idea you've ever had!*

MS: Really?

RR: We'd have to get him, what is it, like a burlap bathrobe and then ... could we just spray-paint him green?

MS: No. I've written six books, you know.

RR: ... Your best idea in the cat Halloween costume arena.

MS: Better. (Accidentally flips chopstick in the air and it lands on balcony floor.) Ten-second rule!

RR: Don't do it! It's filthy out here! Eat with your hands!

MS: I thought you'd never ask!

September 8, 2020

RR (sprinting down the hall): Don't turn on the shower, don't turn on the shower!

MS (turns around with interest, then disappointed when presented with jar to open): This could be an Andy Warhol painting.

RR (now with open jar): Thank you!

MS: Or a follow-up to that Alex Colville painting, the one with the fridge? *Naked Man Opens Jar of Spaghetti Sauce for Fully Clothed Wife.*

RR: Uh-huh. (Departing with jar.)
MS (getting into shower): That would be the title.

September 10, 2020

Day 182: I wrote most of a thoughtful post and the computer ate it — my work computer is quite broken right now, and Facebook is really the least of what is going wrong there, but I may not be up to more thoughtfulness. I would settle for getting my work done, which is not really happening. A hero would keep working this evening, struggling at a third of her usual pace for extra hours to make up for the computer's failings, but I am not that hero. I am on my personal computer, writing, sort of. The cat just leaped at his arch-nemesis, the peephole in the front door, and then fell into the bag of recycling waiting to be taken out, and this all feels like a metaphor, sort of.

When I went for a massage last night, the RMT was really startled by how tense I was, which I suppose is an accomplishment of sorts because she must see a lot. She wondered if I could come back next week, which I'm sure is a little bit salesmanship but also — she was concerned. I wouldn't mind going back next week, if the insurance works out. We'll see.

Mainly I would just like to finish this novel I have been trying to write for four years. Earlier in the process, I used to imagine what it would be like to publish it — the cover, what readers would think, reviews. Now I just imagine finishing a draft worth showing someone. A few very generous souls have even offered to read it for me but, like I tell students when I get the opportunity to teach, don't waste workshop time on problems you could identify yourself, and believe me, I have identified some problems.

But I still like it, is the thing. I do. There's a certain feeling I get from my own work, when not only the room and events and feelings of the present moment feel clear to me but so do echoes of what's come before and a trajectory into the future of the characters. I suppose that's just successful realism, but to me it feels *intimate* — even when it's a dark or vast physical realm I'm working in. This is just the fictional world that I'm intimate *with*, I guess, this tiny space made real. I am not describing it very well, but when I *do* describe something very well, I feel that way about it: intimate, close, touched.

September 11, 2020

Day 183: The trackpad on my work computer broke. I don't have a mouse and was losing my mind. My mother, who has been largely alone in her apartment since March, showed up at dawn with a mouse. Which I am crying over — it works so well! It was so nice of her! How will I ever re-enter society?

• • •

I saw this at lunch today for the first but certainly not last time — I assume it will eventually become a pandemic cliché. Large, chaotic family group stands at entrance to a building and very small children — but older than two, and thus requiring masks — scream, "Mama, where's my maaaaskkk?" and Mama doggedly searches through bags, the stroller undercarriage, pockets. I mean, my experience isn't vast but I assume children of four or five are very capable of dropping a mask in a public washroom or throwing it out a window and then asking their parent an hour later in frustration and rage where it is, no? How is this ever going to work? Or am I underestimating kids and this was just one bad scene?

September 18, 2020

Day 190:

> (RR on conference call.)
> (MS in kitchen, making noises.)
> RR: One second, I'll be right back — I think Mark is
> eating the wrong thing for lunch. (Leaves desk,
> yells down the hall until Mark steps away from
> the fridge, returns.) Sorry about that.
> Video caller: It's okay.
> RR: Poor Mark, he used to be able to eat whatever
> he wanted for lunch. Back when I had hobbies
> and friends.
> VC: It would be good if you could get some of
> those back.
> RR: Now I just need the leftovers eaten in a certain
> order. It's all I have — I need that.
> VC: I understand.

Note #1: This is a long-standing friend/co-worker.
Note #2: At least I made the lunch.

September 22, 2020

Day 194: My previous book came out in March 2017 and I finished working on it in October 2016. Before that, I'd had a few gaps in the editing process in which to start the new project, so it was well under way, and then I had four to five months to continue between the end of the edits, although in fact that was the period in which a lot of family stuff happened, so not really. Then *So Much Love* came out and I did a lot of (fun!) promotional stuff for it, my health was terrible, I travelled a lot, and that — along with being employed full time, additional family stuff, and just being a person — was basically it for the year. At the beginning of 2018, I thought I could put together a good chunk of the draft by fall, and I foolishly said this out loud — and then immediately stopped talking to anyone who could follow up.

So, um. Anyway, hi, I finished a draft. It's about sixty-one thousand words, which is about what I pictured, even though it took two extra years. After all that, it's a *first* draft, so it doesn't even bear discussing that it needs to be massively overhauled, but at least it's a thing that ends. I really wanted to write the last sentence tonight, but there's been a whole bunch of other nights where I wanted that and I didn't, so I'm pretty surprised. I'm just going to have to go back to page 1 and start revising *substantially*, but this is really huge for me, so, FYI — did it.

September 23, 2020

Day 195: In a grand reunion tour of my previous Facebook posts, someone from IT was remoting into my computer to try to figure out my ever-mysterious trackpad problems and, since I couldn't work, I was applying peppermint oil to my still-sore neck and then — somehow — touched my eye and got peppermint oil in it. Dabbing delicately at my eye to keep the peppermint tears from wrecking my elaborate bright-blue eyeliner, I tried to message my IT pal to tell him I had to step away from the computer for a moment, but of course, he had control of my computer and I couldn't. So I texted him on the number he'd called me from previously, which turned out to be the proxy number for the land line they tell us to use from work. So now my text has gone to the answering service, to be read aloud in a robot voice, and I have gotten most (but not all!) of the peppermint oil out of my eye and explained the situation and the IT department really does put up with a lot, don't they?

September 24, 2020

Day 196: Remember ages ago when I was talking about CareMongering, the weird world of extremely helpful and extremely annoying people mingled together on Facebook? There's an additional element with CareMongering that I am learning. The posts are mainly by or about people in need, and there are many every day. Because I am me (thorough, interested, maybe a little too into Facebook), I read a lot of them, though by no means all — there's too many. I have helped a few times — a few donated items, a bit of money, occasionally advice — but that's maybe five or six times in the whole 196 days, and hundreds and hundreds of posts.

It's maddening and, I suppose, deadening. Many, many people post to say they need groceries — what a thing, in such an affluent city. Many people try to help, but many others comment to advise or snark about who should get help, or what is the appropriate way to ask, or what kinds of help folks do and do not deserve. What I mean by "deadening" is that sometimes I read a note from someone who needs X groceries to make it to Y date, and then they post something similar again the next week, and someone snaps at them that they already *got* help — how could someone be in need two weeks in a row? Because it's easier to believe that people would lie than that people would go hungry. If they were lying, then nothing is wrong with anything except those people and nothing needs to be done. But they are probably telling the truth; I think most people know that — they just get so sad and overwhelmed they wish they weren't. (Yeah, somebody games every system. Doesn't mean the reason that the system exists isn't real!)

I've been broke but I've never been poor — like, I haven't had a lot of money in certain periods, but that's not quite the same as poverty, you know? And even at the worst times, I got to stand in the grocery store and make a certain number of choices. I couldn't have whatever I wanted, but I got to choose my own brand of cereal, skim milk or 2 percent; I never had to eat ham or a radish (I don't eat pork; I don't like radishes) just because someone happened to have extra. Is that a right or a privilege? *Eating* is a right — is choosing? It feels like that should be, too. I don't know.

Reading through the CareMongering posts and comments is rough. I do it to try to help and I do it to remember what is happening in our city while I'm wondering if my neck hurts because I slept poorly or because I need a better desk chair.

September 25, 2020

Day 197:

> MS: I'm gonna go get lunch early [we get takeout lunch on Fridays, to give ourselves something to look forward to] because I have a one o'clock meeting.
> RR: Sure, thanks. I might not eat with you, though.
> MS: Why not?
> RR: Because I have a lot of work to do and I should eat at my desk.
> MS: Oh, okay.
> RR: What could the other reason possibly be?

MS (shrugs)

RR: Because I'm mad? Because I had a fight by myself while you were in another room?

MS: It's happened before.

RR (makes the face Kermit the Frog makes when
the puppeteer has his hand in a fist)

MS: It might be happening right now!

September 26, 2020

What is more plausible in St. James' Cemetery (above ravine level)
at the supper hour: a stray dog or a coyote? Nearly twenty years in
Toronto and I've never seen an uncollared stray ... nor a coyote!

September 27, 2020

Day 199: Case counts are climbing again in Ontario, but for now
there's a likely brief window where a person can still pay another
person to look in their mouth, so today I went to the orthodon-
tist. I busted my permanent retainer on the weekend and, while
I'm trying not to be too gloomy about a second lockdown, that
does seem to be the way we are trending and I was worried about
letting this go even a week and finding Toronto sliding back
down the "stages" and my ortho rendered "inessential" again.
So off I went, and on the non-pandemic side of things, I'm still
surprised about how much orthodontia I have to endure in my
forties.

I thought this would be a quick gluing down of my be-sproinged
wire, but they actually had to get all the old glue off with a teeny,
tiny jackhammer, which was very unpleasant — it made a horrible

screeching sound, though it didn't hurt too much. The person who invents silent dental implements will make a billion dollars, says me. All the other patients were awkward tweens. One — who got snapped at by his mother repeatedly for wandering within my six-foot bubble because he apparently had no control over his limbs — was actually named Evan, same as my eldest child [cat], so that was exciting. The people at the office like me as their most compliant patient, but some of their patients have to be urged to brush their teeth, so it's not a tough contest.

September 28, 2020

Day 200: Remember at one hundred days, I was really into the milestone and thought hard about what to do, and it was solstice and really meaningful? Today I haven't been outside yet (procrastinated on the walk and then it rained) and the more time I spend alone, the more every awkward conversation I have ever had bubbles up inside my brain for me to analyze. Friends, so many of them were *my fault*. I make so many things weird and hard for other people as well as myself. I have so much to feel guilty and terrible about in the middle of the night, in the shower, when my fingers hover above the keys filling in a spreadsheet. *But* I have been analyzing one particular awkward conversation for years, maybe nearly a decade, and I have come to the conclusion that that *one* was not my fault. The other person made it weird. This is a big breakthrough, and that is how I am celebrating two hundred days. I'm pretty freaking worried about three hundred.

October 2, 2020

Day 204: I sometimes think that when people say they don't want to go to a "bad" neighbourhood, they don't really fear something will happen to them (if you are a reasonable person and do reasonable things, that's unlikely, although of course there are places where it's slightly more likely) but rather they are simply uncomfortable with witnessing people in the act of being poor. And it is, in fact, very uncomfortable to see first-hand how much people are struggling in our city, but I'm not sure if that's a reason not to do it. That's not disingenuous — I'm genuinely not sure what the point of my ever-attentive eyes are. I give about the same amount to charity as most people, I suppose. If I just refused to see, would it matter?

Anyway, yesterday I went to meet a friend (which was so nice) and needed to walk downtown. I hate walking on crowded streets and awkwardly trying to give everyone enough space, so I tried walking through a wide alley for ten or twelve blocks. There was plenty of space, but I felt almost as though I had walked into people's living rooms at times, and the times were sad and difficult. During the pandemic, safe private spaces to rest have become very scarce and perhaps I should have just left the alley for those who needed it more. No one said anything to me or gave me a hard time that I was there, but a few did seem startled and confused by me. Next time I'll walk on the street.

But this one lovely thing did happen, so I can share that. There were these three little yards side by side, two completely barren and one an explosion of colour — the house with kids. A girl of maybe seven saw me walking down the alley as she was walking to her gate and we caught each other's eyes for a second. I couldn't tell if she was coming *to* me and I didn't immediately see an adult, so I took out my earbuds in case she approached me. I'm always trying to ward off kids and dogs during the pandemic, even though I really want to interact. As soon as she hit the gate, a woman who had been sitting in a chair facing the house rose and started yelling at her, "Don't you do that, don't you dare!" and seemed pretty mad, but the girl went out, followed by a smaller boy, about four, maybe. They closed the gate behind them and started walking past the other yards toward a shed — I was parallel to them on the other side of the alley; it was a wide alley. "Don't you throw that egg! Don't you smash it!" And then I could see the girl had an egg in her hand that she was waving around. "I'm gonna do it! It's just one egg!" And from the little boy: "And I'm gonna watch!" The woman, disgusted, appeared to give up. "Well, fine, but then you come right back in."

I had almost walked past by this point, but I jolted to a stop when I realized she was actually going to smash an egg, just for fun. I wanted to see that — the pandemic has been so boring. The kid had her hand raised above her head but when she saw me stop, she hesitated and looked worried — another interfering adult. I smiled and jerked my chin at the egg, and she smiled back and hucked it at the side of the shed and the kids cheered and we all beamed at each other and I went on my way. It made such a satisfying sound.

October 4, 2020

Day 206: The city has lost so much recently but Furama Cake and Desserts Garden is an extra-tough one to see go. I loved this place for so long, since before I even lived in the city, I think — the first Chinese bakery I ever went to, and probably the best. One memory: being super-sick and on my own, not really able to eat, and then one day I woke up and thought, "I bet I could eat a pineapple bun," so I trekked across town to Furama and got one and it was the first thing I'd eaten in days and it tasted like magic.

Anyway, I want the staff to feel supported and appreciated, so I gave a little money. Also I'm sorry I didn't realize they were closing until after it happened, or I would have come to say farewell (and get a pineapple bun).

October 6, 2020

Day 208:

> RR (comes into MS's office, looks hopefully at bookshelf): Do you have our old *Chicago Manual of Style*?
>
> MS: No, I don't think so. (Leans over to shelf.) It's not on the reference shelf?
>
> RR: No, I looked.
>
> MS: Well, it's not here.
>
> RR: Oh no! Everything is falling apart.
>
> MS: I have a *Writer's Market* from 1997.
>
> RR: ... Why?
>
> MS: Well, it's up to you — whatever you want it for.
>
> RR: !!!!
>
> MS (waves around a bunch of other books in an attempt at obfuscation)
>
> RR: No, really, why do you have that?
>
> MS: Well, in case I need to know ... (flips open 1997 *Writer's Market*) ... the phone number and website for *Trucker's Log* in 1997.
>
> RR: They had a website in 1997?
>
> MS: Says here ...

RR: You didn't have the internet in 1997.

MS: I also have a *Writer's Market* from 2002.

RR: I need a *Chicago Manual of Style*.

MS: I have *MLA*?

RR: Which edition?

MS: Oh, this is very recent — fifth edition.

RR: *Fifth* edition?

MS: 1999.

RR: So what happens in here is you take the books
you know I would get rid of, and you hide them.

MS (puts all books back on shelf, returns to desk)

• • •

The reason I was distracted from the internet — surprising — yesterday is that I took the afternoon off to go to the Toronto Islands, which was lovely, and on the way home we shared the ferry with about three hundred little kids plus their teachers coming home from a field trip. Yes, a bunch of human teachers spent Teachers' Day (yesterday was Teachers' Day!) trying to keep three hundred kids from getting lost, punching each other, falling into the lake, taking off their masks, getting too close to other people, or screaming, and still teach them things. Jeez louise. It was a pretty impressive show, although I have to say, some of the kids at the back of the line were definitely punching each other. I was agitated just watching. Thanks, teachers, for all you have to do every day, and then taking on all the extra on top of that. (I bet no one made them take the kids to the islands — they just thought it would be nice for the kids! Which is really next level!)

October 7, 2020

Day 209: Today is the one-year anniversary of the Global Rebellion, when there was a day of spotlight-grabbing blockades and actions in the hope of making the climate emergency unignorable. Around the world and in Canada, many bridges were blocked. In this city, Extinction Rebellion Toronto (XRTO) blocked the Bloor Viaduct for a few hours, which does not sound like a massive deal when I put it like that, but it certainly felt like one at the time. I put a huge amount of time and energy and just belief into preparing for that day, being there, and the aftermath. At this hour one year ago, I was running around on the bridge and in the area, getting information, helping people; cars were stopped; the lines were set; people were singing. It was a sunnier day and I was with my friends, and all things felt possible. Were we saving the world, right then? Of course not. But could we, could *everybody*, if we put our hearts into it? Seemed likely.

This is a less optimistic moment, both in my life and, I think, in the world. XRTO does not exist anymore and it did not die a hero's death. Global XR still exists in many cities but doesn't seem to be up to as much anymore — maybe it's a movement that had its time or maybe it was fundamentally flawed, or maybe one and then the other. I'm not too savvy about these things. There's a part of me that says, "Well, you worked really hard for a year and it ended poorly and things are worse than ever, give up and don't try," which is *very* intriguing (have you met my couch?). But I can't forget how good it felt to try extremely hard, to do exactly what I felt was right, and sing in the sun. I miss it. I've never had another day like October 7, 2019, but I think I'd like to.

October 8, 2020

Day 210: Just before the beginning of the pandemic, there was this condo a friend of a friend thought we could *maybe* possibly be interested in somehow buying. It was a long shot — and did not, needless to say, work out — but in order to even view it, I got entangled with a realty listing service that now, a few times a week, sends me other condo listings that ostensibly meet my specifications. I should really find a way to unsubscribe, but it's a pandemic and I'm bored (what percentage of these posts are some dumb thing I'm doing for this reason?) so I stay tuned, dutifully viewing condos that I (a) cannot afford and (b) do not like.

Honestly, it's great. I'm a writer and a nosy person, and there are so few opportunities to walk into people's homes and just … look around. Of course, many places are staged, so I'm seeing less personality but still not none — I always get to imagine living there, and who would like it, and why. And some places aren't staged. Some people put a deep freeze *lengthwise* to the kitchen island and then just leave all the space in front of it empty, effectively cutting their living room in half. Some people keep Kleenex on the dining-room table instead of serviettes. I love knowing this stuff, which is probably why I will never amount to anything in life. The messiest bedroom so far had an *iron* in it. These are the mysteries that entertain me!

One of the reasons it's hard for Mark and me to even conceive of a new place is that for all the faults of our current place, it's really big. I often see places posted that have the same number of rooms but 80 percent the square footage — sometimes less. I like trying to figure out where they cut. Sometimes it's buffer space, like hallways — we have a long, skinny one and the more modern condos just have rooms opening off each other. That seems maybe really efficient, or loud, or both? Sometimes it's that mysterious "den" that's supposed to double as a bedroom but in reality sometimes does not have a door or walls. I spend a lot of time looking at these pictures, trying to sort out where the space went.

It's going to be wild when I have to reintegrate into society and regularly participate in conversations where someone talks, then I respond to what they are saying, then they respond. I am very curious about other people — I long for other people — but I'm not sure I remember how to interact with them. Maybe just show me photos of the rooms in your home and we'll go from there?

October 11, 2020

Day 213 mistakes:

- I thought day 211 was going to line up with October 11 but then it didn't.
- My mom asked me to pick up a little bag of cat food for her, and since it's a different size than I normally buy (my cats get the humungo size because there's two of them and also they are gluttons), I got confused and accidentally bought the gluten-free kind. I went back to exchange it the next day, but left it late and the store was nearly closing. In my rush, I accidentally grabbed hairball-control food and didn't realize until they'd rung me through. I went *back* to the shelf, trying to be quick and so embarrassed, and couldn't find the normal cat food *at all*. "Oh, I guess you don't even have it — no wonder I was confused." The very nice cashier came over and pointed it out. "You mean that one?"

- On laundry-day night, I found a sock in my pillowcase in the middle of the night. Somehow the sock got partway out of the pillowcase and woke me up (I'm a light sleeper) and trying to sort out what was happening from a dead sleep was mildly terrifying.
- I bought much-too-large Halloween costumes for my cats (they are skinny gluttons somehow). A friend took the whale costume and I await his photos *avidly*, but I still need a taker for the shark costume. Seriously, I'll pop it right in the mail, anywhere, in exchange for only a photo or two — help me out here?
- Squirrels have been digging in my balcony garden pots like idiots — over and over, despite the fact that they never find anything, as there is nothing to find, and they are wrecking good plants. My plants are still going strong and producing, and the squirrels are getting nothing out of their endeavours, so I would like them to stop. My cats love the squirrels (oh God — are all these stories about cats?); squirrels are like cat TV. They know something is supposed to happen, but I don't think they realize it's that cats kill and eat squirrels, so they just watch, rapt. Sometimes I yell at the squirrels to go away; sometimes I yell at the cats to be more fierce and scare the squirrels; sometimes both. This morning, the squirrel was being particularly aggressive and the cats particularly passive and I was yelling at everyone while Mark read the paper. Then the squirrel went after the tomatoes and I opened the door to yell more

effectively and the squirrel *came at me*. I slammed
the door just in time to keep him from coming inside. Alice ran up to the screen and for a moment
she and the squirrel were nose to nose (they are
about the same size — plump squirrel, tiny cat). I
kept on yelling at the squirrel, the cats were ready
to adopt him, and finally Mark snapped, "We're
all useless, the whole family," and closed the glass
door in an attempt to end squirrel–cat relations. I
personally do not cede the argument but Mark is
just waiting for it to get cold and then he assumes
the balcony belongs entirely to the squirrel, but
also it's less likely there'll be another opportunity
for the squirrel to try to get indoors. *We shall see!*

October 14, 2020

Day 216: Yesterday Mark Sampson mentioned in the morning that
he hoped to go out and buy a new pair of sweatpants at lunch. I
was on a video call at lunch, so I heard him leave but we didn't say
goodbye. When I heard his key in the door returning, I actually
said the words aloud, "Oh boy, sweatpants!" and trotted down the
hall to see them. It turned out his other errands had run long and
he had bought no sweatpants. I was *crushed*, and Mark was very
confused. I think maybe no one in history has been that upset at
not being able to look at someone else's new sweatpants. This is
technically yesterday's story but it is also emblematic of where I'm
at with isolation generally.

October 15, 2020

Since August, I've been getting one or two ripe tomatoes a week. The total yield would be enough for sauce, I guess, but since they are so staggered, no dice. It's nice to be still getting tomatoes in mid-October, but one at a time? 2020, you are so weird!

• • •

Coyote report: I went back to the cemetery where I saw the coyote last time and it was absolutely stunning there — the trees are changing, there were almost no people, the weather was gorgeous tonight. I was feeling a bit edgy about the coyote but everyone said it couldn't eat me and everything was so, so pretty. I walked for a while and then I was standing on the edge of the ravine staring out, thinking I was probably being foolish and could climb down and it would be fine — and a coyote zipped by me. It was being chased by a dog, and they were running in big, crazy circles so I wasn't sure exactly what way to go, and also the City of Toronto thing I read said don't run from coyotes, so I tried to stroll away purposefully. Also the coyote did not care about me, as it was a teeny one this time and very worried about the much larger dog. I met a man and called out hopefully, "Are those your dogs?" And he said, "Well, one is, but one is a coyote!" He seemed unembarrassed at having his off-leash dog chasing wildlife in what is actually a place of mourning. The only dog I've ever had was 100 percent untrustworthy off leash in any circumstances — she had to be leashed while swimming in the lake — so I'm not actually familiar with the protocols, but this didn't seem right, so I gave up after a few more exchanges and headed for the gate, which seemed very far away. I alternated between being afraid of the little coyote and being afraid for it. The dog was much, much bigger. I hope the little fellow is okay.

Also, the man said "ky-oat," but back home I always heard people say "ky-oat-tee." Is the two-syllable version the Toronto way?

October 16, 2020

Day 218: First livestream funeral.

October 19, 2020

Day 221: Outlining a novel is tedious, but so is moving a chapter backward in time nine years, and if you do one, maybe you don't have to do the other. I don't know, myself I've never outlined, but I have *heard* it's great and other people's novels don't take as long as mine.

October 25, 2020

Day 227: So Mark and I are carving a jack-o'-lantern for the first time as a couple because pandemic, and it's going okay. Mark was scooping out the innards into a bowl and I was sorting those into seeds, which stayed in the bowl, and the rest, which went into the compost. When that phase was complete, I was carrying the compost bin back to its spot and I said over my shoulder to Mark to put the bowl of seeds in the fridge and I'd deal with washing and roasting them later, post carving. As I set down the bin, I turned to see Mark casually toss a few seeds into his mouth! I actually gasped — if you've never experienced them, raw wet pumpkin seeds are very gross — and squealed, "No, those aren't food!" And he spat them out. When I asked how they were, he said, direct quote, "Terrible. I couldn't even chew them. That's nature's way of telling it's not food." My response: "Did anyone ever say otherwise? They aren't like batter for a cake, tasty before and after." He shrugged, and said, "No. But sometimes you just want to try …" I don't honestly know why he isn't dead at this point if this is how he discovers what is and isn't food.

October 26, 2020

Day 228: Last week, a fly got into the house. I don't know where it came from — there's not a lot of comings and goings, nor a lot of wildlife outside in these temperatures, but anyway: a fly got in. It's a very companionable fly that always wants to be right where the people are, which is more fun for the fly than for us. We made some attempts to kill it, but not very many because we are neither murderous nor speedy. I figured the fly would die a natural death pretty soon, but instead I woke up this morning and now it has a friend, or possibly a brother — a daughter? Did one fly birth the other? I don't know. I hate them both. They want to be on top of my computer screen all the time and it's gross and I hate them.

So yeah, that's what's going on today.

• • •

Do you want to know a secret? I try to never, ever talk about U.S. politics on here, but it is not because I am chill — it is because I am afraid. Possibly next week will not work out well for Biden, and — as I feel it — for the human race. *Am I displacing all my emotions onto the fly?*

Optimism is a tricky thing — let us not examine too closely the memory of me volunteering in Florida in 2004 for the Kerry campaign, because that is a memory that ends with me crying in Florida in the middle of the night. Is it better to be braced for bad news, or to not realize that bad news is even possible, like poor idiot 2004 Rebecca? But prior to that night, I was way happier — I enjoyed optimism a lot more than the alternative. The defensive crouch is so bad for your back.

October 29, 2020

Day 231, day nine of life with the Fly: Walking down the hall, find Mark unexpectedly outside his office door, poised with unused can of air freshener we have for no discernible reason, because we both hate artificial scents.

> MS: *The fly is back. He's in my office.*
> RR: It never left.
> MS: It's bothering me while I'm working.
> RR: ... And the air freshener?
> MS: I'm going to kill him with this!
> RR: ... How? Also, how do you know you can toler-
> ate the scent? Go out on the balcony and spray
> it so you can see how it smells.
> MS: No, I just need to kill him.
> RR: You once almost vomited in the car because I
> put on a moisturizer you don't like.
> MS (stares at the wall for a long time): Okay. (Goes
> outside in socks, sprays, sniffs, comes back in.)
> Perfectly pleasant.
> RR: How do you know it's even going to kill him?
> That's not what it was designed to do.
> MS: He's going to breathe it in and then he's going
> to die. And I'll dance on his grave.

RR: …

MS: He's been buzzing around my head. While I'm working!

RR: You know he's usually doing that to *me*, right? And I cope.

MS: I have other strengths.

(Update: according to distant yelling, the air-freshener plan did not work out.)

October 30, 2020

Day 232: I just want it noted for the record that I like candy corn and also never received it as a Halloween treat — I would have been happy to trade with another kid for it, seeing as it's so unpopular, but it never appeared in anyone's bag, that I saw. I think I've seen it on sale only at Bulk Barn and that's it.

Just while we're getting into it, I like molasses kisses (I think sometimes known as witch's kisses), too, and I did make out very well on Halloween trades with those unpopular candies. There was also a variant peanut-butter version that more people liked but the wrappers were similar and they didn't like to take the risk so I would get both (does the peanut-butter version exist anymore? I think not — at least, I can't find it). I also like liquorice allsorts, an unpopular treat that is more Christmas than Halloween. I like other licorice-y things, but not straight-up black licorice or (horrors) Good & Plenty, which used to be given out as a Halloween treat when I was a child and which I think pretty much no one liked besides my mother, and I think actually are no longer manufactured, proving that not everything in the universe is falling apart.

THESE DAYS ARE NUMBERED

November 6, 2020

Day 239: Stressed about the U.S. election? Me too! Here are some things that are not the election to distract you:

- I have always been afraid of crows but lately they have seemed friendlier to me somehow. Now when they caw at me, I caw back and it feels like a conversation! (Yes, pandemic loneliness but also crow friends!)
- I learned to make a pecan pie! Way easier and exactly as delicious as expected!
- Nice weather!
- I got a terrifying dermabrasion/facial sander thing as a gift-with-purchase and someday soon will work up to using it. Expect a report.

November 8, 2020

Day 241: Does anyone else think today feels a bit like New Year's Day? The U.S. has a new president and vice-president in Joe Biden and Kamala Harris, and with that, it feels important to me to think about what I will be changing, improving, doing differently in this new world. It sounds like a terrible inspirational-poster slogan, but I truly believe that where you put your gaze is where you go, so I have been refusing to follow much press on the misery of the count or the lies of the sitting president — enough creeps to me anyway that I'm never truly out of the loop. I think being angry can easily exhaust my political advocacy muscle, which is as yet very small — emotion isn't the same as action.

But I did watch the victory speeches last night, and even though I didn't think they were truly revolutionary, I was glad I watched. In between the platitudes about being united and everyday families and fighting the virus, I heard some things I don't think are common in this sort of general-interest speech, and I was happy that specific mention was made of transgender people and Native Americans, as well as Black women working to get out the vote — groups that don't often get shouted out and welcomed in. I was happy that Kamala Harris got a separate speech and her own moment to shine — and receive her own applause. I don't think Biden is under any illusions about how the Venn diagram of his fans and hers is an equal spread. But I think if we've learned anything from the last few years — in Canada as well as the U.S. — it is that politics doesn't happen only during election years. My hope that casting a responsible, well-thought-out vote for a good candidate and then they win would ensure a bright future does not seem to be panning out. I feel very worried about the future, and very responsible for it. So I'm glad about Biden–Harris, very glad, but for me the question remains what it always was: How can I help?

Second Wave

November 13, 2020

Day 246: It finally happened — I tried to put a mint into my mouth and wound up mashing it into my mask. I'm honestly shocked this took until day 246!

November 15, 2020

Day 248: So I had this play thing tonight (the *1000 Ways* show) — a theatrical experience, I guess, where you call in and the performers call in, and one other audience member, and you're both sort of part of the show. I was really excited about it and also a bit nervous — they send you a million emails reminding you to show up, that the show cannot go on without you, and so I had built my whole afternoon around being ready to dial the number at the exact right time. Which I did! And entered all the security codes and then a recorded voice told me I was in the right place — whew! But the hold music dragged on and on and it got very late and I realized something was wrong — had I screwed it up? Had I ruined the show? I tried calling all the various alternative numbers, logging out and then logging back in — then I couldn't get back in at all! Finally I reached the box office and they told me the *other* person no-showed and so the show was cancelled, and I realized I was *wrought* with tension. They rebooked me, it's fine, but also — gah!

I've had some opportunities to take it easier lately and people have been extremely kind to me, and I've been feeling really coddled and cared for, and so it's disappointing to learn that I'm still on this wire-thin margin of calm. How much yoga can I reasonably do, honestly?

November 16, 2020

Day 249: Something interesting about the pandemic is that you find out what people find important. Everyone's grief is valid and if you've lost something important to you lately, I'm so sorry — but I have been genuinely surprised by some of the "I cannot do this or that and I'm devastated" comments.

• • •

I got a fancy new teacup and wanted to try it. I rarely drink tea but I'm a woman in my forties so I *own* a lot of tea (the government sends it to me with my licence renewal papers these days), so I set it all up and put the kettle on, then went back to work. When it whistled like three minutes later, I had already forgotten the whole thing and was briefly terrified of the sound, which is likely also an aspect of my forties.

November 17, 2020

Day 250: I got a foundation sampler where they give you a bit of four different shades and I spent a moment trying to figure out which would suit me before realizing I'm just gonna put 'em all on my face. It's a pandemic, I'm wearing green eyeshadow right now, no one sees me, *it's time!*

November 21, 2020

Day 254: Things to do with your partner if you have been isolated together for 254 days, a list (I did an earlier one of these, but we got sick of most of those things, so this is mainly new):

- Go for a walk in the cemetery and find confusingly worded gravestones, then debate how those people are related, since it's unclear; spell out own final wishes and gravestone wording to avoid a similar fate.
- Fight about which YouTube exercise video to do together.
- Google cast members of a TV show you both like and read their Wikipedia pages, then surprise your partner with surprising facts about those people — where they were born, who they are or were married to, what stage productions they starred in in university; if you choose a show with a large ensemble cast, this can be spun out for quite a while.
- Switch deodorants from the one you have used the entire relationship for the mystery and alarm that comes from smelling like a stranger.

- Talk at dinner about what you might want to eat for dinner tomorrow.
- Grumpily assemble furniture.
- Precisely fold the cloth napkins into quarters for absolutely no reason; get upset if your spouse does it wrong.
- Talk about how you slept last night, and possible reasons why. Develop a lot of theories that don't matter because you're not going to do anything about it.
- Get really excited about what might come in the mail, which is almost always nothing, but ask your spouse repeatedly to check just in case.
- Fight about who the cats like best.
- Go for walks in posh neighbourhoods and make a lot of plans for what you'd do if you lived in each of the houses.
- Nap.

November 22, 2020

Day 255: OMG, it's snowing! Also, I think there's something very wrong with one of my teeth, the one the dentist said about last time, "Either this filling holds, or you need a root canal." So that's bad. Also, Uber Eats turns out to be very expensive! Also just bleh — pandemic moods. Are dentists open during this lockdown?

November 24, 2020

Day 257: One of my best-ever Halloween costumes — the concept for which I'll blame purely myself although I had a lot of help with the execution from my friend Kim — was Evil Tooth Fairy. I had a blue tulle skirt and blue tights and slippers and a top, plus fairy wings and a crown. Also a necklace of teeth we made out of Fimo and painted red on the ends so it would be clear they had been removed without permission. I think I put a few on my crown as well. I had a wand in one hand, also with a tooth on it, and a pair of pliers in the other hand. I wore a lot of pretty glitter makeup, appropriately bonkers-looking, and I think maybe a trickle of blood from the corner of my mouth, though what was I going for with that — that I had been biting other people's teeth out? Yikes.

Anyway, it was a clever, horrible costume, and you're welcome to steal the idea or avoid me for a while based on knowing that I came up with that. The horribleness was driven home to me yesterday when I found out my problem tooth will likely have to be extracted, and I kept imagining that creature of my own creation lurking with her pliers. I have never had a tooth extracted, and I don't like the idea. They're my teeth — I grew them! Even the one that has clearly betrayed me!

As I wander around accompanied by twinges of dental pain, I mutter, "The Tooth Fairy is coming for me..." If I were a different sort of writer, I would definitely write this as a horror film treatment.

PS I think we all know each other fairly well by now, but please, please don't tell me any stories about the time you had a tooth extracted and it went terribly. I am far too fragile. If you like, you can tell me stories about times you had teeth extracted and it went great, and what you think made it that way, and I'll try to follow in your footsteps ... that would be nice!

• • •

Just now:

> (Mark enters apartment drenched in sweat, RR
> emerges from end of the hall.)
>
> RR (screaming): *I saw a cat!*
>
> MS (taking off headphones): Wait, what?
>
> RR (runs down the hall): A cat — a cat on Bleecker
> Street! You didn't answer the phone.
>
> MS: I was running …
>
> RR: I called you twice, the cat crossed the street, it
> crossed *Wellesley Street!* It didn't know what was
> going *on!* Let's go find it.
>
> MS: No, I have to finish my workout. Also, it's dark.
>
> RR: The cat came over to me but then it ran off — it
> didn't like me. It shouldn't have been out there.
> Did you know it was me calling?
>
> MS: I can't get at my phone when I'm running, you
> know that. Maybe it was a squirrel.
>
> RR: *I know what a cat is — that is my life's work!*
>
> MS: I'm sure the cat is fine.
>
> RR: It crossed Bleecker Street and then it crossed
> Wellesley and then it crossed Bleecker again
> and went into a garbage area with a gate so I
> couldn't follow it.
>
> MS: So it's with its owner now.
>
> RR: The owner lives in the garbage area?
>
> MS: In the apartment building behind it, maybe.
>
> RR: Why would an owner let a cat out there? That's
> crazy.
>
> MS: Okay.

RR: I waited outside the garbage area a really long time, but the cat did not come back.

MS: Could you please stay away from the garbage areas of Bleecker Street? As a favour to me?

RR: It was fine. I saw one couple making out and that's it.

MS: Fine.

RR: Those also weren't squirrels.

November 26, 2020

Day 259: The *1000 Ways* show "at" CanStage (actually on the phone) was finally last night — once cancelled; once I misunderstood the date — and it was a beautiful experience. I don't want to say too much about it because part of the joy of it was the surprise in waiting on the line, not knowing what would happen and then it happened, but for those who have tickets but are worried about the participation aspect, you do have to talk a fair bit and engage with the process to make it work, but if you go into it willing to do that, you're not asked to do anything very difficult — other than trust a stranger to listen to you, I guess. I was very moved by the sudden, intense engagement and, when it was all over, utterly bereft — if it weren't counter to the intent of the whole thing, I think I would try to find my scene partner, I felt so connected. The show is now sold out to the end of the run, but it's been extended once so maybe it will be again — if it is, please consider the experience. I've never seen anything else like it!

November 27, 2020

Day 260: Discussion question to end the week: Have you ever, since February, or whenever Covid landed on your radar, felt 100 percent sure you did not have it? My household did one total quarantine (this more recent one was self-imposed and incomplete, owing to dental emergency) and for a few hours after we got out of that one, I felt very safe and healthy — and then I walked near a few too many people and doubt crept back in.

The whole rest of the time — the whole eight months — I've sort of thought I could have Covid at any moment. It's dry in my apartment — sometimes I cough or sneeze. More than I used to? Is my throat sore? Or not? Sometimes I just sit there and swallow for a while, to check, which is very weird when I catch myself doing it. Or I could just be asymptomatic — I never seem to express diseases the way my doctors think I should, anyway. I could have all of them, really, all the diseases. Maybe I do.

The newest quarantine has now ended, but because of the trip to the dentist, I didn't get the same rush when I went out quaranfree, which is sad. I did get some roti for lunch, plus cat food, and it was quite nice, but I don't feel like an angel of health and well-being this time. But it would have ended quickly, anyway. Back into the general populace — which is to say, back to being home twenty-three hours a day, and then one hour of walking and errands.

November 29, 2020

Someone painted #LandBack in the middle of the intersection at Bloor and Church, which couldn't have been easy. Took me a minute to realize why there, since it's all stolen land — the Ministry of Indigenous Affairs is just north. So much goes on that I don't know about, but I am glad to see this.

November 30, 2020

Day 263: Having killed a chapter's worth of darlings, my only hope is that I finish the novel, it's good enough to get published, and then goes on to do well enough that I get interviewed somewhere, and that some interviewer thinks to ask, "What if this one chapter had happened completely differently?" and I can finally talk about this ghost chapter that I murdered.

December 1, 2020

Day 264: Remember our upstairs neighbours, the musicians who play so many covers of Red Hot Chili Peppers? I think they are still there, or perhaps it is new people. Anyway, someone, every evening around eight thirty or nine, spends about ten minutes dropping or throwing small bits of metal around. That's okay, it's only ten minutes, and it lends mystery. But there's something else concerning me — do you think I could send them a note? Do you think I could send them *this* note?

Dear Ceiling Friends,

Hello, it's your downstairs neighbour! I'm sorry to bother you, but I have noticed a buzzing sound in our bathroom that seems to be coming through the vent from above. Is something buzzing in *your* bathroom? This is not a complaint! You can have your buzzing thing if you want — it's not like we sleep in the bathroom. You don't even need to tell me what it is, if that seems like sort of a personal question. It's just that it has been getting louder over the past few days and it would be great if you could let me know that *you* know what it is and that you have it under control and ... that it's not ... going to explode ...? Or anything?

Thank you very much!
The Friends Beneath Your Feet

December 2, 2020

Day 265: Mark and I have started listening to the audiobook of *Anne of Green Gables* at dinner because we have run out of things to say to each other and we just can't watch any more TV. I have memorized the novel in a way Mark is not really familiar with. He's not a big rereader and neither am I for adult books, but for kids' novels that I love, I will reread every few years. They are something extra-literary for me, which is why I will never watch any TV or film versions of any of my true faves — I already know what everything and everybody looks like in these books, and it upsets me if the directors don't get it right. But the audiobook is ... okay. The narrator is the actor Rachel McAdams and she's pretty good and she doesn't do any over-the-top dramatizations.

The big kick for me is seeing Mark laugh at the jokes — he doesn't know they are coming, whereas I've known they were coming since 1984. That doesn't mean I don't think they are funny, I wouldn't have reread it so many times if I didn't, but he's just having such a different experience from me. Like when we watch *The*

Mandalorian, I'm just there for the cute baby and Mark is watching complex connective tissue being woven in this enormous *Star Wars* world he's very familiar with. We're watching the same show, but it's two totally different experiences.

December 3, 2020

Day 266: When I was doing crisis support, I was trained to "tone-match" — listen to the emotional register in which someone is speaking and go there with them. Or, if they are at one of the extremes, like very upset or angry, or very ebullient and manic, go just a few notches down, in an effort to remain in their general realm but bring things to a calmer place so that we could have a productive conversation. This is a great tool to not only make people feel heard but to create more empathy within myself — when I speak in a new register, I start to feel it.

However, tone-matching works best when (a) the other person starts the conversation so that I don't accidentally set the tone and (b) they know on some level that I'm doing it, or doing something, to stay with them emotionally. Which, I would think, would be assumed to be the case on a crisis-support call, but maybe not in daily life.

The thing is, I still do it, kinda. There are people I have known for years and years who kicked things off sort of formally and I dutifully matched it ... forever. And at this point, I think we are an echo chamber of not prying into each other's lives or saying very much at all. It's weird, and not what you would gather from these very, very chatty diary entries — but here, of course, I start the conversation, so one can either tone-match me or not, I guess. No one ever seems to respond "how nice," which would be a funny refusal to tone-match.

Anyway, it's hard to know what to do — I get it wrong in both directions: sometimes way too friendly (I'm still smarting because the next-door neighbours walked down ten flights of stairs *carrying a toddler* [the baby can toddle now! this pandemic is so long!] rather than wait for the elevator with me the other day) and then other times weirdly standoffish. I honestly would like everyone to give me a card at the beginning of every conversation — "I am in the mood for X/10 intensity of RR today."

Social isolation has not done a lot for social anxiety, I must say ...

December 4, 2020

Day 267: Oh yeah, I just remembered — after Mark went to bed, I was sitting on the couch, working. Then my phone pinged a new kind of ping, and when I picked it up, it said it had "created a portrait slideshow" for me, which was something I suppose I knew my phone could do if I wanted, but had not expected it to volunteer. So I clicked on it and it started cycling through all these selfies of me getting ready to go out, on vacation, with Mark, with friends. Because of a weird setting I had on my phone for a while, a lot of the "photos" were actually two to three seconds of video, so some were me blinking or giggling or cuddling in close to a friend. And the *saddest* music was playing, just this wistful dirge that made even the photos of me making a face or soaked in the rain very poignant. And I thought, "Oh my God, my phone has spontaneously made my funeral slideshow at 10:00 p.m. on a Thursday — *what does my phone know that I don't?*" And the slideshow ended — me on a hiking trail, I think looking pretty hearty, and on a good note to send people out into the hall, murmuring, "Why did we have to lose her so young?" — and I looked at the settings, and you could choose the music by mood, and it was just for some reason set to "sad." I chose "happy" and tried again — now it was a goofy, fun little birthday-party video, and I didn't seem dead at all.

The moral of the story is that if your phone offers to make you something you didn't ask for, I'd advise against!

December 7, 2020

Day 270: Fantastic news from the Sampsenblums: we got a Wii Fit. There's an unlooked-for bonus with the Fit that I noticed the first time I used it — it's relentlessly, cheerfully critical when I screw up, which is almost always as I learn how to use it. When I used to take in-person fitness classes, the instructors almost never corrected my form or really anything I ever did, even when I was clearly just flailing. I sort of got it — I was the chubby, clumsy one in the back, and maybe they didn't want to embarrass me by singling me out, but it was a form of singling me out to never offer me any feedback; it made me feel like there was no hope I'd ever get it right.

The Wii Fit does not care about my feelings, and it certainly has no concerns I won't get it right — it sternly points out that I put my foot down in the one-legged exercise, criticizes the roundness of my hula-hooping circles, and shows the audience crying when I run too slowly in the race. I'm oddly buoyed by the Fit's faith in me — no special dispensations here.

One more thing (who would have thought a fitness video game could bring up so many feelings, eh?). When we first got the original Wii (sans Fit extension), around 2012, we were *very* excited about it, so if you came over, we'd be all *Want to play Wii bowling with us?* And most people kindly said sure (sorry about that, friends — I've calmed down now and won't try to make you run a race with me in my living room post-Covid). Anyway, to play Wii, you make a little avatar in the game called a Mii (cute, right?) and then that gets saved in the game. Wii sometimes animates the Miis that aren't playing, as audience members or automated competitors for others' games. Which means a lot of old friends from 2012 are popping up in my Wii Fit adventures. Folks who moved away, partners who got broken up with, and, most significantly, my father, who died in 2017, sometimes cheer for me when I get my steps right in aerobics class. I mean, *what?* But also, yes, I will take this — 2020 is the year of taking what I can get and sure, why not.

December 8, 2020

Day 271: I had my consultation for my wisdom tooth extraction today and it was pretty pleasant — I mean, they definitely have to take out the tooth, but the new dentist was nice and it was rather exciting to talk to a stranger in these times. However, I've been having a bunch of new X-rays taken to prepare for this mini-surgery, and both at the previous appointment and this one, the dentist pointed out bits of hardware in my face that I didn't know were there. Obviously I was aware that I had reconstructive surgery in 2007 and things moved around, and the surgeon told me "a couple screws" were added. *Sixteen* screws, my friends, along with multiple plates and wires. He never mentioned the plates and wires at all, and he drastically undercounted the screws.

I've always been slightly demure about this for some reason, but I'll say it now — my 2007 surgeon was a dick. Maybe a good surgeon — obviously, thirteen years later, most of this seems okay without me even knowing it's there, but depending on your personal belief on how much an individual deserves to know about how much metal is in her personal face, he was and likely still is a giant tool.

Everything is fine and, I guess, always was, but OMG — if you have reason to require maxillofacial surgery and like knowing exactly what's going on inside your body, feel free to ask me who I don't recommend you deal with.

December 9, 2020

Day 272: In celebration of the Pfizer-BioNTech vaccine getting approved, Mark taught me how to pronounce "Pfizer."

• • •

RR (looking in cupboard in surprise): Oh, we still have potatoes!

MS (sighing): Yeah, we still have potatoes.

(We bought a big bag of potatoes for a recipe I wanted to make because I mistakenly thought it would require them all. It required approximately one-sixth of them. We almost never buy potatoes.)

RR: I think I don't really understand how much potato ... is a potato.

MS: No, you don't seem to.

RR: But you do.

MS: Yeah, well.

RR: Because you were born with a sense of potatoes ...

MS: ...

RR: On your island ...

MS: Can you get me the broom?

(Later.)

RR (singing to myself): You say to-may-to, I say to-mah-to, you say po-tay-to, I say po-tah-to ... No one actually says po-tah-to, really, do they?

MS: No, I don't think anyone says po-tah-to.

RR: Some people do say to-mah-to.

MS: Yeah, some people.

RR: British people, I guess.

MS: ... Can you get me a compost bag?

We are dangerously close to not needing each other's participation in order to have conversations here at the Sampsenblums. Dangerously close.

December 12, 2020

Day 275:

MS (wanders into the room chewing, holding something in a cupped hand)

RR: What are you eating? I want some, too.

MS (holds out hand to RR, gives her half of what he has): It's raisins.

RR: Oh, never mind, I don't want them. (Leaves hand outstretched for Mark to return and reclaim raisins, which he does.) Why do you put up with me?

MS: I really don't know. (Departs, chewing.)

December 13, 2020

Day 276: Things seem dire here at Casa Sampsenblum: the sun sets at three thirty, the cats are stripping the Christmas tree of ornaments and possibly eating them, our building has hired a security guard who sits maskless in the front foyer and eats chips — which I think actually makes the building less safe and more germy — and tomorrow someone is going to take away one of my teeth and then charge me eight hundred dollars.

I am told that my outlook on life will improve once the tooth is out, both because it will not hurt anymore and because I will not be scared. Mainly the latter, as it does not hurt very much currently and I am extremely scared. We can only hope, because I do not think anyone wants to hear anything further about this tooth. Check back tomorrow for either an extremely detailed report on how I found the tooth-removal experience or else complete radio silence, which means my very limited experience with drugs of any kind did not equip me to stay conscious following the experience.

December 14, 2020

Day 277: Just a quick post to say I had the dental surgery and it went fine! As usual, my extreme anticipatory panic was overblown — the worst part turned out to be not having anything to drink for twelve hours and getting pretty dehydrated. The sedation was so subtle and thorough I was initially confused as to whether the procedure had even happened yet. But then the drugs wore off pretty fast and I wasn't even groggy! However, now I'm on different drugs for pain and I *am* groggy, so I'm going to bed, but I did want to say thanks to everyone who sent good thoughts or kind words and I will try to remember that the fear was worse than the experience next time I'm really freaked out about something.

December 15, 2020

Day 278: On a topic of not my teeth for once ... it's getting real that the holidays will come. Mark and I are privileged that we have a fair bit of time off to enjoy, and each other to spend it with, but it's starting to hit me that this will be a #NoVisitVacation and that's sad. Also weird! We put the tree in a new place this year because we just scooted some of the houseplants behind the dining table, effectively rendering some of the chairs unusable, but that's fine because the tree looks great and we are definitely not having any company. That was what made it real for me — no one but us has sat at our dining table since February, and they won't until ... spring ... summer? Who knows?

Normally when we have holidays in Toronto, we have a bunch of high-energy social events — parties, concert tickets, dinner with friends, my mom hosts Christmas, we have a big shindig for New Year's — and those are spaced out by lazy days at home with books and cats. Also, the end of the year is often coming at the end of a hectic fall with lots of running around and events, so it's great to just cocoon a little bit. This fall, it's been all books and cats, and now the holidays will be all that, too. If we want there to be an "occasion," we have to make it in our living room, and if we don't, it's just more couch time, straight on into 2021. It's really daunting.

I don't kid myself that there's a way around this — I've really pretzelled it over and over, but I don't have a better solution for my household other than "stay home." And it's definitely not torture to stay home with my partner and cats and be warm and comfortable and gaze at the tree. But it's a huge loss from what I'm used to and ... I miss you, friends. Come sit at our table when this is all over. We'll move the plants back.

• • •

RR: I need to talk to you about the butter dish.

MS (immediately defensive): What?

RR: I think it's great that you're using the butter dish — it's a good idea. [Mark has recently started putting some butter in the butter dish and keeping it in the cupboard, like Sampsons, instead of in the package in the fridge, like Rosenblums, and I'm forced to admit it's better.] But what goes in the butter dish is a stick of butter.

MS: That's what I've been putting.

RR: No, what you've been putting is random gobs of butter that approximately form a stick.

MS: Well, what difference does it make?

RR: Some of the gobs don't exactly fit, and when you put the lid on, some of the butter gets on the outside.

MS: Oh. (Licks lid of butter dish.)

RR (takes several minutes to pull self together sufficiently to ask whether he was removing visible butter or testing for invisible butter; it was the latter)

(Later.)

RR (near tears, watches Mark put butter in [washed] butter dish in several tiny hunks cut crosswise from the pound, get some on the floor, somehow get the knife near his face, and then turn to her in triumph as if the exercise had gone well): Do you know what a stick of butter is?

MS: ...

RR: There are four sticks of butter in a pound, a stick is a quarter of a pound, cut lengthwise. You can buy by the stick — it costs like seven dollars more. We can just do that. I'm worried about you cutting your face, I love you, do you want to do that?

MS: I'll try it your way next time, then if it doesn't work out, we can buy it by the stick.

RR: Okay.

December 16, 2020

Day 279: Well, green soup eaten lukewarm is not delicious, but I have had a day's worth of nutrients by 2:30 p.m., so that's something. I'm really missing out on the snackiest time of the year, because most delicious treats require chewing and if I want to have a snack between meals, I have to rinse my mouth out with salt water or mouthwash (or salt water and then mouthwash, because salt water is gross), which just doesn't seem worth it most of the time. Upside, V8 isn't as bad as I'd remembered ...

December 17, 2020

Day 280: When we first started getting full-size trees, the cats were very surprised and intimidated and just kept an eye on them. Now, they know the tree can't fight back and they are much more ... well, I found a googly eye in the middle of the floor, is what I'm saying.

December 20, 2020

Day 283: One of my wisdom-tooth stitches has pulled partly out, which I think is fine — the nurse told me they would dissolve soon, so whether they are there or not at this point is, I guess, immaterial. But it's not gone-gone, it's just sticking out, a small bit of thread poking me in the back of the tongue, which feels about as great as it sounds. It doesn't hurt — this whole process hasn't really been very painful, and I have taken only one of my codeine painkillers because they put me right to sleep. But if I lie down in bed tonight and I still feel that bit of thread at the base of my tongue activating my gag reflex with its tiny bit of weird, poky pressure, I'm going to take another codeine in order to just lose consciousness because *agh* I hate it.

On the upside, today I received some lovely gifts. They came in a kind of small canvas tub, and I was like *that looks like a small filing unit*, and then I cleaned out my spice cupboard and filed all my bags of spices in the tub in alphabetical order and I feel really great about this.

December 21, 2020

Day 284: We have two hooks on the back of our bathroom door for our bath towels. A few weeks ago, Mark's hook fell off and he's had to hang his towel in a less convenient spot, and since then I've been vaguely saying that we need to finally read the instruction manual on the drill we've never used and put the hook back up, and Mark has been nodding but definitely resisting. I have no doubt that we *could* learn to use the drill, but I've had it for probably fifteen years and never done so, so there's some ingrained hesitation there. My late father, who gave it to me and originally put in the hooks, is, I think, to date the only person to ever use it, or maybe also our sister-in-law who put up our curtains (or perhaps she brought her own drill?). I realize this is a bad look and really do mean to do better in terms of power tools and home improvement in general. *2021!*

Anyway, also over the past couple weeks, the hinge has broken on the bathroom door to the point where it's really difficult to close, so I asked the super to come and look at it. I couldn't tell exactly what was wrong with it, since it's painted over, but I figured they had to bend the hinge a little or maybe remove and replace the hinge entirely. But as it turns out, *no* — the entire door and frame need to be removed and replaced, which seems terribly inefficient but is apparently the only way for our bathroom door to ever fully close again.

Anyway, this is great news for our desire to procrastinate re: installing the hook or learning to use the drill — the building is definitely not bringing us a new bathroom door anytime soon and it will be a "big job" to install it when they do, and only then can we even approach the task of putting up hooks. Had we put them up immediately when the first one fell down, it would have been a huge waste of time.

What a terrible, terrible lesson.

December 23, 2020

Day 286: I live in a huge, extremely diverse-in-every-way apartment complex. The management puts up generic "Happy Holidays" signs in December, primarily to draw attention to office closures, and leaves it at that. For a few years, someone would cross it out and write "Merry Christmas" overtop. One day, I happened to have a pen and I wrote below, "Do you want everyone who doesn't celebrate Christmas to have an unhappy holiday?" Which is what I think every time someone insists "Merry Christmas" is the only acceptable phrase to say to strangers or write generically. Anyway, the cross-out and write-over never happened again. I don't kid myself that I'm the reason — that person probably moved — but I'm glad. I want everyone to get the holiday they wish for — if it's Christmas and I know that, then I wish them "Merry Christmas." If I have no idea or I forget or I'm writing a sign that lots of strangers might see, I just hope everyone is getting some sort of holiday or break or rest, and I wish you "Happy Holidays." Seems like maximum application, right?

December 26, 2020

Day 289: For Christmas, the cats got a battery-operated bee that shoots treats. Mark got a new ottoman that seems comfortable and some fancy new liquors — also pants. I got some pretty new makeup, a cute pompom hat, and the game Sequence. If you've never played Sequence, it is that delightful sweet spot of board games between so hard it makes you feel dumb and so easy there's no challenge. It also, unlike Scrabble, doesn't leave me feeling the temptation to make "clever" moves instead of moves that will allow me to win. It's very fun!

This year, maybe the best gift of all is the additional week off that my work is providing. I had a work-stress nightmare on Christmas Eve and am feeling so excited about just spending this afternoon on the couch, reading magazines. Lunch and dinner today are both leftovers. The greatest.

I miss my family and friends very much, but I keep imagining "the numbers" going down (it's funny how we have all come to accept that "the numbers" mean one thing now) and all the great things we will do post-vaccine. I mean, Christmas Eve was a new daily high in terms of Covid-positive testing people in Ontario and forty-nine people died that day, so I understand what we are making the sacrifice for. There's been well over two thousand positive tests every day for a while now, so something had to change, but if we all have a #NoVisitVacation and there are vaccinations in the new year, maybe ... then hugs? Looking very forward to it, friends. Hopefully I will be better rested by then!

December 29, 2020

Day 292: We went back to the fancier grocery store (Loblaws) to get nice "party" food to eat at home by ourselves on New Year's Eve, which pretty much everyone seemed to be doing. We also needed Parmesan. Although my standards are often pretty low — as evidenced by thinking Loblaws is fancy — I somehow can't deal with the pre-grated stuff anymore because it's all powdery and weird. I want the wedges to microplane myself. This is the hill I will die on in my forties, although I have also been known to eat cold maple beans out of a can for lunch, so ...?

Anyway, real talk:

> RR: This is two hundred and fifty grams of Parmesan for nine ninety-nine. (Waves small wedge of cheese.)
>
> MS: Okay.
>
> RR: This is nearly a kilo of Parmesan for twenty-two ninety-nine. (Waves giant wedge of cheese.)
>
> MS: Okay, let's get the bigger one. We eat a lot of it. (Reaches for giant wedge of cheese.)

RR (pulls giant wedge of cheese away): Obviously that's the better deal. But this is about what kind of people we are. Are we responsible enough to take care of the cheese long enough to use it up? Will we leave it uncovered in the fridge or let something else happen to it?

MS (succeeds in getting cheese, puts it in cart): If we pay twenty-three dollars for cheese, we can protect it. Put the other one back.

January 8, 2021

Day 302: The following things have occurred:

- I ordered some fish off the internet.
- Mark announced, after almost a decade of co-habitation, that he believed we have "sides" of the coat closet, but I never knew that and hung up my coats accordingly (i.e., at random). I have no idea how he persisted in this belief.
- I saw a hawk eat a pigeon, close up.
- I listened and read and thought so much about those struggling with distance learning this week, and felt very helpless to do anything useful.
- I returned some wire hangers to the dry cleaner. (Fun fact: you can't recycle wire hangers, but many dry cleaners will take them.)
- I suddenly remembered last summer's heat wave and panic-bought another air conditioner from a stranger in my building.
- There was an attempted coup in the U.S.

- I gave a little money to a refugee services organization in the U.S., because when the most powerful and protected are under threat, you can bet it's terrifying for those without either power or protection.

So things are … not going well. I don't even know where my internet fish currently is — it's supposed to be here by now to comfort me. How are you doing, friends? I'll go back to being quiet now … for a bit.

January 11, 2021

Day 305: So, I'm told that perhaps a curfew will be announced for Toronto and Ontario tomorrow. I'm among the likely legion people to whom the inability to go out after 8:00 p.m. will make no difference — I can just as easily do my one pointless circuit at noon and be done. And yet I am pretty anxious about the curfew, from how I remember the parks closure going down. Here in St. James Town, where there's a lot of low-income folks, new immigrants, and city housing, the parks closure was rigorously enforced: the tape went up and stayed up, and no one that I saw touched the parks or equipment, even long after the closure ended. Across Bloor, in Rosedale, where there are many multi-million-dollar homes and nice yards, folks ripped down the tape after a week or so and used the parks with impunity and, as far as I know, just enjoyed the parks and no one gave them a hard time or even noticed they had broken the rules. These are the main places I can walk to, so that's what I know, but I heard of giant tickets in other places, places where people don't have yards and can ill afford tickets.

And that's parks, which although very important are technically optional. Also discrete — one is definitely either in or not in a park.

I'm very, very worried about a potential curfew because I fear it will be selectively enforced, and in a certain neighbourhood a person who is on their way to work but can't prove it would be in a lot of trouble, whereas in another neighbourhood they'd be given a lot more leeway or more likely never seen at all, because there wouldn't be anyone watching.

There are five fire trucks on my street (that I can see from my window — possibly more around the corner) at this moment, which is not atypical. We have a lot of problems here but in general this is a high-compliance neighbourhood where people wear their masks and do the best they can, and many people work front-line jobs. I'm eager to see the government do something good to help my neighbours and not just make their lives more difficult.

Anyone want to tell me I'm worrying for nothing? Or that I'm worrying for something and point me toward something useful I can do about it?

January 12, 2021

Notes on day 306:

- I am basically failing at my no-Facebook-posts January.
- It's really showing what party is running Ontario, in this bootstrappy "if you don't want Covid, work hard and don't have it, and if you get it, you didn't work hard enough!" approach to the pandemic.
- I'm also trying to have a low-sugar January, but my brother bought me a box of Korean treats for Christmas, so every night after dinner I have just one of those for dessert. Except tonight, owing to

me being unable to read Korean characters and a significant difference in how Canadians and Koreans apparently characterize treats, my dessert was crackers, and I'm sad about that now, too.

Also, this:

RR: Did you pull out the drawstring in your pyjama pants?

MS: Yeah, why?

RR: I keep finding it in various spots around the apartment.

MS: It's like one of those garden gnomes ...

RR: That seemed like the best thing to do, did it? Pull it out?

MS: Well, it fell part of the way out ...

RR: So you wanted to pull it the rest of the way out, as opposed to put it back in?

MS: It didn't want to go back in.

RR: And now are your pants staying up?

MS: Mainly yes.

RR: Mainly?

MS: Yes. I appreciate you not laughing at me.

RR: No, I *am* laughing at you.

MS: No, I *would* appreciate you not laughing at me.

January 23, 2021

Day 317: It has been great winter-walking weather in Toronto all January and I. Do. Not. Care. Anymore. I do not want to walk around in a pointless circle and avoid people and then come right back home anymore. You can tell me about the joys of fresh air and exercise all you want — I do in fact feel better if I walk, which is why I still do it, but I don't feel *that* much better. Walking has become medicinal, which is sad. There weren't that many pleasures at the start of the pandemic, but walking was one and it's sad to see it go. Today I stood looking at the cow in Riverdale Farm — one of the more interesting walks available to me — and the cow didn't care and I didn't care, and behind me this family was trying to teach a small child to ride a tiny motorcycle they must have purchased in pandemic desperation because what is that? And the tiny motorcycle had training wheels and made an awful screeching noise whenever it was in motion and the child still couldn't really ride it and kept going in the mud, and the cow and I were both sad (I'm projecting onto the cow, but whatever).

Friends, what are we going to do on day 365? Like ... *what?*

January 28, 2021

Day 322: Our next-door neighbours are moving out. Neither of our immediate neighbours are really interested in speaking to me, but this is the set that is nicer about it, nodding and smiling, occasionally going so far as to say, "Good morning" or even "How are you?" unprompted. They would also let their little girl interact with our cats if they were in the hall at the same time (pre-pandemic) because she wanted to so much, even though it was clear neither parent was very comfortable with the idea (I don't know if it was the cats or me they were uncomfortable with). Also the world's quietest people — until this week, when they've been making rather a lot of noise packing up, we could go months and not hear a single sound from their apartment.

Goodbye, north-side neighbours — I didn't know you at all and I couldn't even eavesdrop because you spoke English only to me and not to each other. I hope you are moving somewhere nice where you are either able to successfully avoid the neighbours or like them better than you liked me. And I hope you are replaced by people of similar or greater sweetness, quietude, and fondness for cats.

January 31, 2021

Day 325: My mom asked me to order some stuff for her and when it came there was a little free sample of skin cream, which she said I should keep, so of course I immediately put it on my face — new things in a pandemic are very exciting! It turned out to be really good and my face felt so silky. So the free sample was working as intended and I looked up the product, hoping to buy it, but it's three hundred dollars.

> RR: So I can't get it.
> MS: No.
> RR: There's no way for me to justify that kind of money on face cream.
> MS: Probably not.
> RR: Even though my face is really silky right now.
> MS (touches RR's face): It is!
> RR: And I tried thinking about the cost amortized, but there's only so much time I can spend touching my face.
> MS: Because eventually the pandemic will end and you'll have other things to do.

Mini Dip

February 2, 2021

Day 327: I went to the dentist today. It was just a routine cleaning, which I might have put off but I was worried about my surgical site and wanted someone to look at it and give me the official all-clear. So I did the cleaning too since I was there, and it was very poky. As I sat there in the chair, being poked by the very nice hygienist, I had a weird feeling suddenly that I should tug on her arm or embrace her or something. It took me a minute to realize that that's what I do with Mark when I'm feeling anxious or uncomfortable, and since I'm almost never near anyone besides Mark, something in me took this proximal person for him.

I did not, of course, harass the dental hygienist — I let her do her work in peace and went home and hugged Mark, the only acceptable person for hugging this year. But wow, this is not the kind of weirdo I was planning to be, when it was under my control what sort of weirdo I turned into, which I guess it no longer is. That is disappointing. (My surgical site is fine!)

February 5, 2021

Day 330: I am coming increasingly unglued in work meetings, partly because they are pretty much my only non-Mark interaction of the day and I get overstimulated, and partly because I'm working on something challenging and new right now and have no energy to conceal my insecurities. I have heard about the calm duck floating serenely on the water while the feet frantically paddle beneath the surface, but that path does not seem to be for me. No matter how much I try to tell myself "serene duck, serene duck" beforehand, I am all wild flipper feet as soon as I unmute.

The bananas thing is, my division is doing a thing where we have all-division meetings every few weeks and, one by one, each team has a representative do a little mini-interview on what their job actually is. I volunteered to go for my team, because after all the readings I've done I am decent at public speaking and mind it less than most — even rather like it, truth be known. I also quite like my job, most of the time, and am happy to chat about it. Except right now, awash with imposter syndrome that might *not* be imposter syndrome (just like you're not paranoid if they're actually after you, it's not a syndrome if you've actually been faking expertise for fifteen years!).

I'm worried I'll get into the big divisional coffee hour and the VP will say, "Okay, Rebecca, why don't you tell us a bit about your role?" and I'll unmute and just start listing budget problems and schedule slips and eventually burst into tears.

February 8, 2021

Day 333: I set out to write my novel non-chronologically but I've discovered that either the story is not best served by that structure or I'm not smart enough to do it that way. Either way, I'm now having to reshuffle the pieces into time order by tiny chunks, which *sux*. The pieces are not even complete chapters in many cases, since I have so many fun, interesting ideas about writing that do not easily lend themselves to restructuring *at all*. Also, some chunks seem to be pretty much homeless in the new order, despite being — I think — really interesting. The Humane Society for Homeless Novel Gobbets is going to be seeing an influx.

February 9, 2021

Day 334:

> MS: Can you put the butter in the butter dish?
> RR: Can't you do it?
> MS (wiping down countertop): I know you have a
> lot of rules about how you like it done, so you
> better handle it.
> RR: I don't have "rules" — I have one rule: don't get
> butter on the outside of the butter dish. Don't
> you think you can handle that?
> MS (knocks over knife block, all the knives fall out):
> No.
> RR: I see your point.

February 10, 2021

Day 335: A piece of writing advice that I either heard somewhere or possibly made up, it's a bit misty now, is "A perfectly accurate map of the world would be the size of the world." Whoever said it (*is it me?*) I think meant to encourage choice and deliberateness in writing. Describing someone's hair or driving style or romantic past very realistically or very beautifully or very whatever doesn't matter if it doesn't illuminate and advance something for the reader. You have to not only write well but write with purpose.

It's good advice, I guess, and I try to relay it when I teach. *But I hate it.* It breaks my heart to leave things out. I think of myself as a hyperrealistic writer — even when I write about aliens or people who can fly, I know everything about them: their lives and histories and stuff on the floors of their cars. I can force myself not to include all of it in the book, but I want to. If I ever write a memoir — which I assume I won't, having shared everything worth sharing here on Facebook — it would be called *A Map the Size of the World*. Which is what my dream book would be. [Edit from the future: So ... it's odd that this book exists now, or will soon. This is, in fact, a memoir after all, consisting of minutiae of hyperreality and, in a way, is my dream book. Although it was edited a *lot*: the original manuscript was more than two hundred thousand words and I didn't include even half of that — you're welcome.]

• • •

Oh, I forgot to tell you that smize (smile-eyes for when the rest of your face doesn't show) are a real thing and totally work. Proof: I got into the elevator yesterday wearing one of my bigger masks, which covers my face from the soft skin beneath my eyes to my throat. Also in the elevator was a parent, also masked, and a baby in a buggy. I'm bad with baby ages, but maybe a one-year-old? The sort of animated, interactive baby? Anyway, the kid immediately looked over at me and was very interested — perhaps also tired of being home with just the fam all the time, like me. And of course I gave him a big smile, before realizing, "Oh yeah — mask!" But in the time it took me to think that, he had grinned back, chortled, and ducked his head — totally recognizing the smile in and around my eyes, which was the only thing he could see. Smart, perceptive baby, no doubt, but also — smize are real! Do it!

February 17, 2021

Day 342: Updates:

- The wheel fell off our laundry hamper. Mark, key witness, is not taking questions at this time, but did throw the wheel in the garbage (which is where I saw it and deduced that it was formerly the laundry-hamper wheel) so I am not feeling hopeful about the fate of the laundry hamper. Or of any of us. [Edit from the future: As of January 4, 2023, the laundry hamper somehow still lives, minus a wheel.]
- I have killed so many darlings in my novel that I am unsure whether any sentences I like will remain in the next draft.
- I'm edging ever closer to cutting my own hair. I have watched several impossible-looking tutorials on YouTube, some of them seemingly designed to make it look hard so you will pay a professional, but I found one called the Double Unicorn Method that seemed doable. Not easy, but plausible.
- I told Mark the best gift he could possibly give me would be to let me read aloud to him Gordon Korman's classic novel *Don't Care High* and he

agreed, but then I laughed so hard I couldn't breathe on page 2 and he took the book away. It's a very good book. If you want, we could Zoom and I'll read it to you?

- My mom asked me to buy her some conditioner at the drugstore (she is on month nine of not going to stores, or anywhere) and I bought shampoo plus conditioner by mistake. I will use it myself, as punishment, and try again this afternoon. Can I succeed in this very tiny quest? *Maybe.*

February 20, 2021

Day 345: I've never been wildly into shopping, though I suppose I like nice things — shopping just takes up too much time I don't have normally, plus money, plus I have plenty of nice things and other ways of being thrilled with life that aren't thing-oriented. Except now I don't, really, have much going on and I'm really getting into that little endorphin rush that comes from a New Object. There couldn't be a worse time for me to become indiscriminately shoppy, since I do not feel very confident in my economic future, but here we are. I have managed not to go bananas as yet, but I spend a lot of time thinking about things I *might* buy.

Also ... I try to find ways to outsource this desire. A couple months ago, Mark mentioned he was getting fed up with reading the newspapers on his phone and maybe he'd get an iPad or something. Yesterday, when I was feeling low, I suddenly remembered that comment and to cheer myself up, researched all the iPad options and then went running down the hall to tell Mark.

RR: They come in rose gold!

MS: Okay ...

RR: I know you probably won't want that. I was just
mentioning.

MS: Yeah, probably not.

RR: There's also silver and kind of a dark grey. That
seems more you.

MS: Great.

RR: You can also get it engraved with your name.

MS: Really.

RR: Or anything you want — it doesn't have to be
your name.

MS: Uh-huh.

RR: It's free, the engraving, so you might as well
get something.

MS: Mm ...

RR: The basic one is four hundred and twenty-
nine dollars, which is expensive but less than I'd
thought. Probably you wouldn't need more than
the basic one, right?

MS: I dunno.

RR: So are you going to get one?

MS: Maybe sometime. Not right now.

RR: Really? When?

MS: ...

RR: Are you going to do anything entertaining?

MS: I am not here to entertain you.

RR: Oh really? I do not recall this from the marriage vows.

February 21, 2021

Day 346: Updates: I cut my own hair! The fabled Double Unicorn! I was at first exultant but after my hair dried (it was somewhat wet when I cut it), it was curlier and also shorter and also weirder. I now have … bangs, somehow? A little bit? It's still mainly fine, but not as good as I originally believed. Like, fine with a couple bobby pins, if I'm being strictly honest. I just wanted to be totally honest about this since I'll probably be seeing a lot of you on Zoom soon and my hair may well be dry for that.

Also, we got Pizza Hut pizza last night and it made both of us mildly ill. This has happened before but I hoped it was a fluke — it seems not. We both do fine with high-end Neapolitan-style pizza, but not the delicious mass-produced stuff, which is probably a very depressing sign of age. As I crawled woozily into bed last night, I announced, "I want to either be able to eat junk-food pizza or I want a bed frame. Young people sleep on mattresses on the floor and eat crappy pizza. We have the worst of both worlds." Mark was largely asleep and didn't answer meaningfully but I am planning to make good on this. [Edit from the future: I didn't.]

February 22, 2021

Day 347: Things I have done on my day off today:

- Scrub cat puke out of rug.
- Watch Mark mop unknown cat effluent in hallway.
- Carry delicate cat across newly mopped floor so she wouldn't get her paws wet.
- Attend work meeting.

- Receive checkup call from doctor to tell them about my good progress.
- Work on tax document.
- Go down rabbit hole of other tax documents, so now my office is document exposition town.

While we are counting our losses in the pandemic, we should have a tiny moment for how Covid ruined vacation days.

• • •

I witnessed a woman become extremely distressed and then extremely abusive today at the pharmacy. She had called for a prescription and asked if the syringes she was getting with it would be "the long ones" and the pharmacist said yes. Then when she got there, she saw they were shorter than she was expecting. The pharmacist explained that the ones the customer kept asking about were no longer available, and these ones being offered to her were the longest available at present. The customer said over and over that she'd gotten the longer ones at this pharmacy before, and that the woman on the phone had lied. Of course, she'd gotten the longer ones years ago, when they were previously available, and the woman on the phone had said only that they were giving her the longest ones available *now*, but the woman was beside herself and couldn't process this information.

Eventually she became incoherent to the point of viciously screaming at the woman in front of her, who wasn't even the person she thought had made the mistake, if anyone in fact had. She was furious at having to pay eight dollars for the syringes she didn't want, and while I was horrified by her performance, I was also somewhat horrified that she might not have an extra eight dollars to spare. She left and I started to request my prescription and then she came back to resume yelling and startled me — I squeaked, and she told me off for my "fake" fear, and I scuttled to the side.

It was tempting to intervene and tell her to let people do their jobs and let the growing lineup behind her proceed, but she wanted so desperately to fight that I didn't think that would work. It was tempting to give her eight dollars, but again, I felt like that would somehow turn into a fight. I actually self-inject medication at home, too, but I use an auto-injector and not a syringe, so I was very curious about why someone might prefer one needle length to another.

The pandemic has gone on *too long* and people are raw and miserable. Today I was initially a little sharp with someone at the bank in an email and he told me to call him so he could carefully explain how I'd had opportunities to remedy the situation much earlier and hadn't, so now it is what it is. I really appreciated him getting me on the phone and talking me through my own errors, and I tried to be a person who could at least hear what he was saying. Sometimes that's the best we can do. The pharmacist and the bank guy are probably both really seeing a lot of folks at their worst these days. Be kind out there, friends, and take care ...

February 23, 2021

Day 348: Today is the fourth anniversary of my father's death. It is very weird to me that he does not know about the pandemic. It is, of course, possible that he *does* know about the pandemic and that he has access to news wherever he is now. If there is some sort of rewarding, good afterlife for Jerry Rosenblum, it will include access to a wide variety of international news sources. In case you've ever wondered why I never seem up on current events but, if you try to explain them to me as if to an idiot (I mean, fair), I actually have quite a lot of context and insight, it's because I grew up with world events being gently explained to me at every turn. There's a part of me that still rebels at the thought of having to understand the news for myself — so I often don't. I want someone to do that for me. It's not a great instinct, but, well. It came from a nice place.

I don't really like the idea of never speaking ill of the dead — no one is all one kind of person all the time, so trying to make a dead person into all good all the time makes them seem ... well, deader, to me. A person with flaws who is occasionally a jerk about certain things is more vivid and alive to me (don't worry, I am not coming to criticize all the dead people — I will stick to my own).

I lived with my dad for nineteen years — plus a few bonus months after university — so we definitely fought a lot. He was a deeply grown-up person, the opposite of me in many ways. He was an older parent, forty-two when I was born — I realized to my shock this morning, as that is how old I am right now and it doesn't feel that old. But it's a lot older than a baby. He played with me, and my brother, and had fun with us, but I don't think he really understood "kid" things. He liked news, and serious books, and black-and-white movies, smoked fish, opera, and tidiness. When I was small, some things we agreed on were animals and cheese — he was always up for taking me to see animals, and he loved our own pets. We all loved cheese.

We also disagreed on tons of things. He never really accepted that small children don't want to go on scenic drives, and my lack of interest in Sir Laurence Olivier at age nine was baffling to him. He loved to walk to the end of piers, which as a child I thought was very dull except when my brother argued about maybe jumping into the water and once we saw a person fishing catch a small shark. As an adult I always enjoy walking out on a pier and always think of my dad, but as a kid I just wanted to get down on the beach so I could swim and dig.

When we took our first family visit to L.A., where my father grew up, we went to a number of piers and it was all very dull. After dinner one day, he told us we were going to Santa Monica Pier, and we groaned in the back seat of the rental car. If you have been to that part of the world, maybe you know what I did not — Santa Monica Pier has an amusement park. I'll never forget my shock and delight at seeing the lit-up Ferris wheel come into view against the evening sky. My father hated amusement parks, but he loved us, and he tried. I miss him very much.

February 24, 2021

Day 349: Today I put the laundry in the washer, put some dryer sheets in my pocket (mistake — I will smell like dryer sheets forever), and walked to the library in the lovely sun to pick up a DVD. I even nipped into a convenience store on the way back to get a pop. As I headed back toward my building to put the wash into the dryer with the now-hateful dryer sheets (and get back to work), I ran into: Mark, out for his own walk! Further proving that there is just one guy! In the world!

February 25, 2021

Both these convos took place within ten minutes of each other:

> RR: Oh, you have a new freckle on your ear!
> MS: Really?
> RR: Hmm, yep. It's not a shadow, it's not a piece
>   of lint.
> MS: Wow.

RR: If you weren't married, you wouldn't find out these things.

MS: True.

RR: Oh no, it was a piece of lint.

MS: Well, good thing you didn't try to publish an article on that freckle in a peer-reviewed journal ...

RR: I'm going to make some more cupcakes tomorrow. What colour frosting do you want? (Hands Mark food dye box.)

MS: How about this one? (Points.)

RR: *Brown?*

MS: Obviously not! My mistake.

RR: No, it's okay. It's just that that's the colour that I thought, well, there's only seven colours, really, I guess they've got to put one more.

MS: Brown? *Why did I even marry you? Brown?!* How did security let you in? Ahem. I'll have red.

RR: You can have brown! Just, what drew you to it?

MS: Just a nice chocolatey brown. It sounds good.

RR: It's not flavouring, right? Just colour.

MS: Colour sort of tricks the eye, though.

RR: So what you actually want is a chocolate-frosted cupcake.

MS: Well, beggars can't be choosers.

RR: You don't have to be a beggar. What you can do is go buy a chocolate cupcake! You don't have to put up with this!

MS: I want a red cupcake! It'll be great. What colour
  are you going to have?
RR: I would also like a red cupcake.

Unrelated: Do you think it's okay to go to a local hotel during the current lockdown? I wouldn't be travelling except on the subway, but I wouldn't technically be obeying the "stay-at-home" order …? *This is a serious question!*

February 28, 2021

Day 353: Hello, I got Thai food last night and accidentally ate a really spicy pepper and am still coughing twelve hours later because my body is mean that way. Is there any way I can go to the grocery store without terrifying everybody?

March 1, 2021

Day 354: Letting go of the illusion that I have non-cat news … This morning, the black squirrel that is the enemy of both cats was back, standing on the balcony, twitching its tail, clearly not in the least afraid. When I came more fully into the room, I realized it was making a loud noise, audible through two panes of glass. Chattering, I guess — some form of squirrel yelling. The cats were transfixed. I banged on the glass and all animals ignored me — I didn't want to open the balcony door because you'll remember day 213 when I did that and the squirrel charged me and almost got into the apartment, but finally I opened the glass but left the screen and yelled at it and it left. The cats were sad. Later I posited to Mark that maybe the squirrel wanted to mate with our cats and Mark did not enjoy that conversation at all — but how does a squirrel know what is and is not a squirrel if it cannot smell them? How does a cat know that it is itself not a squirrel, having encountered only two cats and one squirrel and that's it for the animal kingdom in its limited life? As it turns out, according to the internet, squirrel chattering is a sound of aggression, not seduction, when a squirrel thinks another animal is in its territory — interesting that the squirrel thinks it owns our apartment. Also, the max size of a black squirrel is less than two pounds and our smallest cat is six pounds, so that is probably not a good match.

March 5, 2021

Day 358: So I did the lunch-and-learn interview at work today and it did go well — hooray! It turned out my interrogator wanted to talk more about writing than my job, which was fine with me. She said she was worried about asking me the same questions I always get asked, which I wasn't worried about at all since I haven't had a book out in four years and am not getting interviewed by anyone about anything these days. But she did actually ask me something I don't think I've ever been asked before: How do I name my characters?

Which isn't so simple. I used to do it intuitively — I'd think about the character, who they were and what they were like and, boom, I'd know their name. But as time went on, it became very, very apparent in my work that I grew up in a small southern Ontario town where most people (besides me) are some version of WASPs. My favourite names in the world are Catherine, Sarah, and Jake. A character named Catherine is at the heart of *So Much Love*, someone named Sarah shows up in multiple short stories. I've had to restrain myself from reusing those names. To my shame, I've accidentally used the name "Jake" a few times.

So I've started using different methods — I think about the character, who they are and what they are like, and then I google the part of the country or the world they are from and the year they were born, and start going through lists of names. I go through the meanings of the name and occasionally listen to recorded pronunciations. In a way, I find this a bit artificial, but honestly, the world is better because not everyone is from my little town, and I wouldn't want to write about a world where they seem to be.

What's your favourite name?

March 7, 2021

Day 360: After a dinner that was a really impressive homemade cream-of-mushroom soup plus a dessert of a granola bar with icing on it because I. Am. Mercurial, this dialogue:

> RR: So, I saw that movie *Moxie* is out now.
> MS: Yeah, I watched the trailer. Seemed a little obvious.
> RR: Well, I dunno if I want to watch a movie that's too subtle right now. I don't know if I want suspense, or to feel uncomfortable in any way.
> MS: Okay, watch the trailer and let me know what you think.
> RR: I watched the trailer.
> MS: ...
> RR: I watched it *with you*.
> MS: Oh ...
> RR: Oh my God.
> MS: Ah, you have some mushroom in your teeth.
> (Reaches into RR's mouth, picks out mushroom.)

RR: *Agh!*

MS: Okay, okay, we don't have to watch *Moxie.*

RR: I want to watch *Moxie* — I want to watch it!

MS: Sure, well, we both like Amy Poehler.

RR: And if I have something in my teeth, you can just tell me about it.

MS: Oh yeah, I see how that might have been disconcerting for you.

RR: Yeah.

MS: Well, those can be our two movies for next weekend — *Moxie* and that Salinger one.

RR: I never agreed to that.

March 8, 2021

Day 361: Happy Women's Day for those who choose to celebrate! Unrelated to the occasion, I was listening to a podcast about social skills, and there was a debate about being polite and making others feel relaxed and included in minor daily interactions. One point of view is this is traditionally gendered labour, that women have always been tasked with social sweetness and we should feel free to toss it off and not worry so much about how others feel.

My feminism is that I will be retaining social kindness and also asking it of everyone in my life, regardless of gender (and, of course, there are as many feminisms as there are feminists, so feel free to have your own). It was also gendered labour for a long time that women do the dishes, but when that was discovered to be bullshit, we didn't decide to just let the dishes remain dirty, because clean dishes are an unmitigated good — we just decided to share the load of who cleans them.

I think small kindnesses and social warmth are also an unmitigated good and if women have been doing more than our share for some time, instead of just giving up and doing none, let's distribute the effort more evenly. As a person who has worked my entire career in spaces dominated by lady-identified persons, I cannot tell you how much better it has made my life that people around me forty hours a week are basically interested in my well-being. Maybe we don't talk in depth about our hearts and souls, but we wish each other well, and try to take care and be kind wherever we can.

March 12, 2021

This is it — day 365. At least it's sunny. We ran an errand out in Scarborough this afternoon, which meant taking the subway on my old route to work. It was very, very, very weird to do that a year to the day after the last time I commuted to my actual job.

I didn't think too much about taking the subway overall — I've been on it once or twice a month throughout the pandemic and in off-peak times it's fine, if non-ideal. But I am definitely edgy and uncomfortable and there's enough people who start out with their masks on and then edge them down that I feel like I can't read or zone out (I will get up and move if someone takes their mask off or down). It's so much energy! I wonder what it would be like to commute every day — would I develop a system for monitoring (I learned to sleep to my exact stop when I was commuting regularly) or just give up on truly keeping an eye on folks? I really feel for people who have no choice but to be on the TTC all the time.

I was happy to be out in Scarborough again for the first time in so long. We even got some Little Caesars pizza, which doesn't exist downtown, and ate it sitting on the curb in a parking lot before getting back on the subway. What passes for excitement these days.

March 14, 2021

Day 367: I walked to Philosopher's Walk today to see a friend (in human form! all the way down to her feet!) and along Bloor there are ice sculptures, for some reason. It's cool except (a) one has already been smashed and (b) clumps of people gather around them to try to take the perfect photo. I dislike this sort of thing at the best of times. No selfie clusters!

It is Pi(e) Day and I'm making a zucchini pie (quiche) for dinner and my mom gave me a cherry pie for dessert, so let the good times roll.

March 16, 2021

Day 369:

> RR: What's on your shirt?
> MS (picks at it): Crud? I'm gonna say crud.
> RR: And you're going to leave it, are you? Not change your shirt or anything?
> MS: It's the second shirt of the day, so I'm pretty much done now.
> RR: What happened to the first shirt?
> MS: I was so frazzled this morning, I put my pen in the pocket without the lid and it just went … (Mimes a combination of exploding and vomiting.)
> RR: And did you wash it out right away? Ink will come out if you rinse it right away. Where is the shirt now?
> MS: In the garbage.

RR: Seriously?

MS: It was so much ink. It would never come out.

RR: It would have! If you tried. Did you try?

MS: No, I panicked and threw it in the garbage. I
    wasn't going to tell you, but now that you've no-
    ticed this second shirt ... issue, I feel that in the
    interest of full disclosure, I should tell you the
    shirt is gone. I threw away the shirt because it
    was ruined.

RR: It wasn't necessarily ruined! If you'd just —

MS: You shouldn't give me such a hard time. I liked
    that shirt.

RR: Not enough ...

March 19, 2021

Day 372 of the indoor life, day 4,382 with Mark Sampson, twelve
years after our first date. In general, Mark is the best person I could
have been isolated with or married to. Yesterday he played fetch
with Evan and a tiny sardine head. He has put up with all my
Facebook teasing and oversharing with good grace and has agreed
to my ragbag system, more or less. He is CP style but respectful of
Chicago and also *Macquarie*. At this point, all either of us really
wants to do is quietly watch cartoons but we'd like to do it leaning
on each other's shoulders. Quaranlove.

• • •

Last night Mark and I sat down and watched the Red Canary Song
vigil for the eight lives taken in Atlanta — a man murdered sex
workers of Asian descent (and some bystanders), if you didn't pick

up on this particular terrible news story. It was a beautiful and heartbreaking event, and I felt grateful to be witness to a community taking care of each other and grieving together. Zoom in presentation mode doesn't reveal how many people are watching so I was startled when someone said there were more than three thousand of us there together, from all over North America and Asia. It was a unique moment of connection across the internet. I wonder who the other 2,098 were.

March 21, 2021

Day 374: It is absolutely amazing when I remember having written a chapter in my novel and three months later when I go back to revise it, I find out that instead of a chapter it is the beginning of a chapter four different ways, each time just stopped abruptly and then restarted with a different point of view and some of the details changed, and apparently I thought I was going to fix this at some point. I guess now is that point. Thanks a lot, past Rebecca. You're a jerk.

March 23, 2021

The maddest cat, the saddest me, en route to kitty surgery.

• • •

Reunited! I think Evan was very surprised to be brought home after more than twenty-four hours at the vet's instead of to another chamber of sadness! He at first refused to come out of his carrier and then emerged with wonder but also weariness. There's blood in the fur on his face and throat and the vet guesses he was probably in pain for some time before the surgery to remove his infected teeth, but he didn't show it. I feel terrible about that but also so very joyful to have him back.

March 24, 2021

Day 377: Cat update (I'm not even going to pretend cats are not my constant preoccupation right now). Evan was clearly not himself yesterday evening but he was pretty okay, much as I was post-dental surgery. We had been instructed that he was not to jump and climb on the furniture while he was still semi-sedated, and we should prevent him from doing so by "following him around," which sounded pretty much impossible, since I like to ... do things, but it turned out he knew his limits somehow and was content to move around slowly and sleep on the living room rug.

Evan did not want any pets last night, and I couldn't tell if it was because he was in pain or if he was mad because I'd taken him to the vet in the first place or just a standard grumpiness. But I woke up at 2:00 a.m., wondering how he was doing, and went out and found he had climbed onto the couch to sleep. I was standing there worrying he wasn't supposed to be up there when he woke up and was absolutely delighted to see me. He let me pet him and tried to get onto the back of the couch for better access, but fell over, so I picked him up and he *let me*, which is rare, and I *cuddled him in my arms*. Unheard of! We sat down on the couch and had a lovely few minutes, until he had had enough and bit me gently and tried to lie down to sleep on my foot. Of course I went back to bed because I am a doting cat parent but the bed is better than the couch.

This morning he was furious because breakfast was delayed (to time the medication properly) and also still can't properly meow owing to the intubation scratching up his throat (this operation was something else!) but was jumping agilely all over the place and seemed much more standard Evan. Which is my favourite Evan. Although the late-night cuddly Ev was great, too.

. . .

As a distraction from cats, tomorrow a contractor is coming to remove our bathroom door and frame — and then hopefully replace them. You will remember that the hinge broke in the fall, and because of the pandemic we tried to live with it until December, when the door stopped closing at all. Since then the building has been promising to follow up "soon" and just not … but now the happy day is at hand … allegedly. I don't have tremendous faith, but hope springs … Let's see.

Because I can sentimentalize anything, I'm sad to see the door go. The hooks on the back were installed by my late father, probably the last handyman project he undertook for me. And the poster on the outside, which I don't seem to be able to remove without tearing, was purchased at the poster sale in the McGill Shatner building in my first few weeks of university to decorate my room. It's *Café Terrace at Night* by Van Gogh, because I was very classy as a frosh, you see … I also kept a nine-dollar poster for twenty-four years.

And yes, I will have to take my still-recovering cat, high on pain meds, and lock him in the bedroom while strangers with power tools bang away in the hall. *Fun times!*

March 25, 2021

Day 378: After hours of drilling and banging, our broken bathroom door was downgraded to no bathroom door, then eventually upgraded to one that does indeed close but is … unpainted wood? And the frame is … unpainted metal? It is a vaguely prison-like vibe. I mean, don't get me wrong, I'm excited to close the door and have it stay firmly shut as opposed to swinging open if a cat pats it gently, but this looks awful and I feel like unpainted wood plus shower mist will eventually go wrong. Also, the contractor knocked a small hole in the wall. Anyway, this is apparently below my very low minimum aesthetic standard — surprise! Tell me how to paint things, please!

March 27, 2021

Day 380: Cried when I got the text that my mom's vaccine appointment went fine. Went for a walk with a friend and was so overjoyed to just be out, chatting and engaged, and not cold, lonely, or (particularly) frightened of disease. Oh, what a terrible year that these things seem so strange and beautiful, but at least there are beautiful things.

March 28, 2021

Ev update: Today was his first day without post-surgical pain meds and he appears to feel just fine, and now has more energy because he isn't on drugs. Only two after-effects from surgery: The shaven spot on right foreleg, which I assume was for the IV. He hates it and grooms it viciously. And also hunger, as he cannot have kibble or treats right now — too crunchy. His main meals are wet food, so we thought he wouldn't miss the other stuff, but I think we underestimated how much he was eating because he is forlornly hungry all the time, and was ecstatic when we snuck him a random extra meal last night.

Third Wave

March 30, 2021

I asked my mom what colour frosting she wanted for her birthday cupcakes and she said yellow. She remembers having yellow frosting on her third birthday cake, which her mom carried on her lap on the ferry the day they moved from Staten Island to Brooklyn. The other thing she remembers from that year, 1945, is people celebrating in the street when the war ended. I keep wondering how we will remember now.

March 31, 2021

Day 384: I went for an early morning walk since I saw it was going to rain later and I've been having trouble getting outside once I'm immersed in work, anyway. Because it was early, I still had my glasses on — I wear contacts so much that many people don't even know I'm myopic, but, in fact, I'm impaired enough that I'm not even eligible for laser surgery. There's a thing beyond that, where you get implants in your eyes, but I'm not quite ready to be bionic. Still, my vision worries me, and I've mentioned to a number of people that if I ever lose a contact lens when I'm out, I'd appreciate being taken home since I truly cannot see.

Anyway, despite my efforts to get out before the rain, it started misting on me and of course beaded up my glasses. I stopped at a crosswalk and took them off to wipe on my hoodie and suddenly there I was, bare eyed in public for the first time in years. I have memorized my home so I can go without lenses here, but otherwise, I don't even swim unmagnified (after an embarrassing attempt to join a group of strangers at the beach because someone was wearing the same colour swimsuit as my friend). Now I wear goggles and contacts and am a very unsexy swimmer, but I can see!

Anyway, the crosswalk was magical! All the lights looked like glowing orbs of colour and the cars like boats swishing by in the rain. I saw a dog, but it looked like a fuzzy teddy bear. The zebra crossing was terrifying because the ground was not a distinct concept for me right then, but *Yoga with Adriene* always says "trust the ground, it will be there for you," so I stepped off the curb and crossed the street like the Red Sea and didn't die! Then I put my glasses back on, because it was all too scary, but still — nice to have a new experience.

If you're out with me and I lose a contact, please take me home.

April 3, 2021

Day 387: Mark bravely grocery-shopped alone and I went to meet him to help carry things home. As I walked to the store, I saw a woman with three little kids sitting in front of the Tim Hortons, I guess waiting for someone. The kids, all probably under six, started playing a terrible game: running away from her and trying to get into traffic. I saw the first one do it sort of by accident, trying to evade the mom about an unrelated matter and darting off, and then hearing her tone jack up when he stepped off the curb — I guess he was enjoying the excitement. His sister heard it, too, and came running over to see if she could get in on the action.

I stopped and watched carefully for a minute: I know you can't touch strangers' children ever, or even interact with them during a pandemic, but I figure you can break that rule if a kid is actually going to step in front of a moving vehicle. However, I saw the woman could *just* handle it without intervention — she didn't have a stroller or any way to contain the kids, so every time she sprinted after one, another, giggling, would follow to the road, and then she'd snatch that kid by the hand or some other body part and drag them back, and a third kid would see their time, and she'd sort of have to thump the first two down and run back for the remainder.

It was bad, but she was managing it, and I didn't figure I was in a position to make it better, so I went and met Mark, grabbed the groceries, and we started back. As we walked, I described to him what I'd seen — and then from a distance, we saw a little girl dart across the sidewalk and the bike lane before being hauled back, so he got a demo.

By the time we passed the Tim Hortons again, the mom had lined up the three kids against the wall and was crowding against them with her body to keep them from fleeing again. One kid, who I'm pretty sure had had shoes when I passed the first time, was now barefoot. All were weeping, but that kid was wailing, and the mom was lecturing very firmly that the game with the road was at an end. Anytime anyone tried to stand up, they were reseated. If you had passed this family *only* at this point, you might have had concerns about the mom, but really, I thought she was being restrained. Just before I turned the corner, I saw the wailing kid reach out his arms and she gently pulled him into her lap.

Oh, pandemic parents, you have my heart. And — would you want a rando to try to help you in that situation?

April 6, 2021

Day 390: Today I rented a car and drove my slowly disintegrating computer to my workplace, where I have been only one other time since March 13, 2020. There, IT put a non-exploding battery into the computer while I went up to my office and gathered a few things I had been missing and then, with some extra time to wait, just hung out, enjoyed the vibe, recycled some now-defunct papers, went across to other people's offices to look out the window, and remembered the person I had been when I came there every day.

There were some photos up of colleagues who have left and who I'm no longer in touch with, and I felt sad — they had seemed so much a part of my life and then ... poof, a year goes by and we don't talk and I guess that means we aren't really friends anymore. But sometimes that happens even without a pandemic, really.

I sorted through some old papers and found some schedules for projects I don't even remember, things that I guess I was just finishing up when I left for the lockdown. I hope they ended well. I guess with everything that was going on at that point, my brain didn't write that stuff to disk, as it were.

I enjoyed driving the car on my own, the first time I've done so since September. Scarborough is my favourite place to drive, which I bet is not something many people say — it's just the most familiar to me. The LRT project has progressed a tiny bit, but Eglinton is still bonkers to drive on, but even that didn't upset me as much as any other type of bonkers construction would, because it was familiar. I celebrated having done something — so many days have no events in them — by going to a Wendy's drive-thru, drive-thru being one of the rare possible treats of the pandemic. I got myself a salad, and Mark had asked for a Frosty, so I got us both one. Treats!

Driving home, I passed a store on O'Connor called Panopticon. I thought it might be a stupidly misnamed optician, but no, it was actually a surveillance and security camera store. I'm not sure how Foucault would feel about this development. Then I drove back, parked on the first try, dropped my Frosty on the ground like an idiot, and ran home with two minutes to spare for my meeting. Mark met me at the door, confused because he forgot he had asked for the Frosty and wanting to tell me that the painter was there, painting the bathroom door for a fun surprise; the cats were imprisoned and furious; and also the painter had discovered that what we'd thought were just random brown spots on the bathroom ceiling was actually a tiny bit of mould. So we'd also had a mould treatment and had the bathroom ceiling repainted since I'd been gone. What an eventful, disgusting, wonderful, Frosty-destroying three hours. And then I got back online, went to my meeting, and discovered that schools are closing. Thank goodness, but also oh no. Those poor kids — schools were delayed in reopening after the school holidays in December twice? Three times? Until January 25, and then until multiple no-wait-not-really days in February, I think, before finally a real date of February 16, so they've been back to in-person classes less than two months. Those poor kids ... and teachers ... and parents. What a day. You really can't go back, I guess.

• • •

I have been working late nights and weekends pretty steadily lately, which is not my typical MO but things are just unfortunate and needs must. I did not remember that late-night-worker RR was so dancey.

April 8, 2021

Day 392: Depressingly, my postal code has been ID'd as a "hot spot" — not a cool club or restaurant (remember the old definition of "hot spot"?) but a place where there have been a disproportionate number of hospitalizations (and I suppose deaths) owing to Covid. This stands to reason, as this neighbourhood is dense and poor, and people here have homes and jobs that bring them into a lot of contact. I, of course, am largely outside of that — I do have the exposure that living in an elevator building and sharing laundry facilities brings, and I walk on the crowded streets, but I work from home and don't encounter a lot of what my neighbours do. One I occasionally talk to is an ASL interpreter, and I see many people in brightly coloured scrubs around here, and a few food-deliverers park their bikes out front.

Anyway, all of us lumped together are going to be eligible to get vaccinated starting next week, in some sort of way that I don't understand — does anyone understand it? I'm feeling both un-equal to the task of sorting it out and undeserving of the vaccine itself. I know, I know, the wisdom is if you can get it, get it, and I probably will if the way it works actually works, but the whole system just feels incredible chaotic and bizarre. That's it, that's the post.

April 11, 2021

Day 395: For years I had a phobia about taxis, probably brought on by all those childhood warnings about not getting into cars with strangers. It was an easy phobia to manage, as they go (I have a few), as I don't mind walking and transit, and I *can* suck it up and take cabs when I have to, especially when I'm with others. Then I took a few more cabs and a few more, and gradually the fear dialed way down. During the pandemic, of course, I take cabs only when I absolutely have to — basically when I have to transport a cat. The Beck people might have the impression, because when I call for a cab I always mention the cat so they won't send an allergic driver, that I am someone who leaves home only with cats.

This is not quite true, but I truly don't go many places these days so my three trips to the vet in 2021 represent a huge percentage of my outings, and my conversations with cab drivers, a large proportion of my conversations with strangers. The driver who took us home from Evan's post-surgical checkup yesterday had just been vaccinated and was ebullient. He is over fifty, lives in a hot spot, and drives a cab, a front-line worker if there ever was one, so it was pleasing to see the system work as it should. He said the vaccination — at a hospital in the east end of Toronto — had gone very smoothly and he felt great after. I was so happy to hear his story and it made me hopeful. He wondered why I hadn't been vaccinated yet, since I too live in a hot spot — of course, he knew my address — but I said they hadn't set up the process for us under-fifties. He was very hopeful that it'll all get sorted soon. Such a positive guy — made me feel it was all coming together.

Another cab story: When the cab driver picked me and Ev up from Evan's actual surgery, he confirmed that I was Rebecca, the person who had called for the cab, and then said he had the urge to call me "my beautiful Rebecca," because the wife of the president of his country — Ghana — is named Rebecca and this is how the president always introduces her. I am breathtakingly ignorant of the politics of Ghana but thought it sounded like the president of Ghana is a good husband anyway, and I said I would suggest this mode of presentation to my own husband, and we chuckled. If you're wondering, I looked it up: the president of Ghana since 2017 is Nana Akufo-Addo and his wife is indeed Rebecca Akufo-Addo.

It's hard for me to understand much about the president starting from scratch, but I did take a look at some photos of this other Rebecca, who turned seventy last month, and I do think she is rather beautiful.

April 12, 2021

Day 396: I assume many long-term couples have a lot of nostalgia for the days when they didn't really know each other and thus everything they said was interesting. What were you like in school? Have you read this classic novel, and what did you think? Do you remember your dreams? But eventually you find those things out, mainly, and are left with only up-to-the-minute developments to discover in your journey as a couple, and the pandemic has really slowed down the supply of those. Yesterday Mark talked aloud through his whole decision-making process about whether or not to wear sunglasses on our walk, and I responded that we'd have to get divorced for a while, at least until we had had enough solo experiences to miss each other, whereupon we could remarry. Mark, both not interested and not really listening, said he would already miss me, and I said then he could supply all the conversation for the walk because I had nothing to offer and did not care whether he wore sunglasses or not, and he said sure, "but I probably won't wear sunglasses," and now we are divorced.

Kidding! But for how long? At least if we go with my plan, we will get to have another wedding eventually. The first one was really fun.

April 13, 2021

Day 397: I am probably not the only one who has "favourite characters" who are just co-worker children and pets that crash our video calls, right?

April 14, 2021

Usually when I share a story I overheard, it has a sort of arc or completeness to it, but this one is just a vibe. These two very beautiful young women were walking behind me into the building — like, I try not to use subjective adjectives like that, but they were both *so* striking, and both of the same tall, big-eyed, long-necked type, one blond and fair, one dark-haired and olive, like in a fairy tale. And they were talking a mile a minute, and it sounded like the worst gossip, "Oh, and Sharon is just like that, I *know*!" And then I got into the elevator and they trailed after me and paused, side by side in their ankle boots and snug high-hemmed jeans (how? Why?), and asked me politely if I would mind if they got on with me. Since they had masks and I had a mask, I said sure, so they got on and resumed their talk, and I realized that it wasn't actually mean — just ... I don't even know? They wanted to do a star chart for Sharon; they knew her sun sign but not her rising sign. Would it be weird if they asked her? It would be so useful to know — they could work with her better. And then they got off the elevator.

I think I'm alone so much that I'm forgetting how varied and interesting people actually are, and it just blows me away when I recall. Eventually I'm going to become one of those people who picks up discarded grocery lists outside the supermarket and can't stop marvelling at the wonders of people who buy Tang and fennel seeds.

• • •

Oh gosh, I can't believe I almost forgot to tell you that yesterday I was walking in Rosedale and I walked past a couple sitting out on the lawn of their posh house and their dog was wearing an airplane neck pillow.

April 16, 2021

Day 400: Last night was the sign-up for the first vaccine clinic I was eligible for, that I knew of. I knew because I saw two strangers talking about it on Twitter, and then later my friend Susie mentioned it to me. I worry about people who don't know Susie and don't have time to read strangers' conversations on Twitter. Anyway, the sign-up was pretty hopeless — we were online right at the appointed time and the wait was an hour, but after an hour, of course, no appointments.

Which is fine — I don't need to be vaccinated right this minute. I can wait. It's this need to figure it out for myself, to get out there and … hustle for it … that seems wrong? I would be fine with literally whatever date Public Health wanted to assign me, but it seems like unless I want to keep trawling the internet, trying to figure out when I'm supposed to go, no one is going to assign me any date at all! This doesn't really seem like how it's supposed to work.

Anyway, today I had to rent a car and take my mom to a medical appointment, which was super-stressful, not least because the most straightforward route was closed off by a *sinkhole* on College Street. And nice as it was to see my mom, this was the most time I've spent near her in over a year and it felt really wrong since I'm not vaccinated and she's only halfway, even in the car with windows down and masks on. And I'm not very comfortable driving — and what other sinkholes lurk beneath our roads? — so the whole thing was just very stressful, and I couldn't help but feel that society is crumbling, which was really underlined by the number of illegally parked vehicles. I did get an Impossible Whopper from Burger King while I waited during her appointment, though, which was good.

Of course, I came home to discover that society *is* crumbling, and instead of offering any help or support to human beings struggling a year into a pandemic, the Conservatives are "strengthening enforcement" of the stay-at-home order by giving police officers "enhanced authority." What will this "enforcement" look like? What will they be helpfully preventing people from doing, instead of, like, funding more sick days for exposed workers and extra overtime for health-care workers? Maybe people going for walks will be arrested ...? Maybe in parks? Maybe the unhoused? Certainly not people who were doing much damage, since walking around doesn't operate large-scale business, which is where most of the outbreaks are these days.

Gahhhh ...

April 17, 2021

Day 401: Hello! I slept for ten hours last night and am feeling better! I'm working on a Saturday to make up for yesterday's adventures, but before I got to work, I called the Ontario premier's office to register my dismay over yesterday's announcement about the non-specific "enforcement" and got a real person in just five minutes (bored but civil) to take my message. Then I donated a little money to the Black Legal Action Centre, which has been posting all over the place that they will help Black Ontarians who run into trouble with these new and terrible rules in Ontario that can so easily lead to racial targeting. I'm excited to see police departments refusing to comply in some locations, but it's still a scary, scary time. Take care, my friends.

April 19, 2021

Day 403: In a family whose main athletic activity was turning pages in a book, my maternal grandfather was a bit weird in that he was a competitive swimmer. He held a record for swimming across some channel in Boston for a while, and he trained as a physical education teacher, though he could not ever teach because he wouldn't sign some kind of loyalty/anti-communist oath that the NYC public school system was insisting on when he graduated (pushing teachers around: always in season!). He had to work in his brother's socks-and-underwear importing business instead, which he did not like — nor, I suppose, would anyone. I always thought the upside would be that he worked in the Empire State Building, but apparently the thrill of that wears off rather quickly, and it was a very long commute home to Brooklyn. Once he somehow was given a puppy for my mother at work and brought it home by the subway and the bus under his jacket, and the puppy was very good and did not pee, but it was very long for both of them.

Thinking of my grandpa today because I still follow his old Florida retirement condo complex on Facebook — my mom inherited the condo and still owns it, and I started following the complex years ago to find out about hurricane damage. Anyway, they announced a while back on Facebook that they were tearing up the pool he swam in to renovate and it has been taking months — I saw a photo today and it was so sad, just shards of concrete everywhere. One of the reasons he wanted to go to Florida was to swim year round, and he wound up with a pool just at the edge of his building. The whole complex is far larger than the town I grew up in, and dotted with pools — he was lucky to get a unit close to one. He could also get to the ocean by bus. He swam every day and a couple times, when we visited, we swam with him. He taught my mom to swim and wrote a book about a child who was learning to swim, called *Iggy the Fish*, and my mom taught me to swim and read me the book. I am a poor swimmer, but my grandfather did not live to see it. But I understand the basics, from my mom and from Iggy, and I love the water.

It is possibly a bit alarming that I'm so invested in the updates from my dead-thirty-years grandfather's retirement complex, but my grandfather was a nice and interesting man, and many other things these days are neither nice nor interesting so ... I do what I can. His name was Carl M. Rubin. He didn't like to tell people his middle name.

• • •

I really try not to be grumpy about what other people are or are not doing in the pandemic — we all have our struggles. But I wish people would not let their kids ride their bikes and scooters indoors in public places — it is hard enough to social-distance when not being pursued by a tiny speed demon! This is my dream for FreshCo and Shoppers Drug Mart. Thank you.

April 22, 2021

Day 406: I'm still working on getting a vaccine appointment and while I'm very happy for all who have been or are getting vaxxed, it's quite anxiety inducing to not have this sorted out while seemingly "everyone" else does. There are so many sources of maybe-information — go here, call but don't use the web portal, have you tried just showing up, sign up for the text alerts — and people are pretty nice about trying to help, but there's no one central place where if you put your info in, you go in a queue and then you get a promise that when the time is right and your turn comes, you'll get a shot. There's a feeling that the system doesn't really work, so unless I keep struggling, no one else is going to take care of it.

As mentioned before, one of the most educational things I've done during the pandemic is sign up for CareMongering TO. I registered with the intention of helping out — signing up for a volunteer project, or joining some sort of mutual aid, but that never panned out. Sometimes I offer advice in the comments, occasionally I donate a little money to someone in need, once I gave a guy a plant; most of the time I do nothing at all. But I listen. CareMongering has a bad rap for weird bickering and occasional random Child Services calling — yeah, that happens a lot more than you'd expect (never — I'd expect it never). But I keep hanging around because I've led a privileged existence and the conversations about the actual ins and outs of poverty are something that someone like me is very rarely privy to. It is something I always wind up drawn into.

When someone asks for help, they usually just want groceries or other specific items — sad and startling enough when I think of my own pantry. But some of the cases are more complex and ongoing, and people describe in detail their struggles with the Ontario Disability Support Program (ODSP), Ontario Works, the Canada Emergency Response Benefit and the confusing thing that replaced it, child benefits, food banks, and the extended patchwork of programs intended to help people have the basic necessities of life: food, shelter, heat, clothes, communication technology. There is never any *one* program that will provide all these things, and often there are additional subprograms within whatever the individual is already involved in that could help them more, but they have to know to apply for it, submit the necessary documentation, and follow up. Folks who are struggling with mental and physical health problems, insecure housing, and lack of internet or phone service are exactly the wrong people on whom to load the task of finding all these secrets and following up, but that's where the responsibility seems to lie.

It can be amazing to see people chime in with detailed and specific help in ways I never could, because I have never experienced poverty like that and I don't know how to navigate the system: this is how you apply for a one-time payment to cover moving expenses, this is where the furniture bank is and what they can provide, this is what a rent bank is and what they can do. This is what "your worker" (a term I see all the time and I guess is a caseworker with ODSP?) can help you with and what they cannot. This is the number to call if your worker stops answering their phone. This food bank has halal food. This food bank can deal with vegan requests. This food bank often has rotten food — don't go there unless it's a last resort.

These conversations are a beautiful patchwork of generosity and resourcefulness, but they are scary, too, because they represent a system that is not really working, where a person who doesn't know what to do and doesn't have help will just … drift away. It's been incredibly illuminating and incredibly sad. The vaccine thing, as it applies to me, isn't that important, but it's another aspect of a broken system and, as it applies to others, is very important.

April 25, 2021

Day 409: I loved living in Montreal as a student, but I didn't really experience the whole of the city — my stomping grounds were pretty narrow. But sometime early-ish in my time there, I found out that you could buy things for the Jewish holidays near Namur subway station, so I used to go out there maybe once or twice a year, even though it seemed like another planet. Sometimes friends would come with me, because we were young and time seemed more expendable then and running an errand with a friend seemed like a good use of it. One time, we looked out into the distance and saw a Walmart and a Pizza Hut and thought it would be nice to go to those places that our parents used to take us to but that didn't exist in downtown Montreal. But we were pedestrians standing on the sidewalk and we were staring out at the autoroute, and it was hard to figure out how to get from here to there. The solution, with twenty-year-old logic, was to find a hole in the train fence and walk along the tracks for a bit, and then pop out through another hole — there was probably another way, but I never found out what it was. And then we'd come back that way, sometimes carrying those big jugs of laundry detergent you can get at Walmart and leftovers in Pizza Hut boxes, along with my stuff for the Jewish holidays. Those are some really fun memories!

And then I graduated and left Montreal and also read *Nickel and Dimed* by Barbara Ehrenreich, which came out that same year. The subtitle is *On (Not) Getting By in America* and it's about low-wage jobs and how the employees are treated, and it has a long and terrible section about Walmart, and after that I stopped shopping there. It was a very convenient boycott, since soon I was again living in a pedestrian downtown where it was almost impossible to access a Walmart, and though I did get a car and work near a Walmart for those nine years, I didn't feel I was missing out on much. I have twice been in Walmarts in the past twenty years, both times accompanying friends on errands (maybe my time never got that valuable), when it just seemed like a jerk move to insist on waiting outside, but I didn't actually interact with the store so it seemed okay.

Until today. I never did fully back a horse as I should have in the Great Vaccine Race — I was neither fully in the race, committed to finding a vax appointment as fast as possible, nor fully on the sidelines, accepting the wait for an appointment. I oscillated between being okay with waiting and also following Vaccine Hunters Canada on Twitter, which is a lovely endeavour but not very helpful to me personally in that it blows up my phone constantly with alerts for maybe-possible vaccines that you can't book but just have to go investigate in far-flung corners of the city in the middle of the workday, until I was fully deranged by the end of the week and decided booking *anything* was better than living with myself in this state. So when my friend Laura suggested a very helpful site where you can book Walmart vaccinations anywhere, as long as you type very fast and have the means to get to, say, Malton, I just did it.

Was this a sane approach? No. Was it in line with my values, in terms of big retailers? Of course not. In terms of scarcity of vaccines in the downtown core? Maybe, because by borrowing a car and going out of town, we left a slot for someone who can't do that. But not really, because I don't actually have a slot to give up, so far ... and also, there was no selflessness here; I just wanted it done.

The Walmart pharmacist was very kind but fantastically frazzled — I didn't even get a Band-Aid, let alone a sticker, and when I said I was grateful, she just sighed and said everyone is. I cried like half a tear in the condom aisle and got on with the day. All in all, I thought Walmart was organized and responsible, and I appreciated them, but I still won't go back.

I remain worried for people who do not have an Oscar-speech list of people to thank to get their vaccines because this seems like a thing that people really do need help with sometimes. (I woke Mark from a nap to announce that a town called Malton exists and that he had to go there; that's where he got vaxxed today, too, three hours later at *a different Walmart*. You just have no idea how many Walmarts there are. *Four* in Vaughn alone. It's *wild*!)

April 26, 2021

Day 410: Vaccine side effect report. I feel okay today! My arm hurts, and like an idiot I slept on it, making it worse. I lay on my back to go to sleep last night, and then kept rolling over in my sleep, waking up because it hurt, reset, repeat. Sleep-RR is dumb. Otherwise I'm a little achy and headachy, a bit tired, but honestly, that could be any pandemic Monday, right?

In between sore-arm wakings, I had some wild dreams, which some people have been attributing to the AstraZeneca vax. Who knows? To wit:

- As I was drifting off, I was seized upon by a fury that the lyric in the musical *Rent* "Love's not a three-way street" makes no earthly sense. The problem with loving a musical when you are nineteen is that you still have all the lyrics memorized but you no longer accept them joyfully. I actually woke up fully to be mad about this, and then woke Mark, who agreed that the line is dumb.
- I dreamed that I lived in Anne of Green Gables's house — maybe I was Anne? And people were coming to stay with us, so I had to clean the house, which meant I got to see every nook and cranny, which they don't show on the tour — like the cutlery drawer and everything. Best dream of the night!

- Just before my alarm went off, I dreamed that an old friend and I were being held hostage by the mob and when they questioned us, I found out all this really personal stuff about my friend and I felt bad that he had never told me — and that he was being forced to now! The weird thing is, that is a type of dream I have sometimes, where it's like a movie I was cast in, because the friend wasn't a real person and I'm unlikely to be held by the mob.

April 28, 2021

Day 412: I did not personally have paid sick days until 2016 (except for a couple years in the early aughts). What you do when you don't have them is you wake up feeling ill, and then you think about your expenses at the moment and your current bank balance, and whether some of your expenses are unnecessary or could be put off, and how healthy you need to be to do your most basic work tasks, and whether you could fake it, and then you either go to work or back to bed, accordingly.

Some of this for me was a bit theoretical (or theatrical), because I had a decent financial margin a lot of the time, and I also usually had a flexible job, so if I was worried about funds, I could not work one day but then do extra hours later to make it up. I also had the option of working from home at many points, something none of the essential workers currently in the news have. But even if you know realistically your balance sheet will come out in the black, the process of monetizing illness is going to come into your head every time you wake up coughing and realize you are potentially poorer than when you went to bed healthy.

It's worth thinking about. It's worth thinking, too, about who is on the other side of this — business owners, for whom the pandemic has also been pretty devastating, although I bet if we could see the stats, it would have killed fewer of them than workers. Ontario Premier Ford positions paid sick days as a "burden" on business owners, rather than simply a cost of running a successful business that allows everyone to survive. It's worth noting that many of us *have* paid sick days (even me, now) and our employers don't feel overburdened. Perhaps small businesses have not been set up for success in our society if they are forced to choose between financial collapse and employees working sick. Perhaps that is something the government could look at: Why this is so burdensome for some employers?

I remember what it is like to work for a bad employer, one who thinks anything an employee gets is just a loss for the business. I had a job where there was always a contrivance to stop us from taking breaks — some rush, a delivery, a broken piece of equipment. It was like a game, to see if they could get that fifteen minutes "back" from us. And, of course, if you clocked in one minute late, you got docked like seven minutes' pay or something, but you still had to start work ASAP. It was very much down to the nickel.

At one of my early corporate jobs, on an early assignment I misunderstood some instructions and did a couple hours' work incorrectly — they would have to be redone, and the time was essentially wasted. My supervisor, who was a real jerk, yelled at me. Crestfallen, all I could think of was to offer to give back the money that I had been paid for those two hours of wasted time. It was what my old supervisors at the punch-clock jobs would have wanted: to get something from me for free so they wouldn't have to be "out" anything for my learning curve. Of course, in a big company, that offer seemed bananas and drew my screaming supervisor up short. She said of course I didn't have to give back the money, just be more careful next time, and ended the conversation. Even my meanest office boss did not want to be literally compensated for every moment of unproductive time. A viable, functional business has to be able to have employees make mistakes and get sick, at least until the droids take over.

I guess it's the positioning of the problem as oppositional — if an employee gets a paid sick day, then the employer loses something — that's dangerous. I wish I knew more about what it's like to run a business and what it would take to support business owners in supporting employees properly.

Anyway, it's the #DayOfMourning for people who have died from illness or injury at work. Holding space for those losses today, and wondering ...

April 29, 2021

Day 413: I work with overseas companies as part of my job, and two of my colleagues in India, people I usually speak to every day, are now sick with Covid. It is very hard to behave normally in meetings when I don't know how they are doing. They are colleagues and not friends, although we get along well, and I'm not sure when it will be appropriate to ask their boss if they are getting better. I always struggle to understand the global until it's personal, but it always is eventually.

May 1, 2021

Day 415: While I was on an approximately ninety-minute call, Mark Sampson washed the balcony windows, floor, and railing, and has most of it set up for spring and summer! He also had an unfortunate confrontation with his old enemy, the butter dish, in which the butter dish fell on the floor full of butter and briefly everything in the kitchen was buttered. Mark Sampson — a complicated man.

May 4, 2021

Day 418: If you pay very close attention to that gum ad everyone is raving about this week — the one where the lockdown ends in springtime and everybody runs into the street to see each other — you see that the main group of people runs to the park to chew mint gum and make out, which would presumably be all the single people, but a small subsection of people runs through the streets struggling into blazers and buttoning up shirts and frantically breaks into an office building, whereupon they stand cheering in the foyer and hug their colleagues. And those, my friends, are the people who live with family or partners. We had a meeting today at work where it was announced that we won't be back in the office until at least September, and that is good and right, but I was devastated anyway. Mark is my absolute favourite human being but we are out of material. "How was your shower?" is just not a question that has an answer for even once, let alone for four hundred and eighteen days in a row. I feel deeply, deeply seen by that gum ad. I would break into my office and hug my colleagues if I could.

May 5, 2021

Day 419:

- Rain
- Migraine

- Work
- SodaStream exploded
- Cat petulance
- *Star Wars* puns lost on me
- When was Duolingo planning to tell me about the three genders in Yiddish, huh?
- So tired
- That gum ad is great until you wonder how they shot it
- I just want to have a random conversation with a stranger. I cannot talk to the people I know anymore
- Aaaaaaaaaaaahhhhhhhhhhhhhhhhh

May 9, 2021

Day 423: After feeling like hot garbage for all of last week, I managed to rally somewhat for the weekend, and by sleeping a lot and asking very little of myself, was able to enjoy a few modest activities, like the following:

- Watching a classic 1989 comedy starring "Weird Al" Yankovic called *UHF* for the first time as an adult (me) and the first time at all (Mark). I felt it held up really well outside of a few slightly sour moments, and I had a really good time watching it. Mark just shook his head and said, "This is a really silly movie," but did not fall asleep, so we have to take what we can get.
- I met the new neighbours on our south wall. I hadn't realized the old neighbours had moved out,

and it's very strange that they moved out without us noticing, since the north-wall neighbours made a huge ruckus leaving and we are home twenty-three hours a day but the more recently departed neighbours never did like us, and so our relationship died as it lived: silently and oddly. I saw the new people in the hall with a pram and they just said a warm "Hi" and I was so excited to see that they were going to treat me like a non-enemy that I was about to launch into a friendly welcome, but then I thought maybe it was by being too friendly that I'd alienated the old neighbours, so I firmly stomped on my personality and just said "Hi" back and kept moving. Will I ever see the baby in the pram?

- In further neighbour news, Mark and I were standing waiting for the elevator when I realized we were both wearing "bunny-hug" hoodies with pockets on the tummy (pandemic styles!). My pocket went all the way through — I demonstrated by sticking my hand through — and then the elevator came and we got on, and then I stuck my hand in Mark's pocket. Oh, his pockets did *not* go all the way through. He stuck his hand in the other pocket and shook mine through the fabric. Ah, close enough. "Did you guys want to go to the lobby?" said the other person in the elevator. "Because I only hit basement." *Ah!* We thanked him and said yes, lobby please, and also that we are not normally around other people anymore, but he seemed not to mind. Lesson learned, though — eyes on the prize when out in public.

- I still have a migraine but it's mild now as long as I don't sit in an uncomfortable position or get too tired or stressed. So, you know, the workweek is going to be a *delight*!

May 12, 2021

Day 426: Remember that old Jump the Shark website, which pinpointed the precise episode in which each TV show stopped being good? I sometimes still use that expression about TV shows, conversations, events … "Time to go, they are playing spin the bottle, this party has jumped the shark!" I really feel like Canada's vaccination program has now jumped the shark by declaring unsafe the vaccine that so many of us *have already had* and also taking away the vaccination plan for so many others and leaving no firm alternative in its place. Obviously I don't know all the medical data on Ontario's decision to pause the use of the AstraZeneca vaccine — the one I had a few weeks ago — and I should go look into the clotting issues that might possibly, very occasionally result from it, but I don't want to. I want to *stop watching this show*. To all my friends who are upset this morning, either about vaccines that you've already had and are now worried about or vaccines you wanted to have and now can't, I'm really sorry. (I personally feel great about the vaccination I *did* get — it's the other one that I don't have yet that I'm sad about! I'm also really concerned about the people who were on the fence or had limited access or patience who are just going to give up on the whole process of getting vaccinated for good now. ☹))

May 13, 2021

Every time we do laundry here at the Sampsenblums, we take the sheets off the bed, make the bed up sans sheets, and then remake it with the clean sheets when they are ready. Once, near the beginning of the pandemic, someone was fretting to me that she was afraid to go to her laundry room. I said dubiously that maybe she could hold out, since no one would see her in her oft-worn clothes, as long as she didn't spill anything on her sheets. Confused, she said she had multiple sets of sheets and those were not the limiting factor. Now confused and embarrassed myself, I said of course — I had forgotten about the whole owning-multiple-sheet-sets thing.

I was telling Mark this story tonight as we made the bed post-laundry day so he could get into it, and he burst out, "Who has multiple sets of sheets?" He'd forgotten, too!

"We do!" I told him! "*We* own multiple sets of sheets — they live in the linen closet. We just own only one set of sheets that we *like* and we forgot about the other ones."

"I just forgot because they're for guests and we haven't had guests in so long."

"They're not just for guests! Remember the yellow ones? And the red ones? I think we might own blue sheets, too? But they aren't as nice as these ..."

"Do they even fit on this bed?"

"Yes! We own two different sizes of sheets!"

He looked genuinely baffled.

May 15, 2021

Day 429: I have had so many migraines lately, which I know are caused in part by neck problems, that I finally went for a massage. I got a couple last summer when cases were low, but this felt different and I wouldn't have gone if things weren't pretty bad for me. I know the cleaning practices at this place are really good, but I just avoid almost all indoor spaces besides the grocery store and the drugstore and this is not just shared space but contact! So I got there, hopeful but tense, and the RMT was asking me questions in the little treatment room and I was skittering around like a squirrel. I didn't even fully realize I was doing it, the "six feet apart" instinct has been so fully internalized. Finally he reached out to touch my shoulder, trying to show me an area he wanted to treat, and I fully flinched, and he asked me if I would be more comfortable with a female RMT. I felt so bad! I said it wasn't him, it was the pandemic, and I promised to get my act together. The therapist was very kind and gave me a long talk about the hygiene practices he used, his mask, when he'd received his vaccination, but the thing is I had read all this already on the website and in my head, I trusted him. I just had this thing in my body going "run away, he's too close." This instinct has obviously worsened a lot in the past six months, because I wasn't like this when I was at the dentist in December.

I was able to calm down enough to have a good massage, though he said to me, as every massage therapist I've ever had has said, "I wish you had booked two hours." Part of that is upselling but also, I am a *very tense person*. He also delivered the devastating blow that I need to start sleeping on my back, which I suppose I do briefly in my long nights of bouncing from position to position (I am a bad sleeper), but my main spot is on my left side, which is apparently no good. He said put a pillow under your knees and learn to become a back sleeper and, friends, I tried it last night and it was *rough*. Has anyone successfully learned to do this?

May 18, 2021

I saw a lady fall today. She tripped on a curb and fell flat. I spent so much time on first-aid training in 2019 but the hardest thing I've found is just not freezing. I unfroze pretty fast this time and crouched near her and asked if she wanted help. I promised I wouldn't touch her unless she wanted me to. I was sort of ad libbing because all my training was pre-Covid. I said she shouldn't rush to get up and I could sit with her. A couple guys in neon vests — road maintenance? — came over and offered to help, too. We started gathering her things and she did ask for help, so I offered my arm. The guys were very concerned about her having hit her head but she just wanted to get up — she was embarrassed about lying on the sidewalk, which I totally get, but also, concussions are sneaky. She really wanted me to be the one who helped her, which I also understand — I vastly prefer to seek help from strange women over strange men, too — but the guys were strong and I'm not, so it was kind of a team scoop in the end. I tried to talk her into hanging out with me for a bit, just so she could see how she felt from the fall, but she really wanted to go, and I get it — Covid, embarrassment, her hands were bleeding. She said her pupils had been dilated by an eye doctor, which caused the trip, and she couldn't have been comfortable standing around in the sun. I do hope she's all right. I talked for another minute with the guys in their neon vests — so kind. It was very odd to feel a stranger's hands on my arm like that.

I told my mom this story — she worries a lot about falling, and I wanted to talk through not just fall-avoidance but what to do *if* she falls (don't rush getting up, let people keep an eye on you if you might have hit your head). She said she worries no one will help her if she falls during the pandemic and I reassured her that is definitely untrue. Mark saw a woman fall tonight, too, and as he was moving toward her she was swarmed by so many helpers that Mark just kept going.

A couple weeks ago, I saw a guy overdose on the sidewalk. When I arrived someone was giving him chest compressions but struggling to keep going. He was giving up and I was terrified I would have to step in — I've been shown how to do it once, on a dummy, but I suppose I'm better than no one. As I took my first step forward, a guy riding past on a bike leaped off, dragged his bike over the curb, and started doing compressions, and our man on the ground restarted his shaky breathing. Relieved, I started running down the sidewalk to the drugstore to get a naloxone kit, and then the ambulance came.

What is the point of these stories? That we are still kind and connected in our city, despite all this evidence and pressure to the contrary? That there is a world of roles for us all besides being a hero and doing nothing, if we choose to accept them? Something like that.

May 20, 2021

Day 434:

> RR (complains about a novel she's reading in which the protagonist is constantly internally commenting on how attractive his long-term partner is): I mean, it isn't realistic that it's constantly top of mind. I find you very attractive, but I just don't think about it all that much.
>
> MS: Oh, really?
>
> RR: Who has been with their partner a while and thinks, "Oh, there's handsome Mark." It's just

Rebecca Rosenblum

"There's Mark." And really, you don't always
have a name — who else would be here?
MS: Uh-huh.
RR: You're sort of ... translucent at this point.
MS: ...
RR: Is that how you think about me?
MS: Well ... more or less. It's just your presence that
lights me up — just you being here. And your
absence that would bring me down if you ever
left ...
RR: Aw, that's nice.
MS: ... But you never do.

Second Summer Dip

May 30, 2021

Day 444: Mark made us a lovely dinner tonight, which we ate on the balcony, with nice French bread.

> MS (two-thirds of the way through dinner, gesturing toward breadbasket): I saved you the heel!
> RR: Why?
> MS: ... It's your favourite?
> RR: No.
> MS: ...
> RR: Maybe that's your other wife?
> MS: I guess.
> RR: ...
> MS: Can I have it, then?
> RR: Sure.
> MS: Thanks! (Takes heel of bread, puts butter on it [from now-functional butter dish!]) You know, I always thought I didn't like the heel until I started saving them all to give to you, and then I really missed them.

RR: ... How long ... how long have you been doing
   this? I always thought you foisted them on me
   because you didn't like them.
MS: I was trying to be nice! For years!
RR: Jesus!
MS: ...
RR: Well, it's the thought that counts ... and I guess
   it's good we can learn new things about each
   other at this point.
MS: I guess.

June 3, 2021

Day 448: I had a terrible night's sleep last night — the grey overcast
weather is causing me crazy migraines. Usually, sleep is the best
escape from them, but not lately. I must have slept some, though,
because I had this really vivid dream about someone I used to know,
who was mainly really nice but super-private, then briefly behaved
very strangely, then we stopped knowing each other. Odd behaviour
followed by silence is RR kryptonite — I *hate* not knowing why. I
am actually more comfortable with someone being a full monster
if I understand their motivations (well, maybe "comfortable" is the
wrong word, but you get it). I thought I had largely forgotten about
this particular spate of weirdness, but in the dream last night, this
person re-emerged and gave a full accounting of all past actions,
leading me to suspect my subconscious has been troubled all along.
The dream explanation could not possibly have been right — starting with the fact it did not really make sense — but dream-RR was
thrilled to have it.

How much of my desire to write realist fiction is the desire to
create a world where I will know the reason everything happens?

June 6, 2021

Day 451: I continue to get slammed by migraines *but* the apartment was oddly cool today. We often get our own little weather systems in here — heat will get trapped in our place and it'll be stifling four days after the heat wave ends, or freezing when the wind hits the building at a certain angle despite the outdoor temps being very mild. Today we got lucky and even though it was so hot out, the indoors and even the balcony were lovely. I mean, as long as you didn't exert yourself, so I didn't! I just lounged and read my George Saunders book and took a walk after the sun went down and saw *two bunnies* (in Rosedale, of course — the rich people even get the bunnies!).

June 7, 2021

Day 452: Transit has gotten really weird! Last spring, I was out for a walk, chatting with my mom on the phone, and I said it was nice to at least see some new faces as I walked down the street, and my mom, who wasn't even going outside then, asked forlornly if I saw any old people. There were old people on the street then and more now, but almost none on the TTC. I assume most everyone has succumbed to the desire for fresh air and many elderly have to run their own errands, but few have to go that far afield to do those things, so they just don't — too risky. Old people used to be everywhere on the TTC but now — almost none!

Occasionally you see one, of course. Everyone's risk calculus is going to be different — there were people who thought the TTC was unacceptable *before* the pandemic — but for me personally, I generally find it okay, more or less, on the subway. It's big enough that you can allow each other space ... well, it's rarely six feet, but a bit of space, and people do what they can, most of the time. And if someone doesn't seem to be respecting your bubble, it's pretty easy to scoot away, or even get off and run into the next car.

There's always a person without a mask — most often, someone who has pulled their mask down their neck, so you know they *could* wear one but are just choosing not to. I don't have fights with people on transit unless I absolutely have to, so I choose to flee almost all the time. But actually, other than that perennial one guy, almost everyone is masked, and more and more you see that, by fourteen months into the pandemic, most people have found the masks that fit them and are decently comfortable — fewer and fewer have the saggy, falling-off masks you used to see.

I am far less comfortable on buses, where there's less room to move around or escape people, and if the situation becomes untenable, there's often not another one for ages. And yes, the windows on buses do open but often they *aren't* open, and it's hard to reach over people's heads to open them myself. When I'm feeling really overwhelmed, I've occasionally even been choosing cabs over buses — even without a cat.

I have yet to ride on a streetcar in the pandemic, so no report there.

Without many elderly, nor many visibly disabled folks, the TTC is left with young students (tweens and teens, as well as college or university, out for a ramble, I guess, since there is no in-person school) and young or middle-aged working people. You still do see people with tiny kids, though I think fewer, since they have fewer places to go and I suppose they are worried about risk, too. And overall, the human density is just much thinner and more random. Because few of us are commuting nine to five, the crowds are weird — you set out at 11:30 a.m. or 3:15 p.m., thinking it'll be quiet, but that happens to be the day everyone thinks of that time, and it's mildly crowded. Still, fewer people than on an average day in 2019, by a mile. The TTC stalwarts with nowhere else to go are still there, in higher numbers now owing to issues with the shelters and no libraries or coffee shops or malls, plus the heat wave, and without the dilution of more people who do have a destination, those folks seem to take up more space. The upside, I suppose, is that that space is available, so they might as well have it.

Some people just follow the "don't sit here" signs, but that still leaves sitting back to back with a stranger, actually touching if we lean wrong. I usually prefer to stand in a ready crouch unless the car is quite empty. It's sad, really — the subway used to be my favourite place to read and zone out, but now I feel I have to be so alert. I'm still usually happy to be there, though — a little touch of normal.

June 11, 2021

Day 456: I don't really use major "sharing economy" apps. This isn't a referendum on whether they are good or not, but I'm not personally comfortable with paying to be in people's private homes or cars. It freaks me out. I have other political and economic concerns, but my baseline is I worry about being murdered. This is where the post takes a strange turn because now I want to use such an app. I won't put the name lest I be barraged with (more) ads, but it's easy enough to find. It's like a home-share app but for pools! People list their pools online and you book a few hours, and then you can have their whole pool to yourself. I mean, presumably to yourself — it would be weird if they were swimming around you the whole time ... The app says the owners are generally supposed to be home while you are using their pool, which is already quite weird — like, are they looking out their window at me swimming? Also, there are some questions about bathrooms and changing. I looked at the listings and some of the places are quite ritzy and have cabanas, which I guess cover both needs, but others are just normal houses with normal yards and pools in them and ...? One family said there was a porta-potty for guest use. In their yard! I can't imagine!

I feel like I tell this story all the time, but my family had a pool until I was eight, whereupon it collapsed. It was an *in-ground* pool, so that was no small catastrophe. To my childish mind, it was a lovely pool, but my parents said it was quite decrepit and the house listing didn't even mention the pool as a benefit when they bought it, and I guess when it collapsed, that decrepitude was why. I had only recently learned to swim and relished the full capacity of having a pool, so it was a huge blow, and I've never really gotten over it. I want to use the swimming app but, let's be real, I never will.

June 14, 2021

Day 459: Final moments from my weekend of minor yuck (if Friday evening is the weekend, then so is early Monday morning):

> RR: The new pillow does not seem to be working out.
> MS: I know, you mentioned.
> RR: I did? When?
> MS: In the middle of the night, you woke me up and said, "The new pillow does not seem to be working out."
> RR: Oh ... sorry. It gave me a crazy migraine. One of those lightning-bolt ones. Or ... correlation does not equal causation.
> MS: Yeah.

RR: I could try it again, but now I'm scared of it. It was a really bad migraine. I think I just bought a sixty-dollar cat pillow.

MS: At least Alice likes it.

RR: Yeah, she loves it. I had to take her off it last night so I could use it, and then I put it away after only a couple hours. What a waste.

MS: The great thing about Alice is that she doesn't hold a grudge because she has no long-term memory. If you give the pillow back, she'll be like, "Oh, wow, a new pillow!"

• • •

RR (knocks on Mark's office door): I just wanted you to know I was on the balcony checking the plants, and I found some underpants. I threw them away and washed my hands. That is all.

MS: Oh no. I take it they weren't ours? … I mean, one of ours? I know we don't share underpants. We each …

RR: Do you need me for this conversation?

MS: No.

RR: …

MS: At least we know someone had a good night last night. "Honey, where are your under-pants?" "I threw them out the window in a fit of passion — I don't need them anymore. They belong to the neighbours now!"

RR: I'm gonna go …

June 17, 2021

Day 462: Someone said to me yesterday that she thought the Duolingo Yiddish must be so hard if one didn't have a background in reading or writing Hebrew, and I almost burst into tears. I feel like I've been finding so many things hard lately, and while people are generally kind and supportive, I rarely get told that I'm finding things hard because they *are* hard — it always feels like a me problem, or at least that's how I internalize it. I could have kissed the total stranger in the Zoom chat who told me the free app I am obsessed with is legit not designed for a user like me.

And yet … I do like learning Yiddish, though I'm not making great progress. It's the language of my grandparents and my dad spoke it, too, though of course I didn't learn it in time to speak it with him. My mom was never conversant but I find if I ask her about specific words and phrases, she knows a lot of them, and it's fun to talk about with her. My favourite phrase is *vi file*, which just means "how many" but is pronounced to rhyme with "whiffle" and sounds adorable. My other favourite is *biz margn*, which means "until tomorrow" and is pronounced like it looks, but also sounds sort of like someone's name. I kept thinking about it and thinking about it until I had imagined a whole YA series about a Jewish kid named Biz Morgan, who wants to be a private eye when he grows up but his parents send him to coding camp and … mayhem ensues. I think a lot about Biz Morgan these days. It's been a tough few weeks, but if you need someone to count tables in Yiddish, or make plans with on Sunday, Monday, or Friday in Yiddish (I don't know the other days of the week yet), I can do that. Monday is *mantik*, but the app pronounces it more "moontik," which is just delightful.

June 18, 2021

Day 463: I'm not sure if it's because I don't have children myself, or because I have a great memory for certain things (and a pretty bad one for others) and just strong empathy for anyone with vivid emotions, but I feel like I remember really well a lot of the exact sensations of being a child. Like, when I'm playing with a kid and I can't get it right and the kid is annoyed with me, I am simultaneously the grown-up who loves this kid but actually doesn't want to play restaurant and the frustrated kid who knows the adult doesn't really respect the game and isn't trying hard enough to remember what kinds of toast are on the menu. It's a weird cognitive dissonance — I remember so clearly how it felt to be not grown-up, and yet I can't be other than what I am now: grown-up.

Mark got me this nice body scrub for my birthday. It's raspberry and it looks and smells like showering with jam — the seeds are the exfoliators, get it? So cute and lovely. It seems like it would taste divine and I truly did not mean to taste it but this morning as I was sleepily washing my face, a tiny bit got in my mouth and it was disgusting. I was really sad about it. So misleading! And I remembered being a small kid and my mom washing my face with Ivory soap and how nice that tasted — again, she didn't mean to get soap in my mouth, but when you wash a squirmy little person's face, that'll happen, and I always thought it was pretty good. And we also have Ivory in our shower, so I lathered it up and just licked a bubble and, yes, it does still taste pretty good. So I do still have access to that kid part of me, a little bit.

June 20, 2021

Day 465: I got my second vaccination today. I am very grateful. There's a lot going on for me right now and there were like two days I could actually have made time to do this and I just went on the provincial booking site when it opened to my cohort last week and picked the exact date and time I wanted — poof! It took about twenty minutes, albeit twenty carefully planned minutes. Contrast this with the first dose and a couple weeks of stress and running around and worry (and people telling me, "Oh, hey, haven't you done your vaccine yet? You really should, you know — it's important"). I mistakenly thought something had improved, but I guess not — there are still long lines in lots of parts of the city and people struggling to figure out access. I guess a few people just get lucky every time, and this time it was me. I am aware of my luck. The pop-up hot-spot dose one clinic that was promised to my neighbourhood back in April is opening this week. FFS.

The Metro Toronto Convention Centre Vaccination Site was beautifully organized but creepily empty — I'm not sure why. I'd guess it was operating at about 20 percent when I was there. When I arrived, I tried to show them my QR code that I'd been sent, but the greeter waved that away and just announced they were giving Moderna vaccinations today. I was a little confused — I thought they used Pfizer at that site — but sure, whatever they thought was good for people who'd had AZ in April was fine with me. They really needed me to explicitly agree to Moderna, which I eventually did. I mean, fine, but also, what do I know? I've read a bit on the internet but if these vaccines are approved for use in Canada, should I, a person with no medical degree, really be googling around in hopes of vetting that science? Some people think so — the lady beside me at check-in cancelled her appointment. I went happily in and am now fully vaxxed.

I didn't take a selfie, even though there was a "selfie station" set up — I was feeling sad and I was also alone (Mark was also able to be vaxxed today, but later — it was a great day for the Sampsenblums). I did get a sticker, a Band-Aid, and documentation that the vaccination had happened, all things that I did not receive at my frantic first appointment. Interestingly, now that this is all done, I tried to cancel my second AZ appointment, in August, at that Malton Walmart, and it seems it was never properly booked and doesn't exist — now that would have been disappointing.

June 23, 2021

Day 468: There's been jackhammering all day every day lately and I have so much work to do and it's hard to remember during daylight that I've ever been happy, and I usually post during daylight, so … sorry about that. But in the evening, the machines stop and I'm done work and a magical thing happens. I'm *so* happy. I mean, it's sad that it takes making life really wretched for a time and then stopping to do that, but I'll take it. The cats have also noticed the noise–no noise divide. The weather has also been perfect in the apartment lately — cool and balmy in the evenings, with a breeze. After dinner, Mark usually reads in the living room, and since my writing room is all mucked up with work stuff, I have been writing out there, too. Usually, the cats just do their own thing, but lately they've been coming into the living room and resting near us and we all watch the sunset through the picture window together. I've been calling it the cozy hour.

Just so you know, it's sometimes really nice here.

June 29, 2021

Day 474: In the wake of the news of the mass graves of children at residential schools, I am trying to decide what to do with my day off on Thursday. Though I have had some good Canada Days, most years I don't celebrate anyway, which has mainly to do with personal preference, access options, and not loving statutory holidays (I'll save that for another post). I had no ability or intention to celebrate this year, so it seems disingenuous to say I'm "boycotting," but I'm at least trying to be intentional with what I do with my time. My plans so far:

- Read a book by an Indigenous author (I was also going to do that anyway).
- Research the Oka Crisis (do I know what it was, or do I just think I do? Someone asked me yesterday, and you know, I'm not sure).
- Be sad. You can be aware of a historical truth in a vague way, but when confronted with the exact reality, it's still horrible. Tiny kids were deprived of food, deliberately exposed to deadly diseases, violently beaten, and forced to put in hours of labour every day — many until they died. At one point early in the 1900s, 25 percent of the kids who went to residential school in Western Canada died. Children dying and dying, and the schools just kept on going.
- Figure out what charity I want to give money to and give it. Probably the Indian Residential School Survivors Society, but I should read a bit more. None of the above matters to anyone but me — I'd like to do some good in the world, too.

June 30, 2021

Day 475:

> RR (sitting at table with a bunch of lovely pink peonies; some petals have fallen off): When do we throw out the peonies?
> MS (looks at ceiling, floor, wall): What? Peonies?
> RR: The flowers. (Points.)
> MS: Ah, yes. They've lost some petals. (Comes over to the table, pets a peony, half of it falls off, MS leaps back in alarm.) Well, don't touch them. (Scoops up the petals, carries them to the compost, most of them fall on the floor, he picks them up again.) Just stay away from the peonies.

• • •

Work-from-home fun: Add up all the money you have saved not commuting for fifteen months. Go to the bank, take out that money in cash, then build the bills and change into a person-sculpture. Sit next to them and ask them about their life. Never be lonely again!

July 15, 2021

Day 490: Mark and Rebecca run errands (in a borrowed car). An ambulance drives up and Mark pulls over.

> MS: An am-bi-lance!
> RR: ...
> MS: I said it the Moe Szyslak way.

RR: It's Moe Sizz-lack, not Moe Shizz-lack. If we have to be quoting from *The Simpsons*. Which I do not prefer.

MS: Okay. It's from the "Beer Baron" episode. Moe says, "I'm not here for the am-bi-ance."

RR: ... So he doesn't say "am-bi-lance"?

MS: No, he says "am-bi-ance" and I assumed he'd say "ambulance" the same way.

RR: You are kidding me.

MS: Marry me, marry *Simpsons* references.

RR: That is not a *Simpsons* reference if no one on *The Simpsons* said it. That is a reference to nothing.

MS: I expanded it.

RR: Get out of the car.

MS: Okay, sure, I'll get out in traffic, you can drive yourself to Bulk Barn.

RR: Fine.

MS: Of course, you don't know where you are right now — you're counting on me to get you to Bulk Barn.

RR: ... True. (Sighs deeply.)

MS: I am counting on Bulk Barn to be where it always is.

RR: Where would it go?

MS: I don't know ... ah, there it is!

RR: Are you coming in with me?

MS: Are you going to be quick?

RR: No.

(Coda at drugstore)

> MS: I think I'll wait in the car.
> RR: But who will get the toilet paper and butter
> while I get the prescription?
> MS: That's what I'm getting, am I?
> RR: Yes, please?
> MS: Salted or unsalted? ... For the butter?

July 24, 2021

Day 499: We managed a vacation, which is why I have been quieter on here. It was good, and hopefully I will be back with a positive attitude and more relaxed approach to life, insofar as I am capable of such things. Last night, as I reintegrated with the city, I saw a guy coming toward me on the sidewalk swerving all over the place, muttering to something he held in his cupped hand. As I stepped into the bike lane to give him space, I saw what he held was a wild-eyed baby pigeon. Pigeon chicks are the mysterious secret of cities — there must be millions, but you never see them. This was only the second one I've ever seen in my life, and I've lived in Toronto almost twenty years (yikes).

As man and pigeon staggered on, locked in their intense communication, I figured that was right for a first brush upon re-entry — a little disturbing, a little intriguing, absolutely insoluble, but an interesting story (well, if it isn't, I guess you've stopped reading). That is my Toronto — good to be home.

• • •

A few years ago, a posh restaurant opened in my neighbourhood. Since we are just across Bloor from Rosedale, it somewhat makes sense, but because the actual building was on the St. James Town side, and it opened right around the time the Red Cross was here with emergency services for the people rendered homeless (for years, as it turned out) in the Parliament Street fire, I was angry at the restaurant. It just seemed tonally inappropriate for the neighbourhood — I suppose my attitude was a bit of a NIMBY thing, in a weird way? Anyway, I finally went there for dinner in January 2020, in celebration of Mark and my brother fixing the internet in our apartment, and it was a really nice meal. Overpriced for the food, but I suppose you pay for the pretty room, chatting with the attractive, charming staff, feeling like a fancy person, etc. It sort of worked on me, but I felt weird about it.

Then everything shut down and the place had takeout, but I'm sure they struggled, like every restaurant and especially since they were newer and a lot of their appeal was in their dining experience. We bought a few of their meal kits and they were okay. In more recent stages of the pandemic, they started a biweekly "market" in their outdoor space and that was what I really liked — you could buy restaurant-quality produce and other interesting raw ingredients, and it was a bit pricey, but so much better than what you could get at FreshCo! They had prepared food, but it was the fresh stuff I wanted. In the spring the market was on a weekday afternoon and I would take a late lunch and pop out, but today I was running around in my sweats doing post-vacation errands and saw that the market was today, a Saturday. They said it was a one-off for Christmas in July, which made zero sense to me, but I saw they had scapes and cherries and loads of other lovely things, so I ran in in my high-school T-shirt, lugging my other groceries. Normally, midafternoon on a workday, it's totally empty, but on a Saturday it was crowded with actual fancy people buying lunch sliders and hand pies and I quickly realized I'd made a terrible mistake — too many people, and my T-shirt too clearly had a date in a different century on it. I grabbed as much produce as I could, which was in itself a mistake, because I couldn't move as quickly, and tried to scurry away to the sound of "Feliz Navidad" but I was in danger of dropping my cherries on a hipster who was probably paying my entire salary in condo fees and I felt like a giant loser. It was a weird moment, but I got the cherries.

I think of gentrification as a thing that happens elsewhere, but I'm … in it, somehow, and it's very odd. I feel opposed to it but as I carried my thirty-three-dollars worth of fruits and vegetables past the guys who had been hanging out in the park since that morning, I'm sure they did not feel we were on the same side.

July 27, 2021

Day 502: Toronto swimmers: I have my first-ever swim booking and I'm wild with excitement. It's at my very own community pool, which just opened — could anything be better? The booking system said I need my receipt, which they would email me, then didn't, but no problem — I can get it on the website. They also said I should consider being green, not printing it and just showing it on my phone, but I was not planning to bring my phone and lock it in a flimsy pool locker — even at the idyllic pools of my childhood, locker theft was rampant. What do you all do about this proof-of-entry system?

Also … swimminnnggggg!

You can expect a further post this evening that is either euphoric or crushed, if something does not work out.

• • •

Friends, the swimming was *fantastic*! The pandemic has deprived us of all these beautiful municipal resources and to walk into our brand-new community pool — just down the street, in the heart of my neighbourhood — was such an absolute delight. It's a gorgeous huge pool and changing space, all new and pristine — it has been open less than a week! I'm totally out of shape but I swam hard for my forty-five minutes because I felt so lucky to be there; I couldn't bear to give up any time even though I got really tired. And yeah, they totally had my name on a list and didn't require my receipt! They also didn't ask me for the four dollars they said the booking would cost — not sure what happened there, but I will save my four dollars for next time!

The booking site opens more spaces at the city pools every Thursday morning — I'm sure it'll get harder to find spaces as people get more comfortable doing things again, but if you like to swim, it's worth trying!

August 4, 2021

I have been going to the pool for the first swim at 7:00 a.m. every day and this morning, as I walked down at 6:50 or so, there were a lot of police cars and ambulances around one of the buildings between mine and the community centre, and the cops were in the process of taping off access from the street. I had to cross to get around it, and on the raised walkway out front I could see there was something covered in a large, orange tarp. The something could conceivably have been anything, but given the circumstances, my brain immediately made the leap that a body in a certain posture would fit there. On the other side of the street, a few people were gathering to look at the scene and the man who seemed to have been there the longest yelled helpfully, "Somebody jumped!"

I went swimming and came back an hour later to many more cops and cars, but no more ambulance, and also traffic cut off on part of the street. A cop directed me around. As I crossed, I was very surprised to see the tarp, and whatever was underneath, still in place. I would have thought that it would have gone with the ambulance. I did not like it still sitting there, all alone — the cops and their cars were down on the street, and the walkway is a ways up. Of course, I did not know it was a person — but it seemed like too many cars for anything else.

I went home and asked Mark why they would let a dead person lie there all alone for over an hour and he said cops have to do a thorough investigation into a death like that, in case it's not a suicide, and that takes time, much longer than an hour. Indeed, when I went out to the eye doctor around 10:30 a.m., still tarp, and still cops.

More than three hours. I really hated that. My personal belief system is a version of Douglas Coupland's me-ism, in that I decide for myself what seems most appealing or believable, and that does not include a vestige of a person that clings to the body following death. I myself would like to be cremated and I'm not extremely fussed about what happens to the ashes. But it still just seemed mean to leave a body all alone and exposed to strangers (some passersby were taking photos and, of course, I am writing this) when the person is unable to defend themselves. I wanted whoever was in the tarp to be taken care of better.

I went to the eye doctor and stopped at the library and finally came back and everything was over: tape, tarp, cops, and whatever else was all gone. I went up on the walkway and there was a stain on the cement that could have been anything, and only me and a few flies seemed interested in it at first. I stood there, mourning for the stain, and a man came over to ask me what happened. Then another person came over — I'm not sure why anyone thought a lady staring at the ground would know anything. I said I thought something bad had happened, I thought someone had died, but I wasn't really sure. The second person was unintelligible to me, but the first person seemed distressed and confused like me, and finally he said, "Well, RIP just in case," which seemed right.

August 6, 2021

I was rewatching that Extra gum ad that everyone enjoyed six months or so ago, and thinking fondly of my dream of busting into my office building and hugging my colleagues (the other half of the ad, about making out with people in parks, is less important to me, as making out with my partner is the one thing I have been able to do during the pandemic. Not that it isn't nice, just not a carrot at this point ...).

Anyway, my gum ad–based dream is dead now, as I got laid off from my job. This happened last week but somehow it didn't seem really real until just now when I was watching the YouTube clip and realized there would be no eventual office hugging, surrounded by vines we had chopped down in our joyful exuberance to work together in meatspace once more.

I will, of course, find a new job in time — I don't really have a choice about that — and hopefully a new office to go to (there may come a point where I can't be so choosy, but at the moment I am scrolling right by the "remote" roles I see posted), but I'm not sure I will ever find a happy niche like that one. Perhaps I will end up in one of those workplaces where you say to people, "How was your weekend?" and they say, "Great, real relaxing. Well, enough small talk!" And it's the same every Monday and you realize no one is ever going to tell you what they do on the weekends and perhaps they are all in gangs? I have heard of such places. I would not like them.

I'm being a bit glib. I'm actually pretty upset — I don't even know what day of the pandemic it is anymore. I'm worried about my financial future. I'm worried that fourteen years is too long to stay in a place and now my resumé is weird. I'm worried about all the other folks who got laid off along with me or at other points in this onslaught (hey, friends!). I'm worried about spending even *more* time hanging around the apartment, driving poor Mark nuts (he's been lovely, but the hope was when I finally cut through those vines, I would stay there a while and come home with something new to talk about). I have not been unemployed in twenty years almost exactly, and I don't recall liking it back then, either.

That said, I'm sure I'll be fine and I have a lot of love and support in my life, and I've been on the receiving end of a lot of kindness already. I'm not asking anyone to worry about me or anything like that. But I did want to make this public in case:

- You're in my neighbourhood or thinking of inviting me to something cool during the workday, but don't want to bother me because you think I'm working — I'm not working, I'm almost definitely free, and I'd love to see you/do something cool.
- You see or hear about a cool job posting you'd like to send me.
- You need a favour: Now is the time to ask! I have time and would love to help! I would particularly enjoy doing something that would get me *out of the house*, but absolutely, I will proofread your letter or something, too!

August 12, 2021

Yesterday was a milestone (besides my ninth wedding anniversary) in that I went to my mom's for lunch! It was the first time of the pandemic I was there for anything other than sprinting inside to drop something off or pick something up. When she invited me, I said I was excited to see her and Josey (cat) and also all her stuff, which puzzled her. I had to explain, because apparently she never noticed, that I am extremely fond of all my mom's stuff because when she moved here in 2017, she just took the highlights reel of stuff from our old house and her apartment is basically a time capsule of our family's life. She still has the dining-room chairs that my dog chewed the legs of as a puppy when I was ten, and her fridge magnets are my brother's and my school photos. Her apartment is extremely nice and modern, with a fancy kitchen island the likes of which our home in Mount Hope could never imagine, but it is the stripey couch from the nineties I want to live on. My parents always bought really good furniture, in the hopes of not having to buy more anytime soon, but she has kept that couch longer than anyone — especially anyone with a cat — should, and it will go soon. I will miss it. All the paintings, prints, and sculptures in that apartment are in my earliest memories. She has a tiny, heart-shaped candy dish that can fit only Jelly Bellies. When I saw it, I was excited to finally eat a Jelly Belly, but it was empty — she said sadly it took so long for her to finish the last batch when the lockdown happened, they got all stale and she didn't buy more. It never occurred to me that my mother does not love Jelly Bellies — she bought them mainly for people who came to visit who knew about that dish. I will buy her some more.

In truth I think of my mom's place and her stuff as "ours," even though I have never lived there and my mom has a nice, independent life (perhaps she'd rather a little less independence after this last year, but you know what I mean). It's just a small version of our old house, where I was a kid and everything was everyone's. It's nice to have a little bit of access to that, somehow.

August 13, 2021

I was walking home just now, carrying too many groceries and feeling very hot and frazzled. There was a man ahead of me walking very slowly and it was difficult to get around him because of some weird ways the sidewalks here are laid out (the city planners made a second level somehow, with railings — it's hard to explain). As I tried to shuffle around him, I realized he was talking to himself and not entirely with it, but that was neither here nor there; I just wanted to get round him without inconveniencing either of us too much. I guess he thought I came too close with all my bags, because he made a gesture to kick me. Out of lack of interest or lack of ability, there was no danger of the kick connecting, but I was still really startled — and furious! Try to *kick me?! Jail!* I was not cute about it — just sweaty and mad.

This sort of thing happens to me semi-often in SJT — people who are having a rough time are swearing at someone who isn't there and then I'm walking past, so they swear at me. Other things that come off a little more personal, too — like this guy thinking I was too close, other people who feel I've cut them off on the sidewalk, or otherwise inconvenienced them somehow, light into me. It's not constant but it happens and I always walk away because of course — what would I do? Fight with a stranger on the street? Who am I? And besides, their lives seem objectively more difficult than mine.

But the temperature is very high and this has not been an easy time for me either and even though of *course* it is worse to be the guy who is trying to kick people in front of Tim Hortons, it is not that great if someone tries to kick you, either. I get so tired of being patient and grateful for my lot in life. I wanted to scream at him not to kick people, a fucking toddler knows that, but I just lugged the groceries home and thanked twenty-minutes-ago RR profusely that she had had the foresight to buy Crunch 'n Munch, which is on sale for a dollar. Thank goodness.

Fourth Wave

August 19, 2021

I went with my mom to a bank appointment today (I am not enjoying unemployment, but there are a few advantages, like being free to do stuff during the day). It was semi-stressful, hot, and took for.ev.er. Of course we kept masks on the whole time. When we finally got done what we needed to, and were out on the street walking home:

> RR: Oh my gosh, I'm so thirsty.
>
> Mominator Rosenblum: Would you like a juice box?
>
> RR: Why on earth are you carrying around a juice box in your purse?
>
> Mom: In case I'm out and feel faint and need to raise my blood sugar.
>
> RR: Well, then I can't take it from you.
>
> Mom: Why not?
>
> RR: What if you feel faint and I drank your juice box?
>
> Mom: I have two. It's a big day.

I drank the juice box. It really hit the spot.

August 22, 2021

After 135 days on Duolingo, I've registered for a Zoom Yiddish class. I really like the gamified aspect of the app and the little green owl, but with no one to correct my pronunciation or, indeed, ever talk to me, I just felt I wasn't learning how to actually speak the language. I'm getting to be not bad at reading it, but I'm not sure that was my goal. In these times of remote education, I had the option to take classes from centres of Yiddish learning anywhere in the world, but I chose to go through the Committee for Yiddish via the Jewish Community Centre here in Toronto — which I'm sure is very good, but primarily in the hopes of making a friend to whom I can talk in Yiddish. I think, honestly, that was my actual goal all along.

Which is not to say my Yiddish learning does not proceed somewhat, although mainly textually. It's hard for me to tell you what I'm learning because it's all in Hebrew characters and I don't have a Hebrew keyboard, and I have no experience transliterating, but basically (with the help of Google Translate), *ikh kenen tantsn beser vi meyn bruder* ("I can dance better than my brother") and also *bite shikn meyn epl tsu tsheyna* ("please send my apple to China"). I'm hoping that the phraseology of the JCC course will be somewhat more relevant to my actual life.

August 24, 2021

On screaming: I have mentioned this previously but people in St. James Town and environs are having a rough time in the heat wave. There are more people on the street and they are less okay than usual, and there are usually lots of people out here, even in the worst of the pandemic, and a small but significant percentage are not okay at any given time. It's much worse right now. A feature of any neighbourhood where people are not okay is behaviour that breaks the social compact — things that aren't illegal and don't harm anyone, but also aren't exactly what we've all quietly agreed we're going to do in public. Public undress or odd forms of dress, talking to oneself or to unseen people, public drinking (that one, I guess, is actually illegal, but c'mon), erratic movements or gestures, heckling strangers. Also screaming and other loud noises. We have all, somewhere along the way, made a deal with each other not to raise our voices above a certain volume unless it's an emergency. It startles and scares us when people do it. It's valuable, I think, to have that startle-ability — someone can yell that you've accidentally stepped into traffic and you'll listen and step back, even if it's a stranger — but it's also one of the first things to go when someone is struggling. What I'm trying to say is there has been a lot of yelling and screaming lately, and it's disturbing — not just in the sense that I look up and wonder what's going on, but also it disturbs my heart, because people don't make those noises when everything is fine.

For Halloween 2019, I did a street action with XRTO in the middle of a crowd on Church Street that involved shrieking and running around, which was incredibly fun and cathartic. I don't think I had made a noise that loud since I was in grade school, and probably never in a crowded urban setting. If you have never been to Halloween on Church Street, rest assured we didn't scare anyone, and I honestly think the action may have been more confusing than impactful, but it was fantastic to wail out our climate grief in the middle of a huge crowd and have everyone just hold up their phones to film and watch politely to see what we'd do next. Or maybe "fantastic" is not the right word. It was just good to do whatever and not worry about it.

Maybe the screaming people have the right idea — sometimes it is good to give vent to your emotions. The heat wave is just the most obvious manifestation of a terrible climate crisis. I'm worried about the people out on the street, and all of us. We're also coming around to the anniversary of the end of XRTO, which I still miss. I realize my pandemic losses are insignificant compared with many — many whom I see and hear every time I go outside — but they weigh on me a great deal.

On the upside, for old-school Torontonians only: one of the screaming people I saw was, I'm pretty sure, Zanta — the legendary Toronto street character who wears a Santa suit despite being whip thin and seemingly obsessed with fitness; also, decidedly not jolly and reported to be pretty mean, though I've never interacted with him. He did not appear well, but I suppose he hasn't in some time — and I hadn't seen him at all in several years. He was doing push-ups and yelling in Pape Station.

August 25, 2021

This morning I got up, fed cats, fed self, watered plants, practised Yiddish, went swimming, came home, showered, and then tried putting on a sundress I bought last summer but haven't worn since because it is too long and drags on the floor and causes me to trip. I immediately took it off again because — shockingly — I haven't shot up a couple of inches since last summer. I realize I could have given the dress to someone taller, but I am attempting to make my slogan "Marshal your resources" and one resource I have is this otherwise nice dress that I spent thirty dollars on, so I cut it shorter with scissors. I should have hemmed it — I can't even claim not to know how, because I do, and still have my sewing kit from Mrs. Rostern's class in grade seven, but I just put it on with the cut edge showing, because I had laundry to do and it's *hot*. At least I won't trip now. As I slogged back and forth to the laundry room, at one point the hallway by the elevators had just been mopped and when the elevator came, I stepped toward it and slipped in my flip-flops — didn't fall or anything, just slipped and rolled my eyes at myself — and the cleaner came over and *took my elbow* to help me the rest of the way to the elevator, and that's when I realized that maybe the dress is too big for me all over and not just vertically and possibly she thought I was pregnant and maybe I should have given away the dress before I damaged it with scissors. *Anyway*, it's Wednesday. Happy humpday.

September 2, 2021

Revelation: I asked Mark if he wanted the full story about some people bickering over lanes at the pool or just the TL;DR, and he chose the latter — what is life going to be like now that we both know this can happen? Also, I have finished making dinner at nine thirty in the morning? *Who am I?*

• • •

I am having a weird day. Are all days weird now? Probably. I have a thing that, because I talk a lot and am very friendly, people occasionally tell me secrets. I am nosy and extremely interested in people, but I actually have a healthy respect for privacy — I don't ask a ton of questions about touchy subjects and if you seem tender, I won't push. And I don't really like secrets, except in the silly gossip sense (shamefully, I do sorta like gossip). But sometimes people tell me stuff, anyway — I have a face permanently set on "listening," I think — I also get asked for directions and the time a lot. Once, a classmate I barely knew described her boyfriend's sexual problems to me. Once, a driving instructor told me her fears about her family abandoning her. These are the most extreme examples, from people no one among my Facebook friends would know.

Anyway, someone told me a deeply sad secret today. Again, no one anyone on Facebook would know. I think I responded okay but not great, but maybe there was no great response. Maybe sadness should not be a secret. I've had this huge desire to be out in the world, interacting with other people again, but other people are struggling too, some much more than I am. Humanity, man — it's tough. Still the best thing going, though.

September 3, 2021

RR: Hey, Mark Sampson …

MS: Yeah?

RR: If … someday … at a point in the future … another mattress showed up, we'd just put it on top of the first one and that'd be fine, right?

MS: What? No, of course not. What? Why would that happen? Who would send us another mattress?

RR (voice very high): A sampling company? To review?

MS: No, don't do that. I don't want that.

RR: I think it might be too late.

MS (sighs heavily): I can't watch you every minute, Rebecca.

September 5, 2021

I was staring into the freezer case at the grocery store when the man beside me said, "How does it work?" I smiled warmly (under my mask) and said, "Oh, I don't know how any of it works!" The frozen stuff was very disorganized and I thought that was what he meant — we were laughing at the mess together. But he shrank back in alarm and continued his conversation on what I guess was a very small Bluetooth earpiece.

It wouldn't have been so bad if I had been dressed presentably, but I was wearing my beloved high-school orientation tee, which has finally developed a few holes, and bike shorts. I showered and brushed my hair this morning but that was a long time ago and I've done a yoga class since then (hence the low standard of dress) — I imagine the hair wasn't great. I also have a black eye, which is the real cherry on top here. Your questions about that are warranted; I have them, too. I certainly did not have a black eye when I went to bed last night. Mark maintains he knows nothing and the cats don't typically come in the bed so ...?

I'm really hoping this is something I'll remember as a bad moment or a bad day, and not the beginning of the end.

September 9, 2021

At the beginning of summer, I thought I would be so utterly delighted to have patio and picnic meals I would never for a minute miss dining indoors. Now, after being swarmed by wasps and sitting on hastily erected patios that are essentially in traffic, and really considering my entitlement to not watch people standing two feet away from my dinner screaming invectives, I have come to re-examine that take. I miss indoor dining. I mean, I know it's back, but I miss dining indoors without fear, I guess. Yeah, this is not a take that matters and I'm not going to change any behaviour, probably, nor do I want any rules to relax (at all!). I'm just saying — it was nice.

September 10, 2021

I voted today in the federal election at my advance poll at lunchtime. I had zero wait, but the other numbered lineup (I have no idea what the numbers mean) had maybe fifteen people waiting. The worker said my lineup had been the long one an hour earlier. Either way, it was totally chill. Voting is great — everyone should do it! (But bring your own pen to fill out the contact trace — although with all the comings and goings in the polling place, it does sound a little hard to contact-trace. It's still good that they are going to try! You can also bring your own pencil for the actual ballot. I forgot my pencil and asked if they were recycling the single-use ones and the worker said, "They do what they do," which sounded wild, so I kept mine!)

September 16, 2021

> RR: You haven't told me where to go on my walk.
> MS: I don't know where you're supposed to go on your walk, Rebecca.
> RR: What if I go to the cemetery and see a dingo?
> MS: *What?*
> RR: You know … what are Canadian dingoes?
> MS: Coyotes.
> RR: What if I go to the cemetery and see a coyote?

MS: I don't think you're going to see a coyote in
the cemetery.

RR: I have already seen *several* coyotes in the
cemetery.

MS: So don't go to the cemetery?!

September 21, 2021

Sometimes I wonder what being a Jew who grew up away from Jewish community has wrought. I bought a box of Korean sheet masks for a girls' night. It's a box of six, but there's only five of us. Happily examining my masks, I murmured, "And one for the Prophet Elijah."

September 23, 2021

RR (video chats with friend Carolyn. Enter MS): I
haven't told him about the chocolate yet.

CB: Oh no.

MS: What's this now?

CB: I'm not sure I want to be part of —

RR: I got chocolate on the curtain!

MS: That sounds like a real Mark Sampson move. I
have trained you well, grasshopper.

RR: I don't know how to get it down to wash it.
Gaelan [sister-in-law] put it up but she can't
come back from Nova Scotia to get it down.

MS: ???

RR: She used the drill.

MS: You're asking the wrong guy. You should have
married someone else.

CB: I feel you shouldn't need a drill to wash a
     curtain.
RR: We're going to have to move. We had a good
     run.

September 24, 2021

Last month I went to the optometrist for the first time since before
the pandemic and got a stern lecture about how, since my vision
is *so* bad — my eyeballs are essentially the wrong shape, though
I haven't had any medical issues with them so far — it would be
very easy for something terrible to happen and I must be vigilant.
Annual visits to the opto plus constant near-panic about retinal
detachment were the messages I took away, though they may not
have been exactly as intended.

Today I was supposed to go to lunch with my mom, but on
the walk over, my left eye developed a blurry spot, which is a
symptom of retinal detachment. A blurry spot could be a symptom of a lot of other things, including something being in your
eye or a weird contact lens issue or who knows. I tried going to
the drugstore and spending ten dollars on drops, which I applied
like a weirdo standing on Yonge Street, but in the end the spot
wouldn't go away and I decided I had to go home and change
into my glasses. My mom was worried enough about me that she
said she'd walk me, even though she doesn't usually walk so far
these days. The cats were *shocked* to see her, but also pleased. I
took my contacts out and the problem immediately went away,
so it was the contact that was broken and not my eyeball. It was
a very bizarre waste of forty-five minutes, but my mom at last
got to see the new rug she gave us for Christmas, plus the cats
were happy.

Then we went to lunch at a different spot, now very late, and it was nice except they didn't have anything good for dessert. Annoyed, my mom waited for the server to leave and then pulled a chocolate bar out of her purse and we ate that.

Moral of the story: retinal detachment can be signalled by a blurred or dark spot in your vision, and you should probably panic at least a little if that happens to you, but it could also be something much less scary. Also, my mom is the greatest.

September 28, 2021

Do you live with a person? Do you live with a person you have perhaps called in the presence of witnesses "fascinating" or "the smartest person I know" or "so witty" or "a person I would allow to explain *Star Wars* to me"? Do you now struggle to find anything to talk about with said person? Perhaps I can help! Here is a list of Fun Conversational Topics for People Cohabitating Through a Pandemic, So for Longer than the Earth Has Actually Existed:

- Reasons why a person would kick the doorstop under the bureau every single day that aren't spite
- What do you think other people are doing tonight?
- What these remote controls do, and why they shouldn't be thrown in the garbage
- Things I said when you weren't listening (this one is more of a monologue)
- Why can't I look in that drawer?
- What we did in that hour we were apart
- Is that a drawer you just keep garbage in?
- Things the cats might be thinking, or not

- Foods we own, and when they are going to go off
- I will look in that drawer eventually; you have to sleep sometime, bucko
- Which of our neighbours might hate us
- Things we saw out the window
- Books, I guess

October 12, 2021

MS: At the meeting, it'll be my first time seeing her in physical space ...

RR: *Wait*, I forgot, you're going to *work* ... tomorrow?

MS: Yeah.

RR: Who even am I when you're not around? Who are you? Who is to say we'll still be people if we're not together?

MS: We might just crumble into dust.

RR: Exactly.

MS: Hmm.

RR: So let me get this straight — you're going to wake up, write, shower, get dressed, eat breakfast, and then go to another place? And stay there *all day*? And not come back until night?

MS: Well, late afternoon.

RR: This is terrible.

MS: You might love it — you might enjoy having things to tell me at the end of the day.

RR: What if I gnaw off a foot?

MS: ... You probably won't.

RR: Well ... *Wait*, are you going to make a lunch?

MS: No, there's a lunch at the meeting.

RR: You're going to eat lunch with other people? Like, with your mouth?

MS: Yes.

RR: Oh my God.

MS: Maybe I won't like it, either. I'll have to wear, like, pants and stuff. [Note: Mark was not naked at the time of this convo — he was wearing, as he usually is, cargo shorts and sandals with a button-up shirt.] But I'll tell you all about it after work.

RR: Unless I'm at the hospital having my foot reattached.

MS: Yes.

October 17, 2021

Updates:

- We had our first indoor dining experience in Toronto at our local pub (well, the pub Mark regularly goes to in Cabbagetown — the local SJT pub is a chain sports bar called Gabby's). It was really nice and cozy last night with the rain outside and a fire going inside and the contact tracing and vax record-checking seemed in full swing. The meal was nice and the server was friendly. The place wasn't packed, as it probably would have been on a similar Saturday two years ago, but it was, as my mom would say, "nicely peopled." You couldn't entirely sit six feet from everyone, but it was more or less okay. The best part was a party of four waiting to be seated when a song came on the sound system that had a heavy beat. One person started doing a little knee bend on the beat and then they all started doing it, just four people bouncing in time with the music. Very sweet.

- I finally saw *A Few Good Men* and I will no longer call it *Top Gun*. It was pretty good. It was definitely both a movie of its time and an Aaron Sorkin vehicle, as it considered the adventures of a young, rich, successful, attractive white man to be the most important thing in the picture. Surely it would have been more interesting to centre Demi Moore's character over Tom Cruise's — her life must have been pretty interesting to get her where she was at the start of the film? Or really almost anyone else. But that being said, the film was sharp and snappy and kept me watching, and it would be interesting to contrast the writing with Sorkin's later courtroom procedural, *The Trial of the Chicago 7*, which I also watched and liked a lot better, but it's hard to tell if Sorkin's 2020 film just aligns better with my present-day sensibility or he's improved as a writer. Either way, he still has plenty of annoying features in both films. Highlight of *A Few Good Men*: when Tom Cruise imitates Jack Nicholson's voice with uncanny accuracy.

- I went to see a friend and I took the subway and the bus and then walked for a bit, tralalala. I went by myself and it was very nice and normal to just pilot around the city like the TTC champ that I am and not be (too) frothingly anxious about who had a mask or was breathing near me or was doing anything weird. It felt so natural. Highlight: standing in the bus shelter reading a Sally Rooney story, only half looking up when the bus came, just sort of shuffling my feet to line up so I could continue reading.

October 26, 2021

Swim report — I still love the pool! I've been swimming every weekday morning since it opened, which was also the week I was laid off. It's been a real anchor for me in a tough time.

The community centre has been in SJT as long as I've known it, but the pool is the first new thing I've seen be built here that was directly for the community other than the basketball court that was built about five years ago and torn down this summer. That whole park has been mysteriously destroyed, and the library has been closed all year — it reopened this week. SJT has been having a challenging pandemic, but things are often challenging here. We have seen several condo towers and high-end rental buildings go up, but those don't affect the community at all except with the stress of construction. I thought at least we might get some more stores or restaurants to serve the new inhabitants — we have oddly few places to shop or eat — but that did not happen, at least not so far. I rarely even see the posh people on the streets. I really don't know where they go?

I don't think they are at the pool, but since everyone is barely dressed, it's hard to tell how posh they are. I never thought of myself as a prude but I do find it weird to chat with people wearing so little — but mainly people aren't chatty, so it's fine. I used to get there early because of the traditional Toronto mindset of competi-tion for space, but there are five lanes and ten swimming spots and they are always booked appropriately, and while I do find it strange to just add myself to a lane where there is already someone swim-ming, after a few weeks of early weirdness, everyone just expects it and scoots over. So now I come just on time and there is little time for awkward chat, which is honestly for the best at 7:45 a.m., wearing basically my underwear.

Pool people seem to be racially mixed but mainly white (so, not an accurate representation of SJT in that sense), skewing a bit older, largely men, often weird but benignly so. I wear goggles anytime I get near water so I can keep my contacts in, because otherwise I can't see to even navigate, and I've started wearing a bathing cap so my hair won't dry out in the chlorine. To me, that's already a lot of sealing up my head, but some people have nose plugs and earplugs, so you effectively can't speak to them. Many, many people have exercise equipment they bring into the pool with them, including but not limited to flippers, other small flipper-like things they put on their hands, flutter boards, little foam things they put between their knees, and, one fine day, a snorkel. I do not have anything to bring but am curious, as most of these people are better swimmers than me, weird as they are. Maybe these devices are how you train to be better?

The masking protocols are not really enforced but people are pretty good about it anyway — as soon as you can, after getting out, put it on! It's a nice, quiet, odd bunch at the pool early in the morning, and a great boost to my day. I ♥ the SJT pool!

October 28, 2021

Was reminded recently that in 2001–2, I also tried to invent Facebook. Because I have no real tech know-how, my version did not exist online but rather comprised people talking to each other and talking about other people they knew. It was called the Bureau of People We Know and, owing to lack of other applicants, I suppose I remain head of the bureau. If you were going somewhere or interested in something, there was always someone else in the bureau who might be interested in meeting you to help or just hang out, and there were always so many stories to tell about bureau members to others who hadn't met them (yet). The BoPWK was of its nature smaller and more diffuse, but we didn't sell your data and you got more hugs.

When I joined Facebook in 2006, I was sort of relieved that someone had invented it for me and I no longer had to — it does serve a lot of functions that I had longed for. But yeah, upsides, downsides, man. Long live the bureau.

October 31, 2021

Happy Halloween! I know a lot of people are still freaked out about trick-or-treating since kids under twelve still have no vaccines, but the health officer is saying that the five-to-elevens vax is weeks away, so ... well, not great for Halloween but good news for the December holidays? But cases are still pretty low, actually, and on the other hand, I know a lot of families will be observing tonight, or observing somewhat, after a fashion: bowls of candy on the porch or in the yard. I haven't heard as much about the inventive candy chutes from second-story windows as last year, but I live in hope. As for me, trick-or-treating is banned in my building, I have no costume, the cats hate theirs, and I destroyed the festive decorations on the pastry I made, but once upon a time, I was more seasonally appropriate!

• • •

I had such a wonderful weekend! Imagine that! What a thing to say!

Friday afternoon was the #RBCIsKillingMe street action down at Bay and Wellington — asking the Royal Bank of Canada to divest from fossil fuels — and my first time protesting in about twenty months. I was very nervous but it felt so good to be taking that kind of action to protect our future again, and just to be out there with people who think like that. It was a small, windy, cold affair, but one with beautiful music, an amazing painted mural on the street, and some really good vibes. Also we managed to hold the street for three hours with only a few people shouting obscenities, which is honestly fab in my limited experience. It was so nice to see folks and do something, even if my role was basically just to be there. My mother, who has a fair history of activism, calls this "being a body" and it is important, as numbers matter at these things. As I try to get away from the ableist language of "stand up and be counted," I find myself going back to her expression.

Then I went home and some pals came over to eat pizza, as we weren't quite ready to eat in an indoor restaurant yet but wanted to see each other. Mark had the afternoon off and had been hanging out with a friend all afternoon but, lured by the promise of pizza, they came back to ours and suddenly there were *five people* chatting and eating in our living room. It was sort of like a mini party! Magic! Evan got so excited he started running around like a nut and eventually knocked over a lamp! A floor lamp!

On Saturday we went over to other friends' place (will the at-home hang be the theme of this phase of the pandy?) to play cards and eat cheese, and though everyone else was drunk and I was sober as always, I could *not* keep it together. I never knew when it was my turn, I couldn't keep the rules straight, I got cheese everywhere, and I wound up lying on the floor with the puppy at every opportunity.

But my team won at cards so it's fine, I guess. I think I was drunk on happiness because I have been so lonely and I was surrounded by friends all weekend and it was just utterly the best.

Today Mark and I rented a car and drove around looking at nice leaves like I used to hate when my parents made me do it as a child and that was honestly extremely nice — we really lucked out on getting the kind of sun that just gleams through leaves perfectly. We bought a quiche and came home and ate it. Perfect weekend.

November 4, 2021

Where we're at:

MS: How was the laundry room?

RR: Fabulous. How was your walk?

MS: Great. (Hugs her.) How is your lunch?

RR: This is just a bowl of vegetables with peanut butter on them.

MS: Are you out of lunch stuff?

RR: Yeah. I was going to have eggs but then I realized I needed all the eggs to make brownies. Brownies are more important than lunch.

MS: I guess.

RR: Does life have meaning?

MS: Absolutely. (Walks away.) As long as you have no follow-up questions.

If you are looking for good news, I can report that the word for "fifty" in Yiddish is *fuftsik*, which is almost certainly the cutest number in any language.

November 6, 2021

If you started the "Sampsenblums are out of eggs" story earlier this week and wondered how it ends, hold on to your hats:

At No Frills today, there was a lady with her entire torso in the egg fridge, inspecting every carton and blocking everyone else's access to eggs, with a queue forming behind her. There are many days when I'd have patience for that, but today was not one of those, so I left Mark to deal with it. At the checkout, our cashier asked if we really wanted our carton of eggs, as it was missing two. When I looked up, the carton was not missing two *eggs* but two of the little cardboard pockets that hold eggs — that part of the box was gone entirely. Mark was acting surprised as anyone and upon later deposition, claimed to have no idea how this had happened or why he hadn't noticed. When I scrambled to go get another carton of eggs containing the full twelve, he helpfully told me to hurry.

Tiny Dip

I have been struggling with vertigo lately. Vertigo, if you have never had the pleasure, has a lot of levels — at its mildest, it's really a non-issue; basically like being rocked to sleep when the bed isn't moving. At its worst, it is completely debilitating — you can't walk or even stand. I've known some people at that level, and it takes a long time to get under control. It's a very weird condition and often not well understood.

Anyway, my thing is often at the mildest level and, indeed, goes away entirely for months at a time, but lately has been more of a force. It's called positional vertigo, which means I'm fine in any one position — walking on the level, sitting in a chair, lying completely still; it's the moving or changing angles that's challenging. It's still not *that* bad — I can do what I need to do — but, man, rolling over in bed is great and that is off the table currently.

Anyway, on Friday night I also just randomly broke out in hives, and that's when I started to feel that life is against me. At first I thought something had bitten me as I sat quietly on my couch watching *12 Monkeys* (note, very bleak, doesn't really stand up from twenty-five years ago; also, I bet you didn't remember that it is about a pandemic, but it is. Not a terrible film but not really recommended) but then I had welts all over my chest and no evidence of any insects, so I think it's hives.

I don't know why any of this is happening (the vertigo started before *12 Monkeys*, so it's not that). It seems like it could be stress but I don't feel *that* stressed out. Maybe I never do — sometimes I look back on a period of my life and think, oh, that was terrible, but at the time I think I thought it was more or less okay. But honestly, it's so sunny out and I saw some nice friends this weekend, and as long as I don't go from lying down to sitting up or try to wear a low-cut top, everything honestly seems okay for the moment. Tonight I'm going to watch *La Jetée*, which is the short French film that *12 Monkeys* is based on, and one of my all-time faves, and then I'm going to work on my novel. I feel … pretty good? I think? Do you ever feel like you aren't even totally positive how you are doing, your own self?

November 9, 2021

Remember when our next-door neighbours were a young couple who primarily spoke another language, often had a sister or cousin visiting them, had a little baby who never made a sound, and hated me? They moved away when the kid was about one and a half, perhaps eight months ago, to no one's sorrow, and were replaced by a young couple who primarily speak another language, often have a sister or cousin visiting them, and have a little baby. This couple differs only in the fact that they are perfectly pleasant in a neighbourly way — they say normal things like "good morning" and "excuse me" and smile when walking past me, so I adore them. And their baby, who is the cutest thing in chubby cheeks and maybe six months old, is the *loudest human on earth*. I am, to be clear, not complaining, because I will take sweet, friendly people with a crying baby over people with a silent baby who turn their backs to me when I say hello any day. I just feel bad for them. This baby regularly screams from 7:00 p.m. to 10:00 p.m. such that I can hear them through their front door, the corridor, our front door, and I am currently down the hall in my office — still sounds like a very mad baby. I wish them all great peace to thank them for being so cordial. Sweet dreams, tiny neighbour.

November 10, 2021

I feel that Paul Rudd is fairly sexy for a fifty-ish man I am not married to, but also that him being named *People* magazine's Sexiest Man Alive 2021 has less to do with who is the sexiest man in the world than with who buys *People* magazine, which I'm guessing is mainly folks born before 1990 who enjoy having their opinions validated. As my generation comes to alleged financial dominance in our culture, I'm increasingly uncomfortable with having my bad opinions comforted in the hopes that I will buy a supermarket magazine. Not that Paul Rudd is a bad opinion, but, friends, I heard the Counting Crows on the *radio* recently. And I was *happy*. The joke is on the radio station, because I am not really successfully participating in capitalism right now (i.e., I don't have a job or any money to spend on buying the stuff being advertised to me), and all the ads on that station are for mortgages and beer, so I can at least preen that I am a demographic outlier, but come *on*. I will listen to Counting Crows in private and be *ashamed*, as one should. I am going to find a band that formed this year to listen to, and I will never again find a twenty-year-old attractive, because that's gross at my age, but what I hope is that someday *People* magazine will have the guts to make a twenty-year-old the Sexiest in the name of accuracy, and all the people my age will see the cover and say, "Oh, what a cutie, he looks a bit like my friend's kid," and keep walking.

November 11, 2021

Hey, friends, quick q from our convo of the day:

> MS: There's pop for you in the fridge.
> RR: Oh, I know — I drank it already.
> MS (laughs)
> RR: I can always find pop. I'm like that animal that has metal in its nose, so it can always find north?
> MS: …
> RR: What is that again?
> MS: Was this a dream? Is this a dream animal?
> RR: No, it's real, I just forget. I don't know how to google this.

[Edit: it turned out to be birds — it's how they figure out to migrate south for the winter!]

November 14, 2021

Best day! I got up early today to make a video call work with friends with varying time zone and work and fam schedules. Totally worth it to spend some time catching up and talking about hair, religion, Covid, and books. Then I went out to a park and spent a few hours hanging out with more friends *in person* and it was very cold but very worth it. Got home to catch up on a really beautiful and joyful group chat and then pop onto FaceTime to wish our niece a happy birthday.

I think sometimes when I'm feeling low, I should write the ac-knowledgements page of my pandemic and thank all the people who have helped me not end up a little ball under the furniture. It has been a lonely time, but not entirely alone, and the not-alone parts are the best. You are in the acknowledgements, friends, always always.

November 22, 2021

When I was applying for jobs after university, I applied for one hundred and forty-six. Of those, I got three and a half — a retail job near my hometown where I was living with my parents that I later transferred to a different branch in Toronto (that's the half), an internship, and finally a full-time, sitting-down job in my pro-fession that paid enough for me to have only one job and multiple pairs of shoes. I no longer have the job-search diary I kept at the time (I'm an idiot — I should have kept that as an artifact), so I don't know how many interviews I went on — the number one hundred and forty-six just sticks in the mind. I'm sure it was many. Some individual interviews stick in the mind, too, but most have evaporated — I'm sure mercifully. In total the process took just over a year, though for much of it I was doing some combination of the retail job, the internship, and part-time school. I did not enjoy that year, but it was very interesting, nothing truly terrible happened, and I didn't go hungry (I lived with my parents for a lot of it). It could have been a lot worse.

I try to keep that old job search in my mind as I slog through this one, twenty years later (there was an intervening job search after grad school that was really easy and pleasant, for some reason, so I guess that happens sometimes — maybe one-third of the time? Anyway, irrelevant to this note). Now I can send emails instead of letter mail, Zoom-interview instead of showing up at some hard-to-find office twenty minutes early in pantyhose and bus sweat and having a weird conversation with the receptionist, and at least I have some experience to talk about (at least for some of the jobs). Also, I don't live with my parents, which is great (although honestly sometimes I think my mother should start a helpline where people just get to call and tell her what they are worried about and she'll tell them how they're going to be fine — she's very good). The downside is I'm older and a bit sad now, and if someone seems unenthusiastic about talking to me, in my heart I'm like, "Dude, I get it — did you want to just go?," whereas young me would've just pushed through and tried to be more charming. So — there are levels.

When I was single, even when people would say things such as, "I can't imagine why you are single, you are such a great girl!" to which there is *no answer*, I knew the social code was that I should say something positive and not, "I know, I'm sad — I really want a partner." I always did say something semi-sunny and even generally meant it: I didn't hate being single, and I don't hate not having a full-time job. But I don't *love* it, either (being single was much more fun), and you're never supposed to say it even though everyone knows that losing one's job is sort of a seismic life catastrophe. In the job-interview training I went to, we were told not to even admit to being unhappy about having been let go, which seemed odd. I mean, you have to say you liked the job but also don't mind not being there anymore? *Anyway.* I am not loving this phase of my career, is what I am trying to say. This isn't a plea for pity or anything, or even an announcement that things are particularly bleak — today was a good day, as these things go. It's just that, today, someone mentioned normalizing rejection, and I'm like, hmm, what does that look like, exactly …?

November 23, 2021

I have finally come up with some general, good writing advice that I can give to both serious students and experienced writers who are just nervous, as well as people who ask me without having written anything just because ... I'm actually not sure why they ask. I say, "Write it as a writer, and then return to it as a reader and you'll know what's working and what isn't." It's a bit simple and glib, but it's a very abbreviated version of what I actually do, so it's advice that works for me (well, I claim it's working). After all, no matter how many books we write, we'll always have read a billion more (and for anyone who hasn't, I think I see where it's going wrong), and it's much easier to spot a problem on the page than in the jumble of "probably perfect" notions inside my own head. I mean, other people work other ways, but this is just advice I share as something to try. Also, it's hard to think of technical solutions for something that doesn't exist yet. I struggle to explain this to new writers who want to know if their idea is "good" — most ideas are good, if you do something cool with them. Books are really in the execution. So write it and then see! Feel free to borrow this if you meet someone who wants to know if the first step toward literary excellence is cover art or putting their idea in an envelope and mailing it to themselves, or what? I think I finally found a way to say "try writing the book" that sounds a bit fancy.

November 24, 2021

Today at the pool, I walked into the locker room and passed a woman already at her locker. She was making a small squeaking noise, but there is a *vast* range of odd, harmless behaviour at the pool, plus it was 7:30 a.m., so I ignored her and took a locker six feet away (of course). After a few moments, she turned and said, "Can you please help me?" I looked and saw she'd been pulling her sweater over her head and gotten the zip caught in her hair, which has definitely happened to me and sucks, because you are stuck with the sweater held in the air above your head and can't really go in either direction without yanking out your hair. But ... was I really going to touch a stranger's head? It had been so long since I'd voluntarily touched anyone I don't know — I've only just started hugging my friends again. But I couldn't leave her like that, and we were both masked, so I went over and together we very awkwardly unbraided her hair so it could be pulled through the spot it was stuck, and she thanked me profusely, and then we went on our way to swim. It was shockingly intimate, and among the greatest hits of my pandemic.

November 25, 2021

RR (returns home, greets cats, puts down packages, takes off outerwear, washes hands, eventually starts to wonder what Mark is doing, goes to his office)

MS: Where were you?

RR: The mall? It was delightful.

MS: Really?

RR: I told you this. I told you several times. And I texted you.

MS (takes out phone): Oh, you did. I didn't feel the buzz.

(Conversation meanders, but returns.)

RR: Where did you *think* I was?

MS: In your office?

RR: For *three hours?*

MS: I was working!

RR: You came back from your walk and just ...
thought I was ignoring you?

MS: If I was at work, I wouldn't normally know what
you were doing in the afternoon.

RR: I think the ship on "normally" sailed a while
ago.

MS: ...

RR: So if I fell down in the street and had to be taken
to the hospital, you would just never investigate
what happened to me? I'd just be gone?

MS: You could call me.

RR: Phone is smashed in the fall.

MS: Um.

RR: So if I'm planning to get injured, I need to text
you in advance and get a read receipt.

(Slightly later.)

MS: You're grouchy today!

RR: You forgot me!

MS: I didn't forget you — I just misplaced you!

November 26, 2021

I really wish the rhetoric on self-care weren't "ditch your plans,
ghost everybody, be late with everything, don't apologize," instead
of "have an honest conversation about your needs as soon you realize you need to." If we are *all* struggling — and I certainly think
it's most people, these days — then we're not really pushing back
on "the system," just other fragile humans. Saying kindly, "No, that
won't work for me," is more generous than saying, "Yep, absolutely,"
and then putting the phone in a drawer.

This isn't a passive-aggressive sub-Tweet — it's whatever the opposite is. I had a really good week of being able to connect with friends and feeling lucky that people treated me so thoughtfully and kindly. Even the woman who kicked me at the pool today, the only person in the entire athletic complex who knows my name, stood up and bellowed, "Sorry, Rebecca!" I felt so seen (and not even bruised).

November 28, 2021

Here's an interesting thing: I had a challenging thing to do the other day. I worried about it for a few days and then, on the appointed day, I got up early and did it. It went well, which wasn't really down to me, but I will take it. I celebrated by taking a nap. When I woke up, anxiety drifted back in with consciousness — I had disoriented myself by sleeping at an unusual time, and I'd been in the habit of worrying for several days, so my brain took a minute to sort out that the subject of worry had been happily resolved. It was such a nice moment when I came fully awake and *fwoosh* — no more anxiety. I mean, about that particular thing — there's still plenty to worry about in the universe, of course. I liked the feeling so much I lay there in my sunny bedroom, dialing back through memories of the autumn, trying to remember other things I had been worried about that had since been successfully resolved. There were a few of them. I feel like I don't do that enough — I fret about things and then solve them and forget about it: on to the next! It's nice to savour when a problem isn't a problem anymore. I really recommend this.

November 29, 2021

If you do something silly in a job interview, you could let it go and hope no one noticed or that it didn't matter. Or you could immediately point it out and then cover your face with your hands. *Guess!*

• • •

Here's a long shot: Do I know anyone who has access to a Toronto Lions Club that is selling Christmas cakes? The Lions Club is a service organization and a charity, though I have to admit I don't know what they support. While I don't know if I've ever personally known very many Lions, it was ubiquitous in my hometown and all through my childhood, and my parents would pick up their fruitcakes at the bank or the garden supply store in December. We almost always had these cakes in December, until 2017 when my dad passed and my mom moved to Toronto. There are Lions Clubs here, too (they are everywhere — I saw the symbol when I was in Japan), but not every club does the cakes, and it seems too hard to figure out.

Possibly they do not realize that for people who dislike the taste of booze (*even* if "all the alcohol evaporates"), Lions Club fruitcake is the only acceptable fruitcake. And no, neither making it myself nor having no fruitcake are acceptable outcomes and, yes, I am Jewish. No further questions at this time.

November 30, 2021

I came into the locker room at the pool this morning and took a locker six feet away from a dude putting his stuff away, standing in his Speedo.

Another dude came into our aisle and did a double take when he saw me. "Is this the men's change room?"

The other guy and I chorused, "It's unisex."

"Oh, okay, sorry," said the second guy, and then he wandered off.

This was the first time, since I started coming in July, that anyone had mentioned anything about the all-genders changing area. The first time I encountered such a thing, years ago in Regent Park, I was startled for one day, and then it didn't register anymore. You use the lockers and sinks out in the open, but there are private changing stalls and toilet stalls. You already see a lot of people's flesh in their bathing suits, and I haven't seen anything extra in the changing area. I suppose it would be nice to shower without my suit, but even at pools with single-sex changing areas, most people shower in their suits, in my experience. Who knows who is secretly harbouring resentment for not being able to get their junk out in front of others at the Wellesley Community Centre pool, but I've never witnessed a problem. The set-up is pretty good.

The other thing: If you are going to be a dangerous person, you are going to be a dangerous person — you do not need a certain type of bathroom structure in which to enact that. I have been flashed *four* times during the pandemic alone — on the TTC, in the park, and on the street. Completely unlike my pleasant all-genders changing space at the Wellesley Community Centre, where there are many weird people, including yours truly, but I've never seen a dangerous person, nor more flesh than a Speedo reveals. It's safer than I've often felt on the subway, TBH.

December 1, 2021

(MS stands in front of mop closet, trying to unwrap plastic from new mop.)

RR (wanders down the hall, sees MS and mop): Did you spill something?

MS: No, but I'm about to.

RR: Really? How do you know?

MS: I defrosted the freezer, and when I try to get the water out, some always gets on the floor.

RR: Ah.

(MS appears to be destroying mop in the quest to get the wrapper off.)

RR: Do you want to use the scissors?

MS: No, don't be silly — I want to use my teeth.

RR: You don't know where that plastic has be—

MS (gnaws wrapper off mop): It's been in my mouth, now. (Hands RR shredded plastic, marches away triumphantly, mop held high.)

December 2, 2021

RR: I was talking to X and I said Y, and they thought that was really good.

MS: Uh-huh.

RR: And then I thought, is that a little too good to just say spontaneously? Is that something you actually told me?

MS: Oh yeah, totally.

RR: Oh no, I'm sorry. I'm a thief.

MS: Don't worry about it. I've accidentally passed off clever things you've said before as my own, too. This is an open-source marriage.

RR: That's a great attitude. I agree!

MS: ...

RR: What a nightmare to be married to someone
not smart ... nothing good to steal!

December 3, 2021

My friend Jessica found a website for the Lions Club in the Beach,
selling cakes online along with a range of other things. Seventeen
dollars and I could pay by PayPal. I'm super excited about this plan
but also a bit daunted as the pickup options are really tricky. When
you order a fruitcake from the Lions Club in the little town where
I'm from, you can pick it up whenever at the bank or maybe the
library, or just get a pal who is a member to bring it to your house
when they are passing by. When you order a fruitcake from the
Lions Club in Toronto, you have a few three-hour windows when
you can pick it up from an upholstery place in the Bluffs or, if you
don't have a car, a single two-hour window at night where you can
go to their clubhouse in the Beach. If you pick that option — as I
did, because of the car thing — you will receive (a) directions that
don't make sense and (b) a *password* for the door. And that's when
you begin to hope that, while in a sleepy rural area, the Lions Club
is a pleasant service organization, maybe in Toronto they are actually the Stonecutters. *Full report next week!* (Small PS: Sometimes,
like when I spend several hours negotiating with strangers and going to the Beach in the dark in order to get a baked good, I wonder — is the weird thing about me that I do this stuff, or that I talk
about it in public?)

December 4, 2021

From the Festive Shenanigans Files: So we probably shouldn't even have been ordering delivery food to start with, certainly not at the supper rush on a Friday, so maybe this is my own fault? But the Swiss Chalet Festive Special was for many years a cherished tradition with my work peeps, and I still wanted to have it even though I don't live anywhere near a Swiss Chalet, and so we ordered it last night. A few things to note that will make what follows make more sense: (a) if you've never had it, the Festive Special is already kind of a lot of food, and (b) we ordered a "family special," which is four portions, because it was a good deal and I like Swiss Chalet, and because I'm not into cooking lately if I can get out of it, so hooray leftovers.

Obviously, it was going to be a long wait time — the website said seventy minutes, so after about that long and no food, I checked the site again and it said "delivered," but there was definitely no food outside our door or messages on my phone, which seemed bad, so I called the helpline and asked. There was a long hold, and the person said the food was just five minutes away, but they also sounded really uncertain and encouraged me to call back if it didn't come soon.

Reader, it did not. Fifteen minutes later, I called back, and was placed on a different, even longer hold. If you have ever tried to watch the very depressing TV show about academic life *The Chair* while Swiss Chalet hold music plays on the speaker of your phone, you know my pain. Also, Mark, who was extremely hungry, was starting to go to pieces emotionally. As we approached the two-hour mark on the order, I got a call on the other line, and since I figured I would be on hold forever, took the call. It was a man named Scott, calling from the sixteenth floor to report having received our food for no discernible reason! My phone number (and apartment number) were on the package, so he kindly called me to collect it. I left Mark with my phone to report all this to the Swiss Chalet helpline if I ever got off hold, and went upstairs to collect dinner.

Upstairs, Scott told me he had recently ordered Swiss Chalet and had been hopeful that his order had been re-sent accidentally so he could have eaten it again, but since it was clearly addressed to me, he called. I told him he was a good person. At the time, I thought him having ordered it recently explained how it got mis-delivered, but in the cold light of day ... not really?

I lugged the dinner downstairs (did I mention we also got four pops? It was heavy), where Mark was just hanging up with the Swiss Chalet switchboard.

> RR: Did you tell them we got it?
> MS: Yeah, but they were extremely uninterested.
>   They already sent a replacement order.
> RR: What?
> MS: It was already on its way by the time I got
>   off hold. And they credited your account the
>   money, too.
> RR: But we have the food now.
> MS: I said, but she was like, yeah, yeah, the new
>   order is coming.

We sat down and ate our dinner, which was delicious if not particularly warm, and put the other two dinners in the fridge. Just as we finished doing that, four more dinners turned up at the door, so we put those in the fridge untouched. Our fridge is now wall-to-wall Swiss Chalet and we cannot buy groceries — I guess there are worse things. When I checked online, I saw that they had credited not my credit card but my Swiss Chalet account, which I hadn't even realized I have, with money to buy four *more* dinners, bringing us to three times our yearly total in Swiss Chalet consumption at some point in the near future.

I wouldn't tell this story if I didn't feel like Swiss Chalet made a good-faith effort to solve the problem (though had the first order honestly been lost for good, we would have eaten at 10:00 p.m. and Mark would have burst into tears) and that they are generally a pleasant brand. But *jeez*. Also, we have a lot of extremely perishable chicken at our place if you are in the neighbourhood and would like to have dinner with us. [Edit: the extremely obvious answer, to give one of the dinners to Scott, was eventually pointed out to me, but it was the next day by this point and I felt weird about it and didn't follow up — I really feel this was a missed opportunity to be kind.]

Fifth Wave

December 8, 2021

Now seems like a great time to share the story of the time I was chatting with my mom and mentioned my alarm that some public schools have or had nativity plays for all the students.

> RR: That seems so inappropriate! What do the non-Christian kids do?
>
> Mominator: You had one of those. At your school, grade one or grade two.
>
> RR: I did? I don't remember this. What did I do?
>
> Mom: You were in it. We went to see it. It was cute.
>
> RR: I was? You let me be in a nativity play?
>
> Mom: Sure. There wasn't anything else. You would have had to just sit there, otherwise.
>
> RR: Well ... what was I?
>
> Mom [it is not clear to me if my mother, who grew up in a more Jewish context, knows the nativity story very well]: ... A sheep.
>
> RR: A sheep! Did you make me a costume?
>
> Mom: You had a towel over your head.

RR: That doesn't sound right.

Mom: That is what they said to give you to wear. It
was very cute in the play.

RR: That doesn't sound like a sheep. Maybe I was a
shepherd? I think I was a probably a shepherd.

Mom: You were a sheep. A cute sheep.

December 9, 2021

Dear furious screaming baby next door who is very, very audible through the wall: yeah, me too, kid. Me too.

December 10, 2021

Hello from a weird, gated boatyard on the beach where it seems like a drug deal should be about to go down but I am actually attempting, fruitlessly, to buy a fruitcake? Was that funny? Oh man, I am getting cold. What a weird night.

December 11, 2021

Okay, here is what happened with the fruitcake, which, while I did end up getting it *and* not getting murdered (what Mark calls win-win), I think we can all agree was one of my worst ideas.

As you may recall from a previous post, I was supposed to pick it up from the Lions' beachside clubhouse during their holiday party, but since the clubhouse was literally on the beach, far from the main road, and I had to go after dark, I felt dubious about finding it. A friend wound up mapping out the whole route for me, like a hero. Honestly, thank goodness she did, because it was pitch-dark on the path and I was *very* concerned about being murdered. I had to use my phone flashlight to even see where I was going. Midway along, I switched from worrying about murder to worrying about slipping in some wet leaves and falling and spraining my ankle, and having used up my phone battery on the flashlight, needing to wait until morning to be found. I was still worried about the chances of violence, but honestly, what would a murderer have been doing, sitting alone in the pitch-dark and pretty cold Beach park? Just waiting for some idiot to walk by in search of cake?

So I got to the Lions Clubhouse gate, just as my pal's map-video had shown me, but there was clearly no party going on. I also couldn't figure out how to get inside. The place seemed dead. But then I saw there was one car beyond the gate and as it went to drive out, I stepped up to it, hoping the driver would talk to me because they were the only humans in evidence. When the driver rolled down their window, I put on my mask and said I was there to buy a fruitcake, but that this was clearly not the right place, and then the man said, "Believe it or not, it is!"

He got out of the car and said he would call some mystery number I did not have that was associated with the fruitcakes, explaining to me as he dialed that he had ordered some too and driven there from *Brampton* (apparently the Brampton Lions do not sell cakes). He handed me the phone and I spoke, I admit somewhat hysterically, about my journey through the murder park, to a woman on the other end who maybe was more focused on the cake issue. I was really freaked out about the park.

During this conversation, a third potential fruitcake buyer had emerged from the shadows, and once we had all acknowledged each other and our various fruitcake needs, the woman on the phone said she didn't know what was going on or who had promised us night cake, but she would go home, get the cakes we'd ordered, then drive down to us at the Beach. This seemed as good an offer as we were likely to get.

The three of us chatted a while about what we like about fruit-cake, and also what a weird situation this was, but since that was the limit of what we had in common, the conversation petered out pretty quickly. I texted Mark that I had no cake but, since I was no longer alone, the situation was now less risky (he had been maybe 5/10 concerned) and texted my friend that "I roil in a crowd of angry fruitcake buyers" (melodrama settings on high), and settled in to wait.

Eventually another Lion called back to say that the website we'd ordered from had been left active from a previous year (*I had figured this out already!*) and that we should wait inside the gate, in a very icy boatyard. Inside, we scattered to opposite corners and I briefly got my hair caught in a tree. I could no longer see the other person who had come on foot (it was very dark), but I had something I really wanted to ask him. Finally I turned my face up like a *Peanuts* character and yelled, "Other cake buyer?"

"Um … yes?"

I followed the sound of his voice to a stack of canoes.

"When we leave here, can I walk back with you through the park? It's really dark. I'll wear a mask."

"Sure, that would be fine."

I was so happy and relieved. I also felt I had to ask right away in order to get ready for the next phase of the evening, but then we stood in the boatyard for another half-hour, until a *very* frazzled and sweet woman came and brought our cakes. She had brought her husband, too, in case it was a prank or a scam, because she, like us, saw no reason to be at the Beach after dark, transacting treat purchases, but someone had set this up as a legitimate plan, albeit in a previous year.

The Brampton guy drove away, his wife having never exited the vehicle or spoken to the rest of us. With me and the other guy ready for our power-of-numbers walk back through the park, the husband noticed our lack of car and demanded that they drive us out to a main road. I tried to demur, even though I desperately wanted no more park, then quickly gave in. (MS: You got in a stranger's car? RR: It was the safer option!)

As we drove to the subway, more chaos:

(1) To make conversation, I asked the lady Lion about her accent, which I thought sounded like Mark's Cape Breton relatives, but turned out to be a speech impediment. Then I apologized and did not speak again.

(2) The Lion couple got in a fight over a lost phone.

(3) When we got to the subway, me and the guy gave profuse thanks and scuttled away, and then, to my surprise, the guy scuttled away from me as well without saying goodbye. I thought we had got along all right for strangers who had met in the dark trying to buy cake, but I guess not. Of course, I rejoined him on the platform a moment later, but since he seemed so done, I felt I ought not walk by him.

(4) This trapped me between him and two men having a drunken fist fight. I was only mildly troubled by it until one clonked the other's skull on the tile wall. At that point, two more drunken men intervened, entered into complex peace negotiations, and eventually resolved the whole thing and they all left happily. None ever got on the subway.

I had time to watch all this because there was one out-of-service train and then the next was significantly delayed. When I finally got on, service was then halted when I was (just! Still quite far!) walking distance from home. I *really* didn't want to walk, so I hung around the train for a while but, after a long sulk, stormed home.

Mark was there. We had each been out about three hours. Mark had gone to a bar with a pal, had drinks, dinner, and a good time. I had done exclusively what is above, and it had taken three hours. I had left out some stuff for my dinner but Mark had put it away, thinking that since it was nearly nine, I must have eaten already. I hadn't, so I did, and then I had some cake, which was good, but *not worth it.*

OMFG.

December 17, 2021

Today an acquaintance who has always been kind to me mentioned she was upset because her grandchild has asked to use gender-nonconforming pronouns. She suggested it was the school's influence for teaching trans materials and that children cannot know they are trans, although this would be fine for an adult. I do not enjoy arguing with my friends (but what sort of jerk does?) and pandemic isolation has made me desperate to have just pleasant conversations, so I was paralyzed until she pointed out I was conspicuously silent. I finally said that it wouldn't do any harm to accept a kid's gender identification — perhaps they'd change their mind later, perhaps not, but accepting it (even if only on the surface) would be supportive and wouldn't take anything away from anyone.

It was *so hard* to say that, even though it wasn't a big statement, plus I am cis and well protected and there was really no risk to me, even if she lashed out viciously — she didn't; she responded kindly and the subject eventually changed. It's hard to disagree with people you like. But it would be so much harder to actually be the vulnerable child in this convo, who will be having lots of much more challenging chats for a long time. I don't think I changed anyone's mind today, but we had a civil conversation about a fraught topic, and that counts in the good column for us both, I think.

December 18, 2021

As I was walking down the sidewalk today, a food-deliverer blocked my path, straddling his bike and looking around in confusion. I was not impressed. Finally he dragged his bike off the curb and over to the back of a van for a repair service. Just as I was about to — at last! — stride triumphantly by, he tried the back door and an old man popped out. Think Billy Crystal in *The Princess Bride*. "Oh, thank you, thank you!" said Billy Crystal. "It locks from the outside and there's no handle on the inside, so I was trapped!"

The deliverer must have heard him trying to get out and was following the sound when he paused. You just never know what people are up to.

December 21, 2021

There's more Covid Omicron variant cases now than there were of the original variant (what Greek letter was that? Alpha? I never knew!) back in March and April 2020. Everything is getting cancelled — all the fun plans we thought we had for a better holiday season this time around, all nixed. Another low-interaction holiday lies ahead, I guess, but somehow this one is worse because (a) it's the second one and (b) it was supposed to be different. But also hospitals are cancelling non-emergency surgeries and a lot of people are sick, so I should have a little perspective on the fact that I don't get to get any hugs. Or maybe just a few? Let's see ...

December 23, 2021

I got my booster yesterday, mainly thanks to my friend Jamila holding my hand (figuratively — no holding hands in real-life Omicron times, OMG) and helping me get my act together. I'm sort of ashamed of how easily it all worked out in the end, considering what others are going through. Anyway, a few notes on the process (the TL;DR is that the "every drugstore is an independent, vaccine-providing entity" thing is stupid and also I am breaking up with my boyfriend, Galen Weston):

- The way I got the shot is that I got up in the dark and lined up at my local Shoppers and was given a same-day appointment. Eleven hours later, when I came back for the appointment, the pharmacist who had given me the appointment was still there, working in a set of scrubs that appeared to be cut out of a garbage bag somehow. I asked her if she had been there the whole time and she said, "Haven't had a chance for a break yet!" I hope she did not mean literally no breaks at all, but I'm worried she did. She also said, as soon as I walked into the pharmacy area, "Hello, Rebecca." It is her pharmacy (Shoppers Drugmart pharmacies are franchises) and I have been coming for over a decade for many, many prescriptions, but we have few direct dealings, and I had never known her to know my name.

I was reminded why this particular Shoppers pharmacy is so good (I know some aren't) — it must come from the top down.

- In the night, another nearby Shoppers, whose wait-list I was on, messaged me that they had appointments available. The message came in at 1:00 a.m. They asked that I please remove myself from the wait-list if I didn't need it. I tried to do that this morning, but the page 404'd. Argh. There were actually no slots left in their schedule (I checked) so it's not like they are holding one for me, but still — argh.

- As with the other two shots, I have had no side effects so far except some arm soreness and weird dreams. It was a real epic night, dream-wise.

Anyway, let's vote Ford out and implement some other system than "push health-care workers to the limits of human endurance." Take care out there, friends!

December 25, 2021

Merry whatever, pals. Hope you are doing okay.
#MerryEnoughForAllNormalPurposes

December 26, 2021

Something that has meant a lot to me through the pandemic has been sharing stories here on Facebook. It has been a gift to me to have a safe place to write through my experiences, and friends to share them with — and friends to help explain, advise, comfort, or laugh as needed. The expression "writers write their way through adversity" means different things to different writers (and is utter nonsense for some, I realize), but this has been a way through for me.

Wanting to share something most days, and trying to put together something that would make sense and be interesting relatively quickly, and then reading people's feedback and comments again and again over such a long period has also made me think about the ways in which I tell a story. Although I haven't been publishing work in a professional way in a long time, I am always working on the next thing, and thinking about it. How do I write about human beings, and do the ways I write about myself and my life reflect in how I write fiction?

I had a breakthrough listening to my mother tell a story in which she mentioned how she had met all of the protagonists and how they knew each other and also what religions they practised and where they went to school. I love the way my mother tells stories, though I admit I appreciate her more as I get older.

> RR: I think I learned my storytelling style from you!
> Mominator: What do you mean?
> RR: The way you include so much detail, and tangents, and how everything is related to everything else. I think you are a lateral storyteller, like me!
> Mom: What's that? (She seemed really worried about this development, like it was a criticism.)
> RR: Like your stories grow sideways, to take in more connections and detail. They jump from connection to connection — you see everyone's point of view.

Mom: I think some people just wish I would get to
the point ...
RR: But what *is* the point, when we are just sitting
here talking about this? We are just trying to entertain each other, and share something about
our lives, to know each other better. What other
point could there be?

She seemed satisfied with this. I certainly wasn't criticizing, because I don't think there's a hierarchy. Some stories are long and
some, I think, are *wide* — there isn't much distance between where
you start and where you end up, but they expand at the edges for
detail and connection. It depends on what you need to tell, and who
wants to know.

Does this distinction resonate?

January 1, 2022

I'm having a weird little sore throat/tiredness/vague yuck such as I
get in times of stress (December was thunderdome here). This year,
of course, it is time to panic and crack into my very expensive rapid
antigen tests. Negative. I actually do not know if I can grocery
shop now — I mean, I guess I have a minor cold or something, or a
faulty rapid antigen test? Mark appears healthy (we have discussed
getting him a T-shirt made that says "Always fine" so he will not
have to respond to questions), but perhaps he is carrying latent cold
spores? Evan actually sneezed a bunch earlier today, too — maybe
Alice can go to No Frills?

Anyway, happy 2022 — we are off to a roaring start.

January 3, 2022

Notes from indoors: well, I'm still sick but not very. It seems horrifying now, but in 2019, I might well have gone to work in this condition and sat in my office and if someone came in, just waved at my tissue box and said, "FYI, I'm a little sniffly, so stay away from my germs." That sounds scandalous in light of recent events, but let's be real — most of us did it back in the day. Probably better that no one will ever do that again, but the past is the past.

Of course, now is not 2019 so I've been staying indoors, which suuuuuuckksssss … Since I live in a building, no outdoor time at all for me — I didn't quite notice my symptoms or understand the situation on day one, but I'm doing it now. Also, in light of today's closures, missing today's swim means no more swims at all for at least two weeks (but who are we kidding — more than two weeks, right?). (If you haven't been following the news closely, note: Omicron is bad in Ontario, schools are going back online *again*, no more indoor dining, no more rec centres, yada, lockdown, yada … I mean, you know, right?)

Anyway, I started doing another Thirty Days of Yoga (yep, there's one every year) thanks to a nudge from a pal, so at least I am getting some exercise. And of course there's the cardio from fear every time I cough a little harder or sneeze too many times in an afternoon. This is actually the first time I've been sick in two years, so it's a real wild ride.

Tomorrow will be day five since my first twinge of a sore throat, so I suppose that means if I feel better, I could go outside Wednesday, which would be *great*.

January 5, 2022

Okay, here is the rant: in November and December, I went through the interview process with a bunch of interesting jobs, and didn't get any of them. It's fine — I felt the processes were fair and I kinda see how they could find better candidates than me and everyone was nice (well, one time …), but it was a ton of work. Anyone who says "don't overprepare for interviews" has not job-hunted in a while: tests, presentations, writing samples, not to mention the pop quiz "tell me what you know about our organization"–type stuff. It was exhausting. Right around the holidays, when it was beginning to dawn on me that if I had gotten any of these gigs, I would have heard by then, I started feeling weirdly itchy … and then a little more. Yes, I did not get a job for Christmas, but I did get bedbugs. Technically, Mark also got bedbugs but unsurprisingly Mark is immune to bedbugs, as are cats in general. So it is very much like I alone got bedbugs. If you have never had the pleasure, the way you get rid of bedbugs is that you clean and launder (or throw away) everything you own and then wait for the exterminator, all the while sleeping in long pants, a turtleneck, and two pairs of socks (one pair on your feet and one on your hands) and *still* they find ways to bite you. This, as you can likely guess, is also exhausting. My greatest fear was that I would get Covid and become bedridden while the bugs were still there, and thus be eaten alive, but that did not happen — we had *one* (one!) day where I had neither bedbugs nor Covid. Yep, I did wind up testing positive, although not until today, when I feel largely fine and had big aspirations about going for a walk. How my dreams have shrivelled. I am obviously not going for a walk, but I guess the upside is neither am I bedridden. I am mildly enraged at the injustice of it all but nothing has bitten me lately, so … there's that. The building insists on two exterminator visits, so all my remaining possessions are still in plastic bags

(I threw a lot away — nothing defeats capitalism like vermin). I've been so ashamed about the bugs and now Covid — it must sound like I spend all my time licking strangers and rolling around on street mattresses, but I assure you mainly not, and I have no idea how either of these things happened.

I will now share the *only* things I've learned from these experiences:

- Every six months or so, take all the linens and mattress cover off your bed and vacuum the mattress, the box spring, and the frame — top and bottom. Worst case, it'll be a minor waste of time and you'll just get rid of some dust, but best case, you'll stop an incipient bedbug infestation before it starts (advice from the exterminator).
- If you test positive on a home Covid test, call your family doctor and ask that this be put in your chart, even if you don't need an appointment or any help (advice from my MD pal).

January 6, 2022

Update: I am now almost entirely well but Mark is pretty sick, continuing to get most things done while wrapped in a blanket and demanding "children's chewable cyanide." He took a lunch nap and a pre-dinner nap but is upright for now. My brother brought us a bunch of NyQuil and DayQuil, so that helps. I spent a few hours on hold with the EI people — which is a *wild* ride, let me tell you — and otherwise worked on teaching and freelance stuff and took a brisk walk in circles on the balcony; it's about four steps in each direction, but honestly, just being outside was fab. Did you know that the bizarre construction across the street, where they have spent six months destroying a park, jackhammering down beneath it, and then constructing a strange black carapace over the hole, is *still* not complete? That is one of the things I learned on my "walk." Pretty much the only thing. The baby next door has reached violent-overthrow levels of screaming rage and her parents have taken to hanging out in the hallway outside their door, which is outside our door. They don't sound upset, but surely inside the apartment is nicer than outside? Unless the baby is now entirely in charge? Maybe she is ... maybe she is.

January 9, 2022

Friends, I left the house for the first time in, I think, seven or eight days. It was a little blurry when I first started showing symptoms, but we locked it down fully early in the week and I have been going steadily bonkers since. I talked to tons of wonderful friends and haven't been lonely exactly, but it's just weird to be totally sealed indoors. I was so excited when I found a filthy walnut some deluded squirrel had jammed between the bars of the catio — a concrete bit of the outside world, coming in! So that's tragic ...

We took out the trash, which had been living on the balcony, as well as the compost and the recycling, got the mail, and then I went to FreshCo! FreshCo, the second-worst grocery store in our neighbourhood (above Food Basics!) but it does sell food and is very close to where I live. Since Mark is beyond his five-day isolation but has lagged behind me symptom-wise, we decided not to have him come in with me, so we needed somewhere easy for him to come retrieve me and the bags from, so that was FreshCo.

Anyway, it was totally fine, and we got lots of nice new foods. The weirdest thing I noticed was there were many men shopping solo, which is, I suppose, a return to the earlier days of lockdown in that one person at a time would shop. However, these men were sans list, sans any sort of plan, and instead being operated by a kind of remote control via Bluetooth earpiece by, one assumes, a female person at home. These vacant-eyed men were terrible to shop near since they didn't seem to know anything or even look where they were going, just standing idiotically in the aisle, saying, "Okay, I put a lemon in the bag — should I get another lemon? Two lemons? Okay, I'm looking at it — no, I don't see a bruise. Should I put it in a bag? That's two — should I get three?"

On the one hand, I sort of get it — everyone is emotionally fragile now, food is one of the few reliable pleasures we can mainly control, and I have definitely lashed out at Mark in unpredictable ways because he was slightly off on a certain kind of fruit or cheese for a recipe I really wanted. And then there's the legendary shelf-paper imbroglio of 2013, culminating in Mark's washing his hands of the whole thing by claiming "I don't know what anything is or does." I don't blame anyone for wanting to get it right. But it does seem to me the worst kind of gender essentialism to agree to do a chore only if one doesn't have to learn or understand anything about it — if the mental load in fact remains zero, even if one does have to go to another place and walk around for a little bit.

It is also possible I am *wildly* overanalyzing the first non-Mark, non-screen humans I have seen in a week.

After we wrestled the groceries home, we took a real out-of-doors walk and it was glorious.

January 10, 2022

I'm suffering from a delusion of being bitten by bedbugs. I have not, in fact, been bitten by any bedbugs since the exterminator came

(#blessed) and we actually haven't been able to schedule the second visit yet, which is necessary for prevention or I don't know what, even though they do seem to be gone; anyway, the process is as yet incomplete. The original second visit had to be bumped because of Covid — life contaminated by multiple things is difficult. Anyway, I keep having sudden, intense feelings of itchiness in specific spots that I fear is a bug biting me, but turns out to be nothing — or rather, I guess just a human being can be itchy living in a dry apartment in winter, but I have sort of lost the plot and/or am overreacting. I don't know how itchy a normal person is supposed to be anymore. Possibly I am losing my mind.

In December, before we knew about the bugs but after I was pretty itchy, Mark lovingly bought me a bunch of products to combat the itchiness and is now suggesting again that I use those instead of complaining all the time. I am worried that the symptoms are largely bugs-of-the-mind and will not be assuaged by topical products, but still we had this conversation at breakfast.

> MS: You could just use that spray I bought you.
> RR: Yes.
> MS: You seem determined not to use it.
> RR: ...
> MS: I know you think it is just for feet, but if you spray it on a different part of your body, it will work.
> RR: Okay.
> MS: It's the same active ingredient anywhere — don't believe the foot-oriented marketing. It wants you to believe you need a different product for each body part, but you don't. The spray relieves itchiness, period.
> RR: Well ...

MS: Or you could use the brush. [He got me a dry
brush to exfoliate dead skin.]

RR: Yes, I like that. But I want to use it everywhere,
like my back and my face.

MS: No, you're not supposed to use it on your face.
It's too rough.

RR: Yes, I know that, but I want to.

MS: You can use it on your back.

RR: I can't reach.

MS: Well, I can do it for you.

RR: Really? So around ten this morning, before
I take my shower, I can come into your office
naked and you'll brush my back for me?

MS: If I'm not in a meeting, sure.

January 12, 2022

RR (encounters MS in the hallway): Hello!

MS: You have cat hair all over your shirt.

RR (turns on the light): It's not cat hair, it's people
hair!

MS: You cut your hair again. Why did you do that?

RR: It was blah blah me …

MS: What?

RR: I was trying to say, "It was bothering me" and
"it was bugging me" simultaneously and it didn't
work out.

MS: It was buggering me? No.

RR: No. … Do you like it?

MS (strokes RR's hair): Yes!

RR: Does it seem even?

MS (strokes more): Not at all!

RR: Oh no!

MS: This side is up here, and this side is down here.

RR: I can fix it!

MS: Why don't you just go to the haircutting place
and get a professional to do it? They're open,
you know.

RR: *I can fix it!*

January 14, 2022

I have always been confused about how I come down on the
optimism–pessimism spectrum. I definitely don't see the harm
in complaining about things that bother me — when others say,
"… But I can't complain," I say, "Sure you can, if you want to!" But a
lot of the time, I'm pretty hopeful, too: you never know what's going
to happen, but maybe something amazing? Maybe. I'm a bit all over
the place, as this account will indicate — I know that, over the years,
I have irritated people for being *both* too positive and too negative,
which is a fun feat. But life is so mixed — I just feel a lot of ways
about things. And I'm very available to empathize with others' sor-
rows, minor or major, just as I am fully here to celebrate their joys.
At least I extend my full emotional weirdness to my friends, instead
of just remaining self-absorbed … is that something? Maybe?

Possibly I have been a little bit resistant to the blessing counters
of late. I *hate* being told to look on the bright side — I feel it's a
slippery slope to nothing having any context: "You shouldn't complain about your headache, you're lucky you didn't die in a fire four
years ago." But the fact remains that things do have context and I
am here in relative warmth and comfort and love, and I am grateful
for that, as I should be. So I will make an effort today, a day where

I'm not terribly grumpy, to *feel* lucky, and then probably a plague of locusts will descend or something and we'll have to talk about that for the next three weeks.

January 18, 2022

Once, a couple of years ago, someone posted something thoughtful and sad on Facebook and I went to put the little love emoji on it, and then an hour or so later they messaged me to ask if I had put the wrong emoji — I had slipped and put the laughing face emoji by accident. Of course I immediately apologized and fixed it. That incident is something that means a lot to me — someone I don't know that well assumed the best of me and kindly and privately checked with me that I probably didn't mean that dickish thing, right? It's about a combination of the energy I normally put into the world and the generosity of the other person. Anyway, that's the ideal, for me, on both sides.

January 19, 2022

When I say the bedbug treatment plan is not going well, I actually can't discuss it further without bursting into tears ... so ... there's that. No questions at this time. It'll resolve, I guess. A lot of the stress is simply logistical, a majority having to do with not having our own washer and dryer. This has been a fact of my life since I stopped living with my parents and I never thought much about it until the last few years, when I realized I really wanted these things. Something to dream about.

Anyway, since I started using shared laundry facilities, I've had this concept in my head called Laundry Nirvana. The dream of

Laundry Nirvana is that everything you own is clean at once — no dirty laundry exists in your home at all. The trick is, in order for this to be true, you have do the laundry naked, so there is no fabric next to your skin, becoming minutely dirtied by sweat molecules. Obviously, this is ruled out by using shared facilities.

Sometimes I tell people this and they say kindly, "I hope you get your wish someday," and sometimes they say, "Ha, you are so funny," but what I actually want, while I'm waiting to see if I will ever achieve Laundry Nirvana for myself, is to know that someone else did it. But no one else has ever said, "Oh, what a neat idea — I'm going to do that!" So I'm putting it out there, for someone — probably someone who has a manageable laundry pipeline already — to get naked and achieve the dream of every single thing being clean for one shining moment, and then tell me about it. Obviously, no need to send pictures.

January 23, 2022

Okay, so what happened with the exterminators was their first visit was delayed because of Christmas. In many ways that was the worst because I was still getting bitten during that period. When they finally came, we had to give the cats to my mom overnight and go somewhere ourselves for six hours, but of course there were few options because pandemic and also we were outcasts owing to bedbugs, so we treated ourselves to a hotel and it all worked out. The second exterminator visit was delayed because we had Covid. In many ways that was the worst because we had Covid. Then it was rebooked and the second visit was again delayed owing to the blizzard last week. That was also the worst because we had reserved the hotel again for what turned out to be no reason and we were told the appointment was rebooked for Wednesday, which was *wrong,* and there was a lot of nonsense and then finally they said they couldn't come until *Friday* of last week, which meant we had to redo all the room disassembling and laundry and start over. Since we had already wasted the money on the hotel, we had to go somewhere cheaper or free, which meant the library, since everywhere else in the entire city was or is closed. Mark was on the clock and I had work to do too, so we needed Wi-Fi and places to sit, but even if we hadn't, there were really no other options. So we were going to go to the Toronto Reference Library, but then they had a Covid outbreak and closed their seating. So we went to Parliament Street library, which was the last place I could think of — it's a tiny library and I was worried there might not have been enough seating for us, at which point we could have ridden the subway in circles until the poison faded or just walked around in the minus-twenty-degree weather. But there were enough chairs and tables so we just worked there for five hours and it was okay.

The whole experience was hard but also just really illuminated for me how brutal this city is for those who have the least protection. Like, we had a home to go to after five hours and actually a few people who said if we got stuck, we could go to their places, which I would never do in my potentially bugged state, but it was a kind thought. And we *could* have paid for another night in the hotel if we'd really had to — the budget had been spent but, you know, in an emergency.

The room we sat in to work had five distanced tables, each with one chair. You could sit there and work or read — everyone I saw was on some sort of device, working or playing games or watching movies. I was curious what percentage of people were there to get something done and what percentage just needed a place to be. A few looked like they were struggling and I overheard one man on his cellphone calling a food bank about how long the line was. The picture window I was sitting next to actually looked out on the Davis branch of the Yonge Street Mission, which had a long line out front the entire time we were there. I kept wondering what people were lining up for — it must have been important, since it was a slow-moving line and so fricking cold. When I went outside to stand between two snowbanks and eat my lunch, I tried to watch and see if anyone came out carrying anything, but no one did. I ate pretty fast, because of the cold.

There were also the standard library characters, including a man who fought with the security guard over eating a granola bar, trimmed his nails, then fell asleep face down on his table, snoring. The woman on the other side of me took several hours of Zoom meetings about her work in the IT department at an insurance firm. They were pretty awful, but I figured she must have been stuck, like we were. Mark said at least she had a pretty voice, but Mark is nicer than me and less easily distracted.

And we did hear several people yell at librarians, which is absolutely terrible. Libraries are really one of the last places in the city right now that are trying to uphold a sense of society for everyone, even if you can't pay, and they should be treasured and respected and honoured.

January 24, 2022

How sad can a baby be? Asking for the little girl next door, who was howling like an enraged gorilla before I turned on the space heater and now I can't hear her anymore. I have never lived with infants, and when I stay with them for a few days or babysit, I can just ask the parents how upset is too upset, is X normal, etc., and then they tell me when it's time to panic and I calibrate accordingly. Neighbour baby does not need me to panic about her but she is *so upset all the time*. The parents honestly seem fine, and I hear them chatting and laughing, which is a good sign. But it's hard to hear someone in the depths of despair for hours a day without feeling a little despairy myself. I wonder what she is thinking?

February 1, 2022

So I went back to the pool yesterday after exactly one month off between the New Year's closure, Covid isolation, and the lockdown. It felt like such a long time and also, weirdly, everything picked up exactly as before — has anyone else noticed that time is getting elastic and bizarre?

It was very, very nice to go back. My newly short hair is a challenge to get into a swim cap, but otherwise everything was great. It was nice to see some of the early morning regulars but — as with most of life — I found it awkward. I have seen more of their bodies than I have of almost any of my friends', yet I don't know their names! (I am the only one who ever wraps myself in a towel while we wait to be let into the pool, which I find odd — even if no one cares about the view, it's cold!) Very few people actually talk to me, but they talk to each other loudly near me, so I know a fair bit about them: what they do and where they live and some of their physical aches and pains. So it's good to know everyone seems okay. I worried about the ones I haven't seen so far — hope they are fine!

• • •

Feeling extremely upset about the convoy — the anti–vaccine mandate truckers blockading roads and blasting noise in Ottawa for several days now. I've gone from not completely understanding what was going on to feeling personally implicated. When XRTO blocked the viaduct back in 2019 — about a hundred pedestrians singing on a single bridge to draw attention to the climate emergency — they came at us with riot cops on horseback after about four hours and arrested a dozen people. And that was upsetting but expected; sometimes you feel so strongly you get into the street, but law and order comes after you pretty quick so that there's not too much disruption, I figured, lying on my bench at the police station, waiting for my friends to be released. And now I realize it doesn't really work that way as hundreds of people and trucks get to block dozens of streets for days and days. Law and order is real chill with that, for the most part — two arrests so far.

I kept looking for "how to get involved" but there wasn't really much — people of Ottawa were supposed to maybe do something to help defend the residential areas, but even that wasn't clear to me. Anyway, here is what I came up with (let me know if you have some ideas!):

- Donate. The usual outsider option, but money does help people. I gave to the Shepherds of Good Hope, the organization operating the soup kitchen in downtown Ottawa whose volunteers were harassed by the convoyers — not only did the convoyers yell racial epithets at them and take a lot of the food meant for those in need, I think the soup-kitchen volunteers are just in general having a rough time in the chaos. I also gave to the National Centre for Truth and Reconciliation, because of the devastating discoveries at Williams Lake and how this nonsense is taking attention away from that. If we were going to have people in the street this week, it should be in mourning for those murdered children, not for grown adults who cannot tolerate following a public health measure.

- Say how I feel. My other usual thing. But sometimes I think people change their minds if someone they care about shares their feelings. So: I do not support the convoy. Vaccine mandates are the law right now, but there are ways to find exceptions that are not blasting airhorns until people are driven out of their homes and workplaces. And anyone who says the people with swastika flags are just tagging along and if you want to make an omelette you have to break a few eggs, FYI this is a bad omelette and also so many of the people I love are potential eggs!
- Okay, I don't have a third bullet, but thanks for reading this far. I have gotten pretty worked up, but it was good to write this all out. Let me know if you have any other ideas.

February 2, 2022

Edit: I ended up deleting the post that was here — it was pretty heightened; melodramatic, perhaps? I wrote it after being upset by seeing swastika flags at the convoy rallies in Ottawa on the news and having *several* people say to me, "Oh, you can't let the swastikas get to you, they don't *mean* old anti-Semitic, anti-queer, that kind of Naziism. *These* swastikas mean that being forced to get vaccinated is just like being in Nazi Germany. You have to really look into what people *mean* by swastikas before you get upset." But I will not be doing that. I'm not here to put swastikas into "context." And that request just seems so unimaginably heinous and cruel. The claim that none of the swastika flag-wavers were "real Nazis" also sounded pretty untrue to me, given that Pat King, one of the main

organizers of the convoy, has a history with "white nationalism" —
that didn't sound like a coincidence to a lot of people. I will never
forget the "do your research on what people *mean* by their swastikas" comments: the patronizing dismissal from people I respected
really scared me, maybe more than the flags did.

. . .

Evan knocked down the "not everything is terrible" flowers that
Mark gave me and smashed the vase, so there was a lot of picking up
glass and mopping up water, plus I don't have flowers or that nice
vase anymore, or currently that cat, since he is hiding like a coward.
When the floors dries, I can vacuum, hooray! Only three of my *five*
prescriptions came in at the drugstore and the work I have to do this
afternoon is to look at stuff for my archive again after a *two-year
hiatus.* Did I mention I am assembling my old drafts and letters to
donate to the Thomas Fisher Rare Book Library at the University of
Toronto? I sent off the boxes in February 2020 and then before anyone could look at it, everything shut down and they are just getting
back to me now. It is clearly not the archive people's fault there was
a pandemic, but also I forget everything — both things that I had
planned for the archive and things that happened in my life. They
have pulled everything off the floppy disks and would like me to review. This is going to be terrible, isn't it? They had a student make a
finding aid! For whatever I wrote and saved to 3.5-inch disks in the
1990s and early aughts and then was unable to subsequently review
so I just sent it to the archive hoping it would be of literary value!
Part of being alone all the time is just being ashamed to suddenly
realize other people know I exist ... over and over. HOW LONG
BEFORE THESE UPDATES ARE ENTIRELY IN CAPS? Oh
good, the floor is dry, I can vacuum.

February 3, 2022

The anti-Nazi post is back up — I took it down but maybe the world needs to be reminded to worry about Nazis more than I thought. That's bad, but also this happened: after an older gentleman I've seen many times before at the pool reacted angrily to having to share a lane with me, one of the baffling non-swimmers from last fall also joined our lane and the older gentleman swam away. And the non-swimmer was friendly! He asked me for tips, which unfortunately I didn't have, but I suggested he ask the lifeguards, who are all also swimming instructors and fairly bored with our tedious ten-person lane swims. I saw her giving him some ideas. The next time we paused together at a lane end, he asked me where I live, and, though this is probably bad practice, I was so surprised that a stranger was taking an interest in me that I told him. And we live in the same building! He asked me if I have a family and I just let that go — I told him I have a husband, and asked him about his. He has a new baby! He is so happy and proud and excited! He is also a recent immigrant and as I was apologizing for the state of things here — Toronto is usually so much more fun and welcoming — he cut me off: "My baby was born here!" I said he must be busy and he said yes, it's his first baby. Then he stumbled, and said there had been three miscarriages, and then this baby. I was startled to be told something so personal, but I sort of understood not wanting to leave those lost pregnancies behind in the new happiness, especially if perhaps he is not practised at talking to people about it all. I told him I was sorry for his losses and so happy to hear about the new little girl. He seemed very eager that I should visit him and his wife and baby, and I thought his wife might have another opinion about having a stranger in the home with a surely unvaccinated infant (three months?), unless they are all unvaccinated and don't care, in which case I shouldn't be there anyway ... but perhaps I could bake for them? No neighbour has ever been this forthcoming here, and he seemed quite eager for friendship. I could drop off some cookies or something and that wouldn't be weird, right?

Friends, I've written this twice because Facebook is having a hard time and I've cried throughout both.

February 6, 2022

Anti-vaxxer convoy report: I'm a bit too far away for it to reach us here, but last night we went over to my mother's place, which is much closer to the provincial legislature at Queen's Park, though not directly adjacent. There were a lot of police present and largely things were moving okay, though there were a lot of clogs caused by what, I think, were mainly just normal cars trying to navigate the blocked streets. The cops were letting only residents' vehicles onto residential streets and checking ... maybe ID? Not sure. I was pretty worried about getting hit by a car just because people were so befuddled and antsy and mad in some cases, and I was just highly anxious. But nothing bad happened. There were many helicopters flying around, I guess some news and maybe some police or Orange, I'm really not sure.

As the evening wore on, you could tell convoy people were getting drunker, as there was more and more drunken scream-singing of semi-political obscenities — we were on a blocked street but you could hear it from pretty far away. I thought taking the subway home would be safer than walking, but there were a few young, unmasked white men drinking yellow beer on the platform, one wrapped in a defaced Canadian flag and yelling belligerently. I couldn't exactly see what it was defaced with and I didn't want to look too closely, lest I give him a pretext to yell at me.

All in all, nothing bad really happened, but for all the times people have said I live in a "bad" neighbourhood and should be afraid, this was pretty much the most scared I've been in Toronto.

And of course, we spent the evening with my mother, who is almost eighty and whom I worry about so much, and these pro-testers are asserting their rights to make sure there are no stores, no restaurants, no libraries or community centres she can go to where she will feel confident that people are masked or vaccinated or taking any measures to protect each other's health. The only other people I've seen recently are my new neighbours and their tiny, perfect baby, even more vulnerable. I am just devastated that so many people think even a basic law to keep each other safe — I saw someone have to leap out of a crosswalk in terror last week as a driver ran a red light — is too much to ask.

I am very sad. It was nice to see my mom, though. And that baby — OMG, A+.

• • •

The baby is *outstanding*. Of course we went inside. I said I wouldn't but I was not equipped to turn down hospitality and the possibility of seeing a baby and we kept our masks on. She is a squish ball and was wearing a *hat*. When she woke up, she seemed against it but very quietly, like I am sometimes against the sun coming through the curtains, turning her face away and scrunching her eyes shut. It was cuter when she did it. Her dad did this thing where he tapped her gently on the cheeks and lips and she smiled and stuck out her tongue — he told us she really uses her tongue a lot.

Friends, you might have guessed what I did not: that the family are refugees. When I pictured being pals, I imagined telling them cooking tips and where all the best parks are, and maybe helping them find library books for the baby. Well, it's freezing out and they are having trouble taking the baby out in the cold, so no parks, plus our local library is shut and only the dad really speaks English, anyway. Their questions were a lot more complicated than recipes and parks, and while I had hoped to help them with the task of being Canadian, I started to wonder if I am even good at it myself?

It doesn't matter, I can still be nice — a nice person is better than no nice person — but if you know how to get a day-labour job in the city without a car, HMU! Or whether refugees can go into the U.S. with just a permanent resident card? (Apparently, other family members were evacuated to the U.S.) Or, hell, what should a tiny baby be wearing to make her not scream if she goes outside on a cold day? I had no advice on really anything, unfortunately …

February 7, 2022

All is chaos, but today I was walking on Bloor and I suddenly said to myself, "Sarah Polley … Sarah Paulson … two different people!" So at least I've got that under control now. Although up until today, that was a hell of a resumé for the Sarah Paulleyson who lived in my mind.

Dip???

February 10, 2022

My smaller cat is *wild* about the smell of chlorine. Normally I come back from the pool and go directly into the shower, but sometimes I stop to pet her and she goes into a nuzzle frenzy. Unlike her brother, she is not a biteyhead — she bites only when she is truly overcome with emotion, positive or negative. Sometimes when I smell so good she just can't stand it, she tries to bite me — this happens with the chlorine. She also doesn't truly know *how* to bite, so this mainly just involves her opening her mouth very wide and then bonking me with a tooth. It is very obvious that Alice in the wild, or even as an outdoor cat, would have died long ago, but oh man, she is sweet.

• • •

Saw M, my new neighbour/friend, at the pool today, as I had hoped. He came late again, and it was just me in my lane, swimming back and forth with the grumpy older gentleman. When there are two people in a lane, you can sort of have half of it to yourself and ignore the other person — more people than that, you have to swim proper laps up one side, down the other, so that you don't get in each other's way. When M arrived, I paused in the shallow end to say hi and chat for a sec. GOG spotted us from about halfway down the pool and stood up, throwing his hands in the air and shrugging enormously. Since it seemed he would not come closer, I looped my finger in the air, indicating we would have to swim laps now. He shrugged again and flopped backward, swimming away to the deep end again. "Oh, he minds!" murmured M beside me. I was sorry, obviously, to have annoyed someone, but also secretly delighted to have a pal commenting in my ear on the odd pool behaviour. It has been six months of intense interior monologue about the pool denizens (and obviously sharing it with you fine folks) and it was exciting to have someone there with me, reacting in real time.

I did not, sadly, get to share all our good ideas for baby things with M, as he left early, saying the baby had been up all night and he was tired, so we didn't walk home together. I told him I had some stuff I wanted to tell him and he said anytime, and we left it at that. I feel a little bit odd that I have a dozen potentially helpful ideas for him and his family waiting to spring on him whenever I get a chance, but, well, it's all very pure hearted.

Gosh, how hard it is to make a friend, and how deeply I want to!

February 11, 2022

(RR in an early meeting)
Meeting Pal: Oh, your husband just walked by.
RR (glances behind her at open door): Uh, okay?
MP (seeming agitated): Well, he was there! Tell him we say hi!
RR (yells at wall): *Hi, Mark!*
MP2: Oh, my husband's name is Mark, too.

RR (has very few hours in the day where there are
people besides Mark to talk to, *not interested*):
Uh-huh.

(Other things are discussed, meeting ends, RR
exits office and goes into the kitchen and gasps
in alarm; MS comes out of his office.)

MS: What was that gasp about? [Our walls are thin.]

RR: Evan was on the counter! With a knife!

MS (not interested in Evan's turn to the dark side):
So your meeting saw me in my towel after my
shower today ...

RR: Ooooh ... no ... so that's what that was. I'm sorry.

MS: So that's a few new people who have seen me
without my shirt. At least the towel did not fall off.

RR: At least that.

MS: Close your door, Rebecca.

RR: You say that like this is an ongoing problem.
This has never happened before. We've made
it through the whole pandemic so far with no
flashings until today. I didn't even think of it.

MS: You heard the shower.

RR: It didn't register. I'm really sorry.

MS: ...

RR: Can I put this on Facebook?

MS: Yeah, okay. But make me look heroic. (Rides
off on his mighty steed.)

• • •

Went a bit deeper into downtown than usual this morning, and it
was tense and trucky — or maybe it's totally normal and I'm just
afraid of trucks now? I'm sure it's been said before but no harm in

continuing to consider how all the stores along Bloor boarded up and, in some cases, cordoned off their front windows before the Black Lives Matter protests two summers ago, despite there not being any threats of violence or desire to overthrow the government. I walked along there at the time and it was like a ghost town — some of them had posted awkward little messages of good cheer on their hoardings before running away? Downtown today is normal enough and nothing is boarded up that I can see, even though the convoy in Ottawa has been setting off fireworks in populated areas and harassing businesses and terrifying residents and generally making it very clear that they mean harm. Anyway, a popular refrain from protests I have participated in myself is "Whose streets? *Our streets!*" and I see that as very much the concern at this time.

February 15, 2022

Love forever — getting-ready-for-Valentine's-dinner edition:

> RR: Oh, wow, you're wearing a jacket and tie?
> MS: Sure, why not — when do I get the chance anymore?
> RR: True. Well, you look great!
> MS: Thanks … Oh.
> RR: What?
> MS: I just remembered there's something wrong with this jacket.
> RR: …
> MS: It doesn't have any buttons. (Flaps the front.) I can't do it up!
> RR: What happened to the buttons?
> MS: They've gone … away.

RR: Did you put them somewhere?

MS: I dunno — probably. I haven't worn this jacket in a long time.

RR: I guess no one is going to notice tonight. It still looks nice.

MS: Okay.

RR: But that was an expensive jacket! It would be good to have buttons!

(MS shrugs.)

RR: I mean, in a way it's good that all of them are gone, so you don't have to worry about matching them. You could just buy whatever new ones.

MS: That's true — it's like a stopped clock being right twice a day.

(At dinner.)

RR: So about the buttons.

MS: Wait!

RR: Are you going to buy new ones?

MS: *Wait!* (Rummages through exterior and interior pockets of the jacket.) I have ... one button!

RR: You can use that to gauge the size when you go shopping for new buttons.

MS: At the ... store? Button City? Like Spatula City?

RR: Well, there was a Fabricland under the Bay, but it was replaced by a Dollarama. Actually, maybe Dollarama has buttons.

MS (indifferent): Yeah, maybe.

RR: You can do this! You can buy buttons and sew them onto your jacket!

MS: I don't know why you believe that. I haven't sewed anything since grade eight home ec class, when I made that fuzzy soccer ball.

RR: Why did you make that?
MS: Because it was *very practical*, Rebecca.
RR: But ... what did you do with it?
MS: I took my C+ and I went home.

Valentine's Day was magical and I am the luckiest!

February 16, 2022

One of the advantages of working from home is that if your skin is about to moult off your body from a combination of winter, forced air heating, and pool chemicals and you are dying of itchiness despite constant application of every known moisturizer *and* suffering vivid flashbacks to when you had bedbugs two months ago, you can pause in your work as many times a day as you like to take off all your clothes and examine yourself in the mirror to check for bites. (*No bites yet! Touch wood!*)

The downside is that the more you do this, the more normal it seems. Going back to working among non-husband, non-cat co-workers is likely the most necessary thing for me, and likely the steepest slope.

February 17, 2022

Welp, tonight, toward the end of dinner, we were chatting about not much and I got confused and somehow just said, "Rebecca!" So the level of discourse is basically cartoon character or toddler now. How long before it's basically *all* that?

February 18, 2022

Had brunch with *friends* today, and it was amazing. I know not everyone is feeling up to it, and you gotta go at your own pace, but if you can see your way clear to connecting with a few people you care about in the flesh, man, you should. You have no idea how lit up I feel.

Bonus feature: one pal brought me some Froot Loops mini boxes she didn't want, and as I took them out of my bag at home just now, a memory I had completely lost came back to me. Mark and I didn't have a Jewish wedding, but we had vague awareness of some customs, so as we ran down the hall after they pronounced us husband and wife, Mark gave me a mini box of Froot Loops he had smuggled in from the breakfast buffet at the hotel, with the idea that the first thing I tasted in our marriage should be sweetness. It was very odd but perfect in that they were more transportable than, say, honey (which is maybe what you are supposed to have?) and also, I love Froot Loops. In the chaos of that day I completely forgot about that until just now, looking at the little box. Thanks for the blast from the past, Z!

February 21, 2022

Mark and I observed Family Day with just my mom, since no other relations are currently in town, and we drove to see my dad's grave since his *yahrzeit* (deathaversary) is on Wednesday — I'm sure he would understand the needs of the workweek. His grave looked pretty good, considering it's February. We were also going to remember him by shopping at his favourite grocery stores but forgot they'd be closed for the holiday, so we just ate at Swiss Chalet, which we all recall was a restaurant he felt pretty much fine about, and came home. The weather was nice and we got stuck in convoy traffic only briefly, and it was a really nice day.

February 23, 2022

Cases have been low all this month — although by low, I mean around two thousand or so a day, which would have seemed like an utter catastrophe and possibly the end times a year and a half ago. How Omicron has changed me. A lot of people I know have been sick and just gotten better right away and hopped along, the way I did in January. It was extremely strange to be scared of something for nearly two years, do everything I could to prevent it, to organize my days around avoiding it, then have it happen and ... meh, it was okay. It was hard to know how to feel. But I also know people who really suffered long term with Covid and a few who have not so far gotten over it, so ... wow. Even though my Covid experience was basically feeling slightly below par for a few days, I still feel that little internal tremble, the way you do when you look in the rear-view mirror and realize you almost hit someone. I got lucky, and maybe if I'd been sick with Covid at a different time, when my immune system was at a different level, the outcome could have been different. I just can't know.

I continue to take precautions, to wear my masks — I still kinda hate them, but less than I used to — and if anyone offers me a fourth dose of the vax, I will take it. During the pando, I have been taking any vaccine offered: I got all the flu shots and all those stupid hepatitis B shots. I just want to be safe from as many things as possible. Hep B turns out to be mainly sexually transmitted, which I didn't know initially — I just got offered a vaccine by my doctor when I was upset about the false alarm with Canadian Blood Services and said I'd take it. I don't think the pharmacy gets a lot of married ladies in their forties signing up for that one. Oh well, can't hurt, but I probably should have researched it more. I used to look into medical treatments at least a little before agreeing to them.

I used to not be much of a crier and now I cry when people are rude at the supermarket and once, though I choked back the tears, in a job interview. I used to have a lot of settings: fun party Rebecca, serious professional Rebecca, private introspective Rebecca, talking to the cat Rebecca, etc. Now I think I just have Me Right Now. I have gotten so bad at filtering things, though I occasionally wonder if I was kidding myself before about being good at it and I never was? But whatever energy I had for pretending to feel something other than what I feel is being more than expended on looking for a job, doing freelance work, trying to keep in touch with a million people via a million apps instead of just seeing them casually around, keeping my distance from strangers, swallowing to see if it hurts, aggressively asking my mother how she is doing, worrying about people I see on the street, worrying about all the people I don't see, trying to carefully figure out a good way to be helpful and non-intrusive and non-patronizing, and looking for phantom bedbugs.

I am more … porous now. Like any of the other things, this isn't exactly a new problem (well, phantom bedbugs are new) — just something that was exacerbated by so much time alone, fretting about illness and the fate of my fellow humans and what I did wrong in a weird conversation I had once in 2006. Now I feel like the separateness of other people is so much less than it was — oddly because I've been kept apart from them for so long. When I go down the street and see people struggling, or suffering, or just doing something odd — crouching in the bike lane and taking a big pile of lemons out of a backpack — I feel like I'm involved, or I need to get involved. Every conversation that I overhear but can't understand, every tragedy I see but don't help with feels like a train

I see pulling away but that I was actually supposed to be on. Two examples:

- I took the subway to run some errands today. There was a subway disruption but it was at the stop I was getting off at, so it didn't matter, except I was rushed off with a tide of people instead of wandering off in a trickle. As I was cresting the escalator with the disgruntled masses and a TTC officer was directing us to the door (I could see the door — he didn't have to yell), I saw that beyond the red-tape barrier, a person was sleeping on the floor. They were curled up in the classic sleeping-on-side position, except that they were just on the hard subway station floor. Their pants had slid down partway to reveal their underwear and some of their bum. I was glad the TTC officer, standing a dozen feet away, hadn't kicked them out, but it was still pretty miserable. And then the tide pushed me on and I was out the door. I wonder if the person was really sleeping, though — I mean, they didn't have a set-up; no blankets or mat or anything. They looked a little bit like they had just collapsed there. I wished I could have interacted with the person on the floor but in reality, even if I'd had an opportunity, I'm not sure what would have been the right thing. I would have had to try to wake them to determine if they were actually sleeping or unconscious or something worse — and probably they were just sleeping and would wake up and want to know what I wanted? "So sorry to bother, just making sure this is a chronic emergency and not an acute one! Please feel free to go back to sleep on the dirty floor if you like." Clearly that's a train I should have been on but utterly lack the qualifications for.

- Heard in the elevator yesterday:

> Guy A: You were gone for a long time, man. Did you just get back?
> Guy B: Yeah, over a month. We were down in Pennsylvania, rehearsing. But he never came, not even one rehearsal.
> A: Oh man, really? Classic. So what was he planning ...?
> B: Just figured he'd do it on the first night of the show. And that's why he fell in the hole.
> A: Gotta come to rehearsals to know where the hole is!
> B: Right? 'Cause there's always a hole.

And then I had to get off the elevator. I will never know who "he" is, why he's important enough to miss a month of work, or why there's always a hole. Another missed train.

February 27, 2022

Imagined dialogue in the future, with someone — who knows, some young person, not yet born:

> Young Person: So it was a total global pandemic, millions sick, thousands dying, all over the

world, and everyone was trapped at home? What did you do all day?

RR: Well, honestly, mainly worked. Almost everyone who could just did their jobs from home and those who couldn't still found a way to get to their workplaces and protected themselves as best they could.

YP: But with all the fear and chaos and people dying, you were just … working? Doing spreadsheets?

RR: Um … yes?

YP: But what about the kids — how did they go to school?

RR: Sometimes they just did it on the computer, like over Zoom.

YP: But who watched them — the little ones, I mean? So they didn't break the computer or run away or whatever?

RR: Their parents, or whoever was home.

YP: Oh, so those people didn't work. They got a leave or whatever.

RR: … No. Most of those people also worked.

YP: How?

RR: I don't know.

YP: All the time?

RR: Mainly, yes. Sometimes employers tried to be flexible, but …

YP: What about all the terrible things that happened, all the grief? The police murders of Black citizens? The discoveries of the bodies of Indigenous children who died at residential schools? All the people who were grieving for those terrible things? And the people who died of Covid!

RR: It was an incredibly hard time, and it was harder because people were often alone, isolated at home, unable to grieve in community.

YP: But they kept working.

RR: I'm sure individuals took time here and then … but basically yes.

YP: And all this time, you knew the earth was heating up, you were reaching a tipping point on carbon emissions?

RR: Many people knew that. I'm not sure how many.

YP: But mainly they …

RR: Kept on top of the spreadsheets, yeah.

YP: Even when the war in Ukraine started?

RR: Well, things were getting a bit ragged by that point, but sort of.

YP: *Why?*

RR: Well, there wasn't any other way to survive, really. Everyone was pretty clear on needing to work to support themselves and their families.

YP: Really? They would take away your means to feed yourself if you didn't make spreadsheets?

RR: Well, not a one-to-one correspondence, but eventually, that would be the down-the-road ramification.

YP: Wow.

RR: Yeah.

YP: What was on these spreadsheets?

Acknowledgements

Thanks to Russell Smith for proposing and ultimately acquiring this book, Laura Boyle for the absolutely perfect cover, Vicky Bell for the thoughtful copy-edit, Ashley Hisson for the thorough proofread, along with Erin Pinksen and the rest of the Dundurn team for all the work of making a manuscript into a book. Also many thanks to Samantha Haywood (and Megan!) at Transatlantic for arranging the sale.

I am so grateful to all my glorious Facebook friends, as it was in my ardent pursuit of conversation with you all that I created the posts that would become this book. So many times you changed my mind, brightened my day, or showed me something new. Even if all social media flies into the sun, I hope we never stop talking, friends. Special thanks to Shannon Whibbs for the title idea.

Other pals who talked me through the pandemic and the editing of this book — people I would talk to forever — include The Elegancies (Fred, Melanie, and Zainab). I'm also indebted for writerly kinship and general (and specific) friendship from Julia Zarankin, Carolyn Black, Kerry Clare, and Maria Meindel. I consider myself so conversationally lucky.

When I pulled down all the posts from March 13, 2020, to the end of February 2022, they were 206,000 words. To get the manuscript down to submission level — 90,000 — there was only one person with the patience, verbal dexterity, and interest in my life, and that is my mominator. Thank you for doing the heavy lifting of pulling the manuscript together, and for letting me write about you so much, and for being so interesting and wise when I call you constantly.

Of course, no one gets written about in this book as much as my husband, Mark, and while he isn't *always* that funny in real life, he mainly is. Thank you for letting me share your foibles with the world, or at least whoever wants to read this, and for having such interesting foibles.

About the Author

Photo by Claire Sibonney

Rebecca Rosenblum is the author of two short story collections, *Once* and *The Big Dream*, the chapbook *Road Trips*, and the novel *So Much Love*. Her work has been shortlisted for the Journey Prize, the National Magazine Award, the Danuta Gleed Award, the Amazon Canada First Novel Award, and the Trillium Book Award, and her first book won the Metcalf-Rooke Award. One of her stories was made into a short film and her novel was translated into French and Polish. Rebecca works in publishing and lives in Toronto's St. James Town with her two cats and her husband, the author Mark Sampson.